Kant's Theory of Form

KANT'S THEORY OF FORM

An Essay on the *Critique of Pure Reason*

ROBERT B. PIPPIN

New Haven and London
Yale University Press

Designed by Nancy Ovedovitz and set in Times Roman type by
Brevis Press.
Printed in the United States of America by Edwards
Brothers Inc., Ann Arbor, Mich.

Library of Congress Cataloging in Publication Data

Pippin, Robert B., 1948–
    Kant's theory of form.
    Bibliography: p.
    Includes index.
    1. Kant, Immanuel, 1724–1804. Kritik der
reinen Vernunft. English. 2. Knowledge, Theory of.
3. Causation. 4. Reason. I. Title.
B2779.P54   121   81-70669
ISBN 0-300-02659-5   AACR2

10   9   8   7   6   5   4   3   2   1

*For J. D., G. H., S. M., D. H., T. S.,
and S. R.*

What they undertook to do
They brought to pass;
All things hang like a drop of dew
Upon a blade of grass.
                    W. B. Yeats

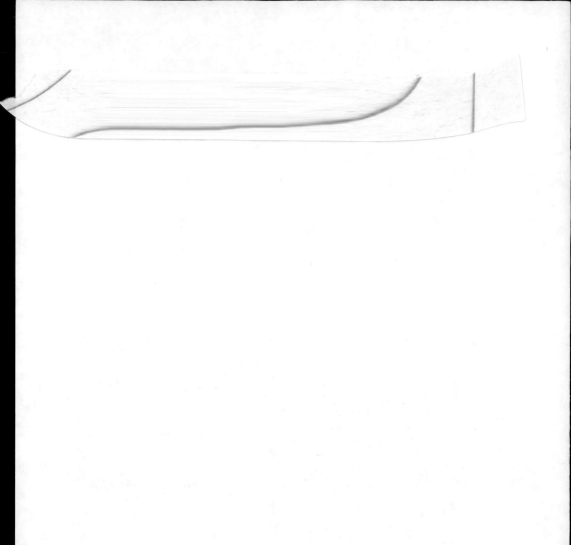

Contents

Preface

In the *Prolegomena to Any Future Metaphysics,* Kant, in clear frustration that the central philosophic position of the *Critique of Pure Reason* had not been understood by his contemporaries, suggests that we consider that position a "formal idealism." That is, as I shall suggest in detail in what follows, quite a useful hint. In the first and most obvious place, such a characterization expresses well the overwhelming importance of the notion of "form" in the first *Critique.* Many of its most important claims are continually expressed in the language of form and formality. Kant's theory of intuitions is a theory of the "forms of sensibility," his theory of pure and empirical concepts is a theory of the "forms of the thought of objects," his characterization of his own case for the "possibility of experience" everywhere insists that the "unity" necessary for that experience, the "unity of apperception," must be regarded as only a "formal" principle, and he seems to have entirely rewritten both the Deduction and the Paralogisms in frustration that this point, among others, had not been clearly made. His whole account of the "objectivity" of certain pure concepts depends on understanding them as indispensable "forms," or "rules," by virtue of which, and only by virtue of which, human experience can occur. In his theory of a priori knowledge or even all a priori "reflection" in general, he always claims that such a priori results are only accessible "formally" for human beings. Indeed, this emphasis on formality is probably what most of all distinctively characterizes his theories of a priori cognitive, moral, and aesthetic judgments.

This book is about Kant's theory of the "forms of experience." In one sense, it is thus a limited commentary on Kant's foundational claims concerning the forms of sensibility, and the forms of the thought of an object, or his theory of intuitions and concepts. More broadly, it also includes an account of the "formality" of Kant's methodology in general, at least insofar as that methodology is explained, defended, and worked through in detail in the first *Critique.*

The project was originally undertaken for two reasons. One has to do with what, following Herder, one could call the "meta-critical" problem of the *Critique,* or: how to explain adequately the status of the results arrived at in Kant's transcendental philosophy. From the initial publication of the *Critique* up to the present day, it has never been easy to explain just what Kant's "new" methodology in philosophy amounted to. Kant himself was faced with charges that his philosophy was simply a version of Berkeley's "idealism," that whatever was of value in his "new discovery" was simply a restatement of Leibnizian rationalism, or, at the very end of his life, that what he had done was to introduce a new way of reasoning about the relation between the "ego" and the "non-ego." Later, his transcendentalism was characterized in even more "absolutist" or metaphysical terms. Then, as the pendulum of German thought swung in the other direction, his theoretical methodology was reinterpreted as a reflection on the presuppositions of science and mathematics, or, later, as a complicated version of "transcendental psychology." More recently, this enigmatic transcendentalism has been interpreted as a kind of philosophical anthropology, or even a "laying of the foundations of metaphysics"; and more recently still as an "analysis" of the deepest presuppositions involved in our "concept" of experience, at least to the extent that analysis of the use of that term can reveal such presuppositions. Along the way in all these accounts, Kant's theory of transcendental reasoning and argumentation has been called everything from a discovery of the Absolute to a disguised version of "verificationism." In the face of this diversity, it seemed to me that no progress at all on this issue could be made without a detailed examination, in Kant's terms (at least as much as possible) of the most obvious and fundamental aspect of "transcendental reflection" — its formality, Kant's claim to have discovered only the "forms" of experience. A decision about the various idealistic, rationalist, metaphysical, psychological, logical, and linguistic characterizations of this feature of Kant's project would depend on as detailed and comprehensive an analysis as possible of what Kant had to say about that feature.

Second, the issue itself seems to me an important ancestor of many extraordinarily influential subsequent characterizations of philosophic methodology. We are accustomed by now to think easily of distinctions between philosophy of science and science, philosophy of history and history, philosophy of art and art, and so on. Indeed, we are so accustomed that many potential difficulties inherent in such distinctions — or indeed, in the very distinction itself between "theories of knowledge" and the actual content of knowledge — do not arise once such distinctions are operationally assumed. While it is no part of my intention to prove it, I think that many aspects of a good deal of post-Kantian thinking about philosophic methodology (and especially about this issue of its formality) are decisively influenced by the way he formulated it, at least in its most abstract form. If Kant did indeed stand at the end of a long tradition of philosophic speculation, many of his original assumptions about philosophic methodology stand at the beginning of another, and much of what is important in that new beginning has to do, again, with this claim about "formality," and the connection between reflection on such form and a priori knowledge. At any rate, I hope to show that there are some basic difficulties in at least Kant's notion of the forms of experience, and would hope that those difficulties would suggest further, more general problems in theories conceptually, even if not historically, tied to his.

The following is thus a restricted commentary on a special topic in Kant, and as general an analysis of the ramifications of that topic as fidelity to an historical text will permit. I have also become convinced that many of the controversies prominent in the secondary literature on Kant often depend on how his transcendental formality is interpreted, and accordingly, that it was important to note the relevance of that topic for many of those discussions. This seemed to me an important and potentially useful point of view for assessing both the classical and contemporary literature, and both the Anglo-American and European literature. I have tried to avoid being guilty of Paton's stinging criticism of Vaihinger — that he started out to write a commentary on Kant, and ended up writing a commentary on the commentaries — but I have made extensive use of that literature as a way of presenting and clarifying my interpretation.

This project began a few years ago as a dissertation, and although it has subsequently been rethought and completely rewritten, it still owes much to two teachers who, in different ways and from different perspectives, influenced much of my interpretation of Kant and German philosophy. I am indebted to Stanley Rosen for teaching me how to read historical texts in a philosophical way, and for his support, suggestions, and encouragement, both in the early and late stages of this project. I am also most grateful to Thomas Seebohm, whose scholarly and philosophic help on Kant, and whose continuing support, have been invaluable.

I owe a special debt of gratitude to the Alexander von Humboldt foundation. Together with a sabbatical and leave from the University of California, San Diego, their generous grant made possible an extended stay in Germany, and the final work on and writing of this book. During that year, I was fortunate enough to hear Professor Gerold Prauss's lectures in Cologne on "Apriorität in der Erfahrung." I am grateful to Professor Prauss, as well as to Professor Gerhard Funke of the Johannes Gutenberg Universität in Mainz, and to Eric and Sara Sandberg in Mainz, for their hospitality and support during my stay in Germany.

A section of chapter 4 appeared previously in Studies in History and Philosophy of Science, and a section of chapter 5 in Kant-Studien. I want to thank the editors of both journals for their permission to reprint here.

I am also grateful to Karl Ameriks, Gerd Buchdahl, Nicholas Jolley,

Fred Olafson, and Mark Wilson for their helpful comments on various portions of my interpretation, and especially to my colleague, Henry Allison. Our frequent conversations about Kant over the past few years have proven extremely valuable in the preparation of this study. I am also much indebted to Maureen MacGrogan, editor for Yale University Press, for her help and support, and to an anonymous reader for his careful and incisive comments. The imperfections of several chapters, especially 2 and 3, would have been even greater than they undoubtedly still are but for his helpful criticisms. Finally, I owe a special debt of gratitude to Catherine Asmann, who patiently deciphered earlier versions of the text, and typed the final manuscript.

1

Introduction: Transcendental Philosophy

Matter and Form. These are the two concepts which lie at the basis of all other reflection, so very inseparably are they bound up with any use of the understanding. (B322 = A266)[1]

1. Kant's Revolution

One reasonable way to prepare to write something extensive about Kant is to consult, in as much detail as one's time and estimate of the importance of such things permit, what other commentators have had to say about him in the past two hundred years. As reasonable as such extended homage to the muses of scholarship is, it can also be quite discouraging. First, one faces the forbidding, almost unbelievable quantity of material. Heidegger reports that nearly two thousand articles about Kant had been written before his death in 1804.[2] And when one considers the sheer number of philosophers who have existed since then (especially the number now writing), the fact that many of them felt obliged to write about one of the greatest books in the philosophic tradition, and finally the number of schools or movements that have "returned" to Kant, one's imagination is greatly strained to picture just how much is already written — some very well written — on every conceivable topic in Kant's philosophy. Such a magnitude is so obvious that many recent books on Kant begin (like this one) with some brief apologia as a preliminary response to the understandable weary sigh that must greet every new study. If there was once a confusing, tangled transcendental jungle, by

1. Immanuel Kant, *Kritik der reinen Vernunft*, ed. R. Schmidt (Hamburg: Felix Meiner, 1954). References to the *Critique of Pure Reason* are to the standard first- and second-edition pagination, and follow the quotation. Unless otherwise indicated, references to other works by Kant are to the volume and page number of *Kants gesammelte Schriften,* ed. Königlich Preussischen Akademie der Wissenschaften (Berlin and Leipzig: de Gruyter, 1922). Aside from not following his practice of italicizing a priori, I have mostly used Norman Kemp Smith's translation of the *Critique of Pure Reason* (New York: St. Martin's Press, 1929), although I have occasionally substituted my own translations.

2. Martin Heidegger, *What Is a Thing?* trans. W. B. Barton, Jr., and Vera Deutsch (Chicago: Henry Regnery Company, 1967), p. 58.

1

now so many paths have been blazed through it that one suspects that there can hardly be a tree left standing.

When one actually has waded through much of this scholarship, a more specific kind of discouragement occurs. Not surprisingly, an enormous amount of repetition does exist; commentator after commentator echoing each other in making some distinction, exposing some defect, or summarizing some argument. In short, one hesitates; both because one suspects that the ideas that tempt one to write such a book in the first place must already have had some adequate treatment in that vast library of books on Kant, and inspection of some large portion of that library confirms that such worries about redundancy are indeed well founded.

However, in one fairly obvious sense, such a continuous repetition of basic Kantian problems is to be expected and even welcomed. However one interprets the fact, it is clear that the dominant interests, language, even "style" of philosophy change quite a bit from time to time. And it is certainly true that Kant's philosophy is fundamental enough to have had something useful to say to the cluster of problems, and the kind of technique, that dominate the philosophy of any given period. Consequently "rethinking" Kant in a variety of different contexts, with different emphases and from different perspectives, can often be quite helpful, both for understanding him and for philosophy itself. There is indeed a great deal written about Kant. But the "Kant" of Maimon, Reinhold, Herder, Fichte, Hegel, Cassirer, Cohen, Vaihinger, Natorp, de Vleeschauwer, Heidegger, Kemp Smith, Paton, Sellars, Strawson, and Prauss seems to have had quite a variety of different things to say. The volume of Kant scholarship can be at least as much an indication of the usefulness of attempting to reinterpret him as it is an apparently intimidating barrier.

Second, and more important, the recurrence of many of the same problems in much of the literature can be helpful in itself. An overview of the tradition of Kant literature, now so extensive, can help reveal both just what it is about Kant's version of philosophy's task that has influenced and interested so many thinkers, and what aspects of his project seem continually to frustrate a full, coherent explanation and defense of that project.

On the one hand, in keeping with many of Kant's own descriptions of himself, his tremendous influence on the history of philosophy has been as a "critic," even an "all destroyer." This is especially true of his often decisive arguments in the Dialectic against the rationalist enterprise, and of his more controversial case against empirical skepticism in the Transcendental Aesthetic and Analytic. But these criticisms were also part of a general philosophic strategy at least as influential as any specific arguments about God, the soul, or causality. That strategy involved Kant in a virtually single-handed, bold attempt to reformulate philosophy's task in the era of modern natural science. Of course, many of the consequences of the scientific revolution were already apparent to the "father" of modernity, Descartes, and to many others in the newly developing rationalist and empiricist traditions. Such men had already decided that philosophy's classical, self-appointed task as "first" philosophy, the investigation of being or the highest kind of being, or final causes, must, at the very least, be substantially reformulated in the light of the criteria of knowledge advanced by the new science (Spinoza, Leibniz), or discarded in favor of a new philosophy of the first principles of *knowledge*, or "method," not being (Descartes, Locke). Philosophy should now provide the secure foundations of knowledge, protecting us from doubt, error, and useless speculation, while engaged in an enterprise "prior" to the sciences, since the latter had to presuppose and could not themselves defend such principles. Much in Kant, of course, continues such an attempt, but with a decisive reformulation.

For Kant claimed that the proponents of this new epistemological turn were still far too closely tied to the substantive metaphysics of the tradition; that, especially, they conceived of their project as dependent on an a priori theory of "mental substance" or on an inconsistent "psychology" of the understanding in order to support claims about the first principles of knowledge. Simply put, Kant denied that this was necessary, and argued instead that philosophy's epistemological methodology could be a priori and foundational only as "formal." Of course, this formal methodology was not merely "analytic" in the loose sense of the word, identifying and clarifying presuppositions, sorting out distinctions, and so forth, and it is deeply connected with his own version of idealism. But however complicated the full story of Kantian formality is, one can at least fairly note its decisive influence on subsequent methodology. Indeed, one can see the legacy of this way of construing philosophy's contemporary task in contexts as different as Heidegger's distinction between ontological and ontic, and Russell's argument that logic is the essence of philosophy.[3]

On the other hand, when one surveys the numerous attempts to work out and defend fully Kant's version of this formal, transcendental philos-

---

3. It is, of course, impossible here to establish the precise historical connections between Kant's enterprise and such modern contexts. In the case of Heidegger, the simple claim of great "influence" is easier to establish since Heidegger wrote three books about Kant, and refers to him frequently. In the case of modern philosophy of language, the key transitional figure is Frege. For relevant discussions of this topic, see H. D. Sluga, "Frege's Alleged Realism," *Inquiry* 20 (1977); Stanley Rosen, *The Limits of Analysis* (New York: Basic Books, 1980), p. 18 ff.; Gerold Prauss, "Freges Beitrag zur Erkenntnistheorie," *Allgemeine Zeitschrift für Philosophie* 1 (1974): 34–74.

ophy, one notices repeatedly the same weak spots at the foundation of the edifice, spots that will not stand the strain of much scrutiny. A very important but undeveloped component of his overall account of knowledge, his theory of the sensory manifold as only the mere "material" of cognition; his account of space and time as "pure intuitions" that are also "pure forms" of outer and inner sense; his theory of concepts as forms or rules, "for the thought of objects," and the account of empirical concepts that follows from that definition; his argument for the necessity of a "schematism" for concepts; his account of just what a "transcendental deduction" is, and the doctrine of a "merely formal" transcendental unity of apperception at the heart of that deduction; and the relationship between formally "conditioned" appearances and things in themselves, are all problems that seem to have required the most effort in interpretations and defenses of the Transcendental Aesthetic and Analytic.

Of course, there are always a number of ways to explain such difficulties in a philosopher: a bad argument here, a careless confusion of terms there, an incomplete explanation, a simple lack of interest in certain problems, or, often enough, a long tradition of confusion on the part of commentators could all contribute. Many such explanations are certainly correct in their place.

However, I shall argue that, as is often ironically the case in philosophy, the common source for such traditional problems lies in just what is also so original, insightful, and influential in Kant's approach, his inauguration of a purely formal epistemology, one not tied to empirical psychology or to rationalist theories of mind. In effect, then, the following is an essay on Kant's philosophic methodology and on the consequences that follow from accepting that methodology.[4]

Of course, such a statement of intention must at this point be very abstract. I try to make such a topic more determinate in the ensuing section by discussing Kant's own versions of his transcendental turn, and in section 3 by discussing generally the strikingly different versions of that "Copernican revolution" prominent in the post-Kantian tradition. But before doing so, I also want to continue to discuss briefly the general issues at stake in raising this kind of topic in Kant, why such issues are important, and how they will be treated here.

Aside from the obvious scholarly and philosophic interest in what Kant meant by claiming that his transcendental philosophy was purely formal, and how he meant to justify that claim, there are two more

---

4. As far as I know, there is no book in English devoted solely to the problem of form and formalism in Kant's methodology. There is an interesting, although somewhat uncritical, work in German: Hans Graubner, *Form und Wesen: Ein Beitrag zur Deutung des Formbegriffs in Kants Kritik der reinen Vernunft. Kantstudien Ergänzungshefte*, vol. 104 (Bonn: Bouvier, 1972).

specific reasons that make that issue an important one. The first is systematic, the second more historical. In the first place, while philosophers have always been interested in what was "presupposed" in such domains as ordinary, or political, or scientific discourse or experience, Kant's "transcendental" way of posing such questions greatly altered how that kind of inquiry came to be understood. Kant saw himself as after fundamental "principles" which either "constituted" such a domain (e.g., empirical experience) or which unavoidably "regulated" activity in such domains. Such a way of talking is already quite an innovation, of course. But, more important, he thought that this inquiry was not itself a *component* of that domain, or even one which arose necessarily from problems in that domain. It was instead logically prior to what went on therein, providing and justifying the "foundational" principles without which that domain could not be what it was. In large part (though by no means exclusively) it was due to such an approach that later philosophy could speak, for example, of a "philosophy of history" that was not about history, but about the forms of historical knowledge, a philosophy of art that concerned the first principles of aesthetic judgments, and not art, a philosophy of science that could see itself as the *independent* legitimation of science, and, in the most obvious case, a philosophy of the forms of language, the "pure" structure of propositions, assertion, reference and inference. Recently, of course, the notion of philosophy as such a foundationalist, a priori epistemology has come under heavy attack, for a variety of often quite different reasons.[5] However, if there is something wrong with the notion of such a formal, a priori methodology, it certainly should be apparent in the philosopher who inaugurated a good deal of this way of thinking. Kant presents what very well may be the strongest case in the history of philosophy for the necessity of such a view of philosophic methodology, and anyone interested in the contemporary "crisis" of epistemology ignores him at his own risk.

More to the point, coming now to the historical consideration mentioned above, attacks on an a priori, formal, epistemological view of philosophy, even Kant's own version, are hardly recent reactions. Throughout all of the so-called German Idealist continuation of and reaction to Kant, one issue dominated much of the discussion, especially in Fichte and Hegel (and extending through Marx and Nietzsche): the charge that Kant's account was unacceptably formal, in both his theoretical and practical philosophy, that he had ignored the embeddedness of the human subject in "practice," or history.[6] However, in making such a

5. I refer here to the well-known attempts by Sellars, Quine, Davidson, and others in different "camps," such as the late Heidegger, Foucault, and Richard Rorty in his recent *Philosophy and the Mirror of Nature* (Princeton: Princeton University Press, 1979).

6. There are several passages in Hegel, for example, that stress that Kant was the

case, Fichte, Hegel, and others were obviously not interested in writing long books on Kant. They dealt mainly with his *results,* and offered their criticisms from the perspective of their own positions and mostly in their own vocabulary. Again, though, Kant would claim that these results cannot be avoided, once one considers how they are arrived at, and that criticisms of his "pure" transcendental subject are unfair if they do not deal internally with the details of his carefully presented, intricate arguments.

I believe that such an internal critique of Kant's theory of form, fair to his own insights and positive achievements, can be given, and I shall try to do so in what follows. Of course, that means that this book will have to give a detailed account of Kant, and deal only incidentally with the relevance of his approach to contemporary issues, and to the development of German philosophy after him. However, I hope that the relevance of those issues will be frequently apparent. I shall return to some of them in the concluding chapter. I also hope that the nature of the criticisms offered is clear. Several books recently have dealt with, and often dismissed, the inadequacies of various independent arguments in Kant. Of course, Kant should be taken to task when he is unclear, inconsistent, or simply mistaken, but it is also important that the fundamental issues in his methodological revolution should be addressed directly. It seems to me that Kant is very often right in his critique of the ungroundedness or dogmatism of much prior philosophy, right in his criticisms of the inconsistency of empirical skepticism, and undoubtedly on the right track in proposing a "transcendental idealism" cum "empirical realism" as a reaction to such deficiencies. However, I think that detailed attention to his own case reveals that he went too far in emphasizing the "pure" and "formal" nature of this idealism and that is, in part, what I want to show.

All of this commits me to a number of tasks: (1) to explain what Kant means when he speaks of the "form" and "matter" of experience and especially (2) what he means by the relation between form and matter in experience (a most neglected topic in the literature); (3) how Kant *justifies* his views concerning what the forms of knowledge are, and how

---

preeminent "philosopher of reflection" or "formal thinking." Cf., inter alia, *Glauben und Wissen, Werke,* vol. 2 (Frankfurt: Suhrkamp, 1970), pp. 301, 302, 310–13; and *Enzyklopädie der philosophischen Wissenschaften* (Hamburg: Felix Meiner, 1969), p. 43 ff. In commenting on this approach, Hegel has high praise for the doctrine of spontaneity and activity at the heart of Kant's formalism, as in *Glauben und Wissen,* p. 333, or the *Enzyklopädie,* section 60, and especially the *Zusatz.* But he constantly criticizes Kant for the "indeterminateness" of this principle, and he thereby charges that Kant could not distinguish his position from "empirical psychology" (this, although Hegel also demonstrates that he understands the differe__e between Kant and Locke; *Glauben und Wissen,* p. 333).

they relate to each other; (4) what these arguments reveal about the formal nature of his epistemology in general; and finally (5) to evaluate each of these elements. In approaching these issues, though, it is surely best to begin by attending to Kant's own general remarks about his project.

2. Transcendental Formalism

Although it is not easy to find a completely clear statement by Kant concerning all the dimensions of his transcendental approach, it is possible to find passages where he attempts to point out how that approach is deeply continuous with much of the interests of traditional theoretical philosophy, and just how it attempts to alter many traditional assumptions. Considering these statements of continuity and discontinuity together can help raise some immediate problems to be considered. I begin with some clear statements of continuity.

However revolutionary, one dominant assumption in the *Critique* remains quite traditional — Kant's conception of the *task* of theoretical philosophy. Whatever turn or revolution is effected by the *Critique,* such a philosophy retains its characterization as "reason attempting to know a priori," independent of any contribution from experience. In that respect, the *Critique of Pure Reason* is itself a task *of* reason, now directed on itself, but still markedly different from any empirical science and even from those other sciences capable of a priori knowledge, such as mathematics. What Kant regards as totally new in his conception of reason's a priori task is the methodology employed, and what turns out to so distinguish that methodology is the special object to which reason has now been turned. Thus he writes,

> The concern of this critique of pure speculative reason consists in the attempt to alter the hitherto prevailing procedure [*Verfahren*] of metaphysics, and to do that by completely revolutionizing it in accordance with the example of geometers and physicists. It is a treatise on method, and not a system of science itself. (Bxxii)

This way of describing his project is worth stressing, for, although the very title of the work suggests its critical intention, most of his own formulations stress that he is after *more* success in the tasks of metaphysics, that he retains the belief that it is quite possible for reason to attain a priori knowledge, and that the most important aspect of his revolution is just this methodological one. In explaining why this methodology is to be so different, he had earlier explained,

> Hitherto it had been assumed that all our knowledge must conform to objects. But under this presupposition, all attempts to extend our knowledge by establishing something a priori about objects through concepts, came to

naught. It must therefore be attempted whether, in the tasks of metaphysics, we might make better progress by assuming that objects conformed to our knowledge. . . . We should then be proceeding according to the primary ideas of Copernicus. (Bxvi)

In order to effect this shift in presuppositions, we shall have to determine just what knowledge is, that objects should "conform" to it, and later in the *Introduction,* Kant baptizes this line of inquiry.

I entitle transcendental all knowledge which is occupied not so much with objects as with the mode of our knowledge [*Erkenntnisart*] of objects, in so far as this mode of knowledge is to be possible a priori. (B25 = A12)

And finally, "The critique of pure reason will contain all that is essential in transcendental philosophy" (B28 = A14).

So pure reason can still claim to know a priori, but only as "transcendental philosophy," that is only as knowledge occupied with the "mode of knowledge of objects," and only by proceeding according to a Copernican methodology. This transcendental philosophy will completely revolutionize the procedure of traditional metaphysics and so achieve more success in arriving at "synthetic a priori" knowledge.

In explaining what is involved in this investigation of our *Erkenntnisart,* Kant goes on to assert that "our knowledge springs from two fundamental sources of the mind," sources he names "intuitions" and "concepts" (B74 = A50). Since, as we have already seen, transcendental philosophy will only concern itself with that mode of knowledge possible a priori, he then explains in what sense a priori knowledge about such sources is possible. It turns out that no a priori knowledge is possible about the content of intuitions and concepts, but only about their "formal" properties. As he puts it,

Pure intuition contains therefore simply the form under which something is intuited, and a pure concept only the form of the thought of an object in general. (B75 = A51)

And it is with such pure intuitions and pure concepts, the forms of intuition and the forms of the thought of an object, that transcendental philosophy will concern itself. Put somewhat loosely, Kant means by this notion of form that his analysis will concentrate on *how* human beings experience (again insofar as such modes can be established necessarily and a priori) and less on *what* is known.[7] As he explains about intuitions, human beings happen to be so constituted that "intuition can never be other than sensible, that is, it only contains the *manner* [*die Art*] in which

---

7. Cf. the discussion of this point by Max Scheler, *Der Formalismus in der Ethik und die materiale Wertethik* (Berne: Franke-Verlag, 1954), pp. 29–107.

[*wie*] we are affected by objects" (A51 = B75). Our understanding can supply itself with no content, but is defined by Kant as *Spontaneität*, exclusively a discursive activity, an activity whose "rules" (again *das Wie*) are accessible, somehow, a priori.

Much more will have to be said about what a knowledge of these forms of experience amounts to, but at this stage it is first important to stress how much is involved in this characterization of the formal nature of transcendental philosophy, and how much of the traditional tasks of theoretical philosophy are still present in such claims.

For, as it will turn out, coming to an understanding of these forms of experience will enable us to understand a great deal — for example, why our experience has a certain unified coherence, structure, and determinancy. It thus could, when compared from a sufficiently high altitude, indeed be said to complete the ancient search for a table of categories, a list of the primary predicates of all the beings (at least any being we could experience).[8] When Aristotle, for example, inquired after the conditions under which a thing was one such thing — a whole, not a mere collection of elements — and answered by means of that thing's "formal" properties, properties other things with a different matter could also have, he began a tradition of enquiry and inaugurated a kind of answer that has obvious counterparts in many of the philosophers before Kant (particularly, on this question of unity, a philosopher most influential for Kant's development, Leibniz), and it would be unfair to Kant not to notice such elements in his own theory of form. His notion of these twin forms as necessary conditions of experience is very far from the Aristotelian conception of *eidos* as a kind of *aitia,* but it is certainly not a 180-degree turn from such an issue. Such conditions will account for, or "ground," the "synthetic unity" of our experience, and thus will evidence a connection in Kant's philosophy between the classical questions of form and unity which, while greatly revised, are still prominent. Kant will define knowledge as "a *whole* (*ein Ganzes*) of compared and connected representations" (A97), and his explanation that only by virtue of certain formal conditions can such unity be explained is closer to the "metaphysical tradition" than is often admitted.

This sort of general continuity between Kant and that tradition is even more clearly apparent if one recalls the limitations imposed by him on the definition of "dogmatic" metaphysics. In virtually all of his official pronouncements on the subject (i.e., throughout the *Critique,* in his essay "Über die Fortschritte der Metaphysik," and in his *Lectures on Metaphy-*

---

8. This view is stressed by Gottfried Martin, *Immanuel Kant, Ontologie und Wissenschaftstheorie* (Berlin: de Gruyter, 1969), particularly in his discussions of the relation between Kant and Leibniz.

sics), Kant defined metaphysics (or at least the kind of metaphysics he was interested in criticizing) as an attempt to know the "supersensible," *das Übersinnliche*. Metaphysics for Kant seems to have meant most of all the metaphysics exemplified in that Baumgarten text which he taught for so many years, and that meant an attempt to transcend the bounds of experience and know special *types* of objects, objects which, by their very nature, could not be known by experience; objects like God, the totality of the world, and the soul. That is, "dogmatic metaphysics" (or "transcendental realism") did not mean, at least not directly for Kant, an attempt to ask questions *about* experienced objects that could not be answered *by* experience. As Heidegger, for all the peculiarities of his interpretation, quite helpfully points out, *das Übersinnliche* is only *one* aspect of *das Nichtsinnliche* in general, and it is the latter which should properly be said to be the object of metaphysics.[9] Reminding us of the traditional scholastic distinction, Heidegger points out that besides a *metaphysica specialis,* there is also *metaphysica generalis,* that besides questions about supersensible beings one can ask questions about all "the beings" that do not admit empirical answers; questions whose terms transcend the distinction between sensible and intellectual beings.[10] Such questions would be directly ontological ones, like, What is being *qua* being? What kinds of beings are there? and related metaphysical questions like, What determines that this being is this and not that being, an individual, and of one kind?

Now, as will become clearer later, Kant is not at all raising such questions in the same way as, say, Aristotle; and neither is he "laying the foundation" for a Heideggerian version of metaphysics. At this point, it should just be stressed that the way he does raise these questions and the way he answers them should not be regarded as indifferent to those aspects of the tradition mentioned above. Kant may well be an "epistemologist" of some variety, but, as will be seen, that to which he appeals in order to establish the limits of human knowledge, and the way he interprets his results, will introduce more than incidental, traditional metaphysical concerns into his account; and, again, many of those will involve his understanding of "formality."[11]

9. Martin Heidegger, *Kant and the Problem of Metaphysics,* trans. James S. Churchill (Bloomington: Indiana University Press, 1968), sections 1–3.

10. A very general discussion of this sort of theme in Kant (interestingly enough, as related both to Heidegger and the tradition) can be found in William H. Bossart, "Is Philosophy Transcendental?" *The Monist* 55, no. 2 (April 1971): 293–311.

11. One of the clearest examples of how Kant's criticism of dogmatic metaphysics presupposes his own claims on metaphysical issues is his attack on the ontological argument. His case there presupposes a definition of "actuality" exclusively in terms of the conditions of sensible apprehension. Further, he will limit possible objects of sensible apprehension, and so all "actuality," to sensible *individuals* (thanks to our spatio-temporal forms of sensibility), and so does not end up metaphysically "neutral" on such issues as Platonism/

Even after having stressed this dimension in Kant, however, one no doubt has to admit immediately that there are vast differences in presupposition between the classical search for an ontological ground of the unity and determinacy of being, and Kant's search for the formal conditions for, finally, the unity of subjectivity or self-consciousness. For one thing, as is often reported, the whole notion of nature and natural unity had undergone enormous reinterpretation by the time of the *Critique*. "Nature" had come to mean extended matter in motion, and the question of the formal unity of nature became the question of the unity prescribed by *law*, that is, basically about the organizing potentiality of the subject. In that respect, Kant's account simply represents a comprehensive attempt to explain, justify, and protect from skepticism *this* notion of "formal unity." (It is in this sense, and only in this sense, that Newtonian science is a "presupposition" of the *Critique*).[12] Given this extraordinarily heightened notion of the source of natural order in the scientific laws formulated rationally by the knowing subject, the natural and pressing question becomes the objectivity of such a subjective source, the source of its formal prescriptions. Such is what Kant means by his claim to adopt a Copernican methodology, and it is certainly quite different in many respects from the traditional attempt to describe and explain the formal properties of "anything at all."

But the old search for the "transcendentals" lives on in more than name with Kant. In fact, we have a fairly direct statement by Kant of his own view of his relation to the traditional question of form. In a bristling little 1796 essay written in response to an attack by J. G. Schlosser, Kant makes a very general point about his position on form. The essay, "Von einem neuerdings erhobenen vornehmen Ton in der Philosophie," is a defense against the charge of mere formalism, that his philosophy was guilty of "*Formgebungmanufaktur*" and so "*Pedanterei.*" Kant responds by directly defending the admittedly formal nature of both his theoretical

---

nominalism, as is claimed by W. Stegmüller in his "Towards a Rational Reconstruction of Kant's Metaphysics of Experience," Part I, *Ratio* 9 (1967): 9. I shall try to show this in more detail in chapter 4. For an interpretation of Kant on "Sein," see what is the least known, but maybe the most interesting, of Heidegger's books on Kant, *Kants These über das Sein* (Frankfurt: Vittorio Klostermann, 1963); and also Gerhart Hüber, *Das Sein und das Absolut* (Basel: Verlag für Recht und Gesellschaft, 1955), especially section 35.

12. An excellent reconstruction of some aspects of Kant's relation to Newton can be found in the Stegmüller article quoted above (also part 2, *Ratio* 10 [1968]). Cf. also on this point E. Cassirer, *Substance and Function* (Chicago: Dover, 1953); Gerd Buchdahl, *Metaphysics and the Philosophy of Science* (Cambridge: MIT Press, 1969), p. 51 ff.; Gordon G. Brittan, Jr., *Kant's Theory of Science* (Princeton: Princeton University Press, 1978), chap. 5; and Newton himself, in the *Opticks*, speaking of principles such as gravity: "I consider, not as occult qualities supposed to result from the specific form of things, but as general *laws of nature*," quoted in Buchdahl, *Metaphysics*, p. 52.

and practical philosophy, and toward the end, makes the following
synoptic claim:

> The essence of things consists in their form (*forma dat esse rei,* as is said by the
> Scholastics), insofar as this thing might be known through reason. If the thing
> is an object of the senses, so its form is in its intuition (as an appearance), and
> even pure mathematics itself is nothing but a doctrine of the form of pure
> intuition. With respect to metaphysics, as pure philosophy, its knowledge is
> first of all grounded on forms of thought, under which any object (the material
> of knowledge) may subsequently be subsumed. The possibility of all synthetic
> a priori knowledge, which we are indeed not able to agree on having, rests on
> this form.[13]

This passage reveals clearly that Kant is indebted to the traditional
notion of form as the object of philosophical interest, and immediately
makes clear how much of that notion he has transformed. While it is true
that *"forma dat esse rei,"* it is also the case that this form is now to be
interpreted as a subjective faculty and, by implication here and explicitly
elsewhere, not itself a special "object" of knowledge. Should the object
of knowledge be an object of the senses, its "form" is not a property of
the object, but *is* the intuiting activity of the subject. Nevertheless, by his
association here with the tradition, Kant admits that knowledge of this
form *will* reveal something like the "essence" of the object — for Kant
the universal conditions necessary for it to be an object at all (space and
time). Should the object be an object of experience in general (of
empirical knowledge), then the Kantian enterprise (here called un-
ashamedly "metaphysics") can also discover the "essence" of that object
in the forms of thought. In sum, knowledge of "form" is an indispensable
element in any synthetic a priori knowledge (as the last sentence of the
above quotation makes clear), and form is inextricably linked with the
knowing subject.

The last point is also made emphatically in another passage in the
Kantian corpus concerned directly with the problem of form, the
"Amphiboly of Concepts of Reflection." There Kant defines the procedure involved in much of the *Critique*'s actual work, and especially in
its criticism of the metaphysical tradition.

> *Reflection* (*reflexio*) does not concern itself with objects themselves with a view
> to deriving concepts from them directly, but it is that state of mind in which we
> first set ourselves to discover the subjective conditions under which [alone] we
> are able to arrive at concepts. (B316 = A261)

Here the contrast between objects of knowledge and conditions for that

---

13. Kant, *Gesammelte Schriften,* vol. 8, p. 404. Cf. Graubner's discussion of the passage,
Form und Wesen, p. 49.

knowledge is clearly drawn, and an official name is given to the attempt to "locate" a representation in its proper faculty — "transcendental reflection." As he proceeds to explain the various amphibolies made (especially by Leibniz) in confusing the "transcendental location" of these concepts, he comes finally to Matter and Form, about which he makes the claim quoted at the beginning of this chapter.

> These two concepts underlie all other reflection, so inseparably are they bound up with all employment of the understanding. (B322 = A266)

Now, if our human understanding were intuitive and not purely discursive, we would expect something always to be first given in this understanding, and that thus "matter is prior to form," that the understanding must intuit intelligible objects directly, prior to any attempt to discern the universal form of these objects. Such of course is not the case according to Kant; the only content to which we have access are "sensible intuitions" and so

> the form of intuition (as a subjective property of sensibility) is prior to all matter (sensations); space and time come before all appearances and before all data of experience, and are indeed what make the latter at all possible. (B323 = A267)

Again form is subjective, is not itself an object of knowledge but a "condition" for knowledge, is alone what makes synthetic knowledge possible, and since it can and must be known prior to experience, can only be known a priori.

Here again, with such descriptions as these, the epistemological aspects of Kant's enterprise, his attempt to account for the "form" of all possible *knowledge,* come very much to the fore, as does an obvious, simple problem. That is, as Kant puts it, he wants a "Copernican" methodology in philosophy. Very roughly, that will mean that, just as Copernicus, working with physical concepts (matter, motion, velocity, force, etc.) and with mathematics, could establish the laws of astronomy a priori, and then subsequently observe the "conformation" of nature to such laws, so Kant seems to believe he could also establish a priori the formal conditions for all human knowledge, and subsequently argue that these forms must in fact *count* as the forms of all objects of experience, that they were the "conditions" for anything being an "object" at all. Just as clearly as this enterprise can be called "Copernican," however, it also differs greatly from it, and many of those differences will arise frequently in the following study.[14] That is, one could simply ask, What "corresponds" to

---

14. It seems to me that this notion of "a priori" legislation is much more what Kant had in mind with his Copernican analogy than a view of Copernicus as having "explained the *apparent* motions of the heavenly bodies as due to the motion of the observer on the earth"

Copernicus's *mathematics* in providing a "source" for the determination of such forms? What "guides" transcendental inquiry in its search for them? Obviously, the clearest point at which this kind of problem arises is Kant's attempt to deduce specific categories in the Metaphysical Deduction, to arrive at a table of twelve, as well as in his attempts to deduce specific categories in the Analytic of Principles.

That is, one must ask *how* Kant claims to prove that the forms of knowledge or experience are the forms of *objects* of experience (since, obviously, all questions of confirmation through observation are impossible). In fact, one could generally say that such a problem always emerges in any "epistemology"; that one always is faced with the problem of "that to which we can appeal" in determining what the "forms" or rules for knowledge are. As will be shown in the following section, it is with such problems that the relation between epistemology and metaphysics, or between a formal analysis and material claims, becomes most problematic, and where Kant's case in particular is at its most interesting, suggestive, and, often, bewildering.

Now, I don't pretend that it is yet clear what kind of "object of inquiry" such forms of experience actually are. That is just the question I want to pose, in detail. Here I want only to discuss the general outlines of Kant's strategy, and especially the extent to which that strategy represents more a methodological turn from the tradition than a fundamental alteration of many of its goals. Thus far, it has emerged that the special objects of transcendental philosophy are the twin forms of experience, intuitions and concepts, that such forms always involve the *activity* of the knowing subject (Kant will later explain that he is after the *rules* for sensibility and understanding),[15] *and* that, properly understood, such forms can be said to yield the "essence" of all *objects* of experience ("*forma dat esse rei*"). Finally, there is one further element always involved in Kant's theory of form which requires some comment. Namely, such forms are always "subjective."

Such an emphasis on the subjective status of these forms has already been evident in the passages quoted earlier from the Amphiboly. Again, though, the precise nature of this subjectivity is a complicated topic,

---

in a way similar to Kant's explanation of "the *apparent* character of reality as due to the mind of the knower." H. J. Paton, *Kant's Metaphysic of Experience* (New York: Macmillan, 1936), vol. 1, p. 75. For a more detailed discussion, see J. W. Olivier, "Kant's Copernican Analogy," *Kant-Studien* 55 (1964): 505–11.

15. Much more will have to be said about the relation between form and "activity," but I am here disagreeing with the views of Vaihinger and Kemp Smith. See Hans Vaihinger, *Kommentar zu Kants Kritik der reinen Vernunft* (Stuttgart: W. Spemann, 1881–92), vol. 2, p. 59, and Norman Kemp Smith, *A Commentary to Kant's Critique of Pure Reason* (London: Macmillan, 1923), p. 85.

involving elements of Kant's characterization of his position as a "transcendental idealism," and that unusual discipline of "transcendental psychology." It is also one of the most disputed aspects of Kant's position, particularly in recent attempts to reconstruct a Kantian theory of the "bounds of sense" without the "metaphysics of transcendental idealism."[16] At this point, it is possible only to notice that there is indeed an ambiguity to be resolved in this characterization, one that again concerns the *status* of these subjective forms within transcendental philosophy. For, even though Kant does speak of these forms as "lying ready *in* the mind," does claim that a transcendental psychology of the faculties of the mind is possible, and does argue that previous philosophy had erred in not recognizing the subjective and so ideal status of these forms, he also insists, particularly in the Paralogisms, that he is not offering a rationalist theory of mind *malgré lui*; that these forms, while subjective, must be understood as "logical conditions" and not as special kinds of objects of knowledge, and that even the most important condition for all experience, the unity of self-consciousness, should not be understood as a contingent, or even essential, characteristic of human minds, but again as a logical or formal condition for the possibility of experience. It can be shown, however, that Kant himself does not mean by such a notion of "condition" just the necessarily inherent presuppositions involved in the concept of experience, but does mean to defend principles that function as conditions for the possibility of experience itself, and thereby to establish some synthetic claim about human experience. And thus the ambiguity, for he wants to establish such a claim without making a statement in the material mode about human minds, but instead to establish only the formal conditions for experience. Thus as well, it is not the case that Kant simply retained an old-fashioned, rationalist version of idealism, interspersed with a more analytic, less "substantial" view of his task. Unless we accept an extremely unlikely and extensive version of the "patchwork" theory of the *Critique*'s composition, it must be admitted that Kant thought he could *both* establish synthetic a priori conclusions about the necessary forms of experience, and do so without offering a theory about the "structure of the human mind," without a *merely* regressive analysis of actual empirical knowledge, and without a "saltus," as he puts it (A783), to a knowledge of objects. Kant appears to be no more updating such works as Teten's *Psychologie*[17] than to be anticipating

16. This attempt by Strawson is quite understandable, given his notion of what transcendental idealism is, but he doesn't seem to me to have captured Kant's intent. See *The Bounds of Sense* (London: Methuen and Co., 1966), pp. 38–44. Cf. Henry E. Allison, "Transcendental Idealism and Descriptive Metaphysics," *Kant-Studien* 60 (1969): 216–33.

17. As in the interpretation of T. D. Weldon, *Kant's Critique of Pure Reason* (Oxford: The Clarendon Press, 1958).

the twentieth-century concern with conceptual analysis. What he is doing again comes down to how one interprets his theory of form and his claims for the formality of his enterprise, and one central problem in the *Critique* — the focus for the following — is whether he can accomplish such a complicated task.

The above remarks suggest a number of different, though interrelated dimensions to the problem of form that all should be kept in mind together. That is, when Kant tells us that his new methodology is formal, he means: (1) that it is a priori. This claim depends on others, to be worked out in the *Critique,* which show that knowledge of physical and mental objects can only occur in experience a posteriori, that the mind, when considered unaided by sensibility, cannot know the "material" of nature, nor any "purely intelligible" objects. (2) That *what* is known by reason itself in such a priori knowledge (if it is other than analytic) are the necessary and universal "ways" in which the content of knowledge *is* known, "modes" of knowledge, or "forms of experience." His language is quite clear that, in all a priori reflection, "reason is occupied only with itself" (B708 = A680). (3) He takes this knowledge of the "forms" or "modes" or "conditions" for experience to be a knowledge of the forms unique to human subjects, and he concludes that a priori knowledge of these forms is thus restricted in some way, that this position is thus a transcendental "idealism," that these forms are not forms of knowledge of things in themselves, but phenomena. (4) Finally, to use a more contemporary term, transcendental philosophy is "meta-level." It is not an attempt to increase the material of what we know, but it is about, at a "second" level, the forms of such material knowledge.

Immediately as such various strands in Kant's account are brought together, however, the above-expressed ambiguity again develops. For, Kant's methodology, while obviously formal in ways close to that summarized in (4), is just as obviously more than an analysis of some accepted body of knowledge. As is clear in (2), Kant also wants to defend, as a transcendental philosopher, various synthetic a priori judgments, as well as, apparently, various claims about the human subject, even while still maintaining that such "objects" for transcendental reflection are "mere forms." That is, when Kant calls his new, transcendental methodology "formal," he seems to mean *both* that his inquiry will only be concerned with the logical (or "transcendental-logical") structure of knowledge itself, at a "meta-level," *and* that it will *thus* be about special objects of inquiry, "subjective forms" of experience, which forms are said occasionally to "legislate" a certain unity to experience. The former characterization suggests that Kant only wants to analyze the rules for cognitive activity, remaining strictly neutral metaphysically about "the I or he or it which thinks," and about the general characteristics of objects of knowledge. The latter suggests a much more substantive claim about the human mind (as "*Intelligenz*" or "*Spontaneität*") and so the limits of any possible cognition, as well as about the nature of all objects of experience (as "phenomena" since always "subject" to such ideal forms). Indeed, this dual emphasis in Kant's characterization of the formality of his methodology is quite clearly demonstrated in the different emphases placed on each in the long history of Kant interpretation. A brief look at those differences will help clarify the various dimensions suggested by Kant's notion of a formal methodology.

3. Epistemological and Metaphysical Form

Consider, for example, in what sense the above summary of transcendental philosophy is supposed to establish a contrast between that new methodology and "metaphysics," the traditional designation for a priori, philosophic reflection.

Of course, the difference between such a philosophy and metaphysics often seems to be the whole point of embarking on this transcendental course, but the issue still remains somewhat obscure. It is certainly clear that Kant meant to criticize traditional, dogmatic metaphysics on the questions of God and the freedom and immortality of the soul (among other issues). But it is also true that he often uses the word "metaphysics" to describe what he himself is doing ("better progress . . . in the tasks of metaphysics"), that he frequently tells us that his critical works are not at all the positive parts of his system, but merely propaedeutic for a further, elaborate "metaphysics" of the foundations for natural science and a long-planned metaphysics of morals (thus implying that the tasks of pure reason, perhaps even in arriving at synthetic a priori knowledge, are not at all exhausted by the methodology of transcendental philosophy). And then again he often claims that the only kind of metaphysics left after his critical revolution is a practical metaphysics, based on a *non*-cognitive, even if still rational methodology.[18] So, while on first glance it looks as if transcendental philosophy, with its concern for the mode of knowledge of objects, is simply to replace metaphysics, with its concern with knowledge of objects a priori, at second or third glance it is not clear in exactly what sense transcendental philosophy "turns" us from the tasks of metaphysics.

18. That is, Kant seems to have had so many different things to say about the relation between transcendental philosophy and metaphysics that one could, with at least some textual evidence, claim (1) that the *Critique* is a special kind of metaphysics, (2) that it is only a critique of the presuppositions of all rationalist metaphysics, (3) that it is meant to be only a preparation for a legitimate metaphysics of natural science and/or a practical metaphysics of morals, or (4) that the positive sections of the work are only a "theory of knowledge," and no inherent or theoretical connections with metaphysics of any variety are intended.

Now part of this ambiguity certainly has to do with the fact that Kant really never had the chance to finish his entire, massive project. Given his late start, and the enormous amount of time and energy necessary for laying the critical foundations, we only have the most initial indications of what the full relation between critical philosophy and theoretical and practical philosophy in general should look like (and even those indications were sketched by a man whose intellectual powers were certainly not what they were in the "critical" period).[19] However, we do at least have the announced foundations of the unfinished system, and we can at least direct attention to just what the theoretical task of transcendental philosophy is supposed to be.

As we have seen, that philosophy is fairly clearly characterized by a methodology which assumes that "objects conform to our mode of knowledge" and which has as its special "object" just this "mode of knowledge." But just these formulations themselves have led to two very different ways of understanding the critical part of Kant's system. They have recently (thanks to Heimsoeth, Martin, and others) come to be called the "epistemological" and "metaphysical" approaches to the *Critique of Pure Reason*.[20]

Much of the problem at stake in such different interpretations turns on the question of methodological "priority" in philosophy; at issue is which set of questions should be "prior," should be asked and answered first, independent of others, in a properly grounded philosophy. Put simply, the so-called epistemological view stresses Kant's claim (more properly, his way of completing Descartes's) to have prepared the way for future work by asking first such questions as, What is human knowledge, is there any, what kinds of things can human beings know, how do they gain knowledge? and the like. And the dispute with a more metaphysical view of Kant turns on whether in fact such questions *can* be asked independent of other, more "substantive" questions, such as those concerning the "human subject" or mind, or even what there is to be known in general; and on how we should interpret Kant's own answers to that first set of questions, particularly his claims to have arrived at synthetic a

19. This point is made quite well in Gerold Prauss's introduction to *Kant: Zur Deutung seiner Theorie von Erkennen und Handeln,* ed. G. Prauss (Köln: Kiepenheuer und Witsch, 1973), pp. 11–23.

20. Heidegger, Heimsoeth, Martin, and Krüger are probably the leaders of the metaphysical (sometimes called ontological) school of interpretation. A brief summary of their approach can be found in M. J. Scott-Taggart, "Recent Work on the Philosophy of Kant," in *Kant Studies Today,* ed. L. W. Beck (La Salle, Ill.: Open Court, 1969), pp. 1–71. There are some recent works which are simply impossible to categorize in these terms. Among others, I would include Gerold Prauss, *Kant und das Problem der Dinge an sich* (Bonn: Bouvier, 1974), and Wilfrid Sellars, *Science and Metaphysics* (New York: Humanities Press, 1968).

priori knowledge about *Gegenstände überhaupt,* and to have grounded a new, rational metaphysics.[21]

The former emphasis, certainly present in Kant, begins with the suspicion that human reason is finite, and often even deceptive, that we can pose questions to ourselves that we cannot answer (or in a later tradition, that are not "really" questions), and that we must be sure about the limits of our ability before we attempt such answers. And the latter tradition emphasizes that any answer about such limits must itself be a kind of "metaphysical" answer, more than an analysis of the formal conditions of knowledge, but itself a special kind *of* knowledge.

Of course, even the view that Kant's *Critique* is an analysis of the kinds of claims to know rather than an independent attempt at knowledge often claims quite a bit even for this attempt. One can accept Kant's claim that his transcendental philosophy provides only "the schema of possible experience," and in the *Prolegomena* that "the word 'transcendental' never signifies with me the relation of knowledge to an object, but only that to our faculty of knowledge,"[22] even while one realizes how much such an inquiry can accomplish. Since Kant's idealism intends to prove that these forms of knowledge constitute the possibility of any relation between subject and object, it is clear that Kant means for his analysis to delimit "the real," insofar as reality can be experienced by human subjects. His "epistemology," then, thanks to his idealism, is also a "metaphysics of experience."[23]

However, it is also clear that Kant meant to be very cautious in drawing any substantive conclusions about "actuality" (*Wirklichkeit*) from his analysis of the "conditions for knowledge." He notes constantly that while our knowledge is limited to "phenomena," there is no justifiable way of proceeding from that claim to any about being, or "things in themselves." Hence he often explicitly and deliberately stresses the formal and epistemological nature of his enterprise, writing, "Now it is indeed very evident that I cannot know as an object that which I must presuppose in order to know any object" (A402), and his famous, "and the proud name of Ontology . . . must give way to the modest title of a

---

21. A clear statement of the claim that there cannot be any *"Erkenntnisfrage"* without a *"Seinsfrage"* can be found in Nicolai Hartmann, "Wie ist kritische Ontologie überhaupt möglich," in his *Kleinere Schriften* (Berlin: de Gruyter, 1955–58), vol. 1, pp. 268–69.

22. Kant, *Prolegomena, Gesammelte Schriften,* vol. 4, p. 293. All English quotations from the *Prolegomena* are from L. W. Beck's translation, *Prolegomena to Any Future Metaphysics* (Indianapolis: Bobbs-Merrill, 1950). I have occasionally inserted the German for the sake of clarity.

23. H. J. Paton, *Kant's Metaphysic of Experience.* See also the discussions by Graham Bird, *Kant's Theory of Knowledge* (New York: Humanities Press, 1973), p. 38; R. P. Wolff, *Kant's Theory of Mental Activity* (Cambridge: Harvard University Press, 1963), p. 320; and the *Critique,* B80–81 = A56.

mere analytic of the understanding" (B304 = A247). He even goes so far at
one point as to say,

> The greatest and perhaps sole use of all philosophy of pure reason is therefore
> only negative; namely because it serves not as an organon for the extension of
> knowledge, but only as a discipline, for the determination of its limits, and instead
> of discovering truth, has only the modest merit of guarding against error.
> (B823 = A795)

However, it is by no means clear that we have said very much at all about
Kant's intentions in the *Critique* by describing that work as a "theory of
knowledge." For, although that "analytic of the understanding" is, as we
shall see in much greater detail, certainly meant to be a "formal" enterprise
(that is, not a direct attempt to increase the *material* of our knowledge), it is
not so clear just *what* this kind of formal knowledge is, or how we are to
assess the results of his analytic.

The ambiguous possibilities inherent in this notion of a "transcendental
knowledge" were well exploited by Kant's immediate successors in that
decidedly metaphysical movement known as German Idealism. Rather than
the above claims about the limitations of his enterprise, philosophers like
Fichte, Schelling, and Hegel took instead as their guiding teaching from
Kant such claims as those in the Highest Principle of Synthetic Judgments,
that "the conditions for the possibility of experience are at the same time the
conditions for the possibility of objects of experience." Thus, they reasoned,
it should be possible to complete theoretical philosophy's task of a knowledge of objects in general, but along what they regarded as Kantian lines, by
means of an analysis of the "source" or ground of such objects in the
transcendental subject, the self-identity of the Ego, or "the Absolute."[24] Of
course, as is well known, emphasizing such tendencies in Kant ultimately
required that much else in his project be revised. But it is certainly true that
the directions such thinkers took are clearly pointed to by many of the things
Kant said, and (again as will be shown in more detail) by the problems left
once his own limitations on transcendental philosophy are accepted.[25]

24. Of course, there are other interpreters of Kant who do not go so far as the
philosophers of identity in stressing Kant's "metaphysical motives." See, inter alia, Heinz
Heimsoeth, "Metaphysical Motives in the Development of Critical Idealism," in *Kant:
Disputed Questions*, ed. Moltke Gram (Chicago: Quadrangle, 1967), and his commentary, *Transzendentale Dialektik*, vols. 1–4 (Berlin: de Gruyter, 1969). A brief rejection of
this view of Kant can be found in W. H. Walsh, *Kant's Criticism of Metaphysics* (Edinburgh: Edinburgh University Press, 1975), p. 4. Walsh, though, ignores the fact that Kant
did *call* much of his moral philosophy and theory of science a "metaphysics." Cf. Gerhard
Krüger, *Philosophie und Moral in der kantischen Kritik*, 2d ed. (Tübingen: J. C. B. Mohr,
1967). See especially the important, and unfortunately neglected, essay reprinted in this
edition, "Der Maßstab der kantischen Kritik," pp. 237–68. Cf. also Gottfried Martin,
Immanuel Kant, Ontologie und Wissenschaftstheorie.

25. A detailed examination of the various twists and turns taken after Kant on such issues

Now again, it is not hard to find numerous passages in the *Critique* which can support either view, either that the *Critique* should be viewed as an analysis of the conditions for scientific or ordinary knowledge, or that it offers a novel kind of metaphysical knowledge *about* all possible objects of experience. There are, though, distinct dangers in taking either view to extremes. One such liability is obvious in those interpretations which construe Kant's doctrines of phenomenal knowledge as a phenomenalism, or which attribute to him the view that "to be" *is*, in some sense, "to be experienced." This makes Kant a metaphysician of sorts, but quite a bad one. (It is also a characterization of his position that most infuriated him. See chapter 7.) Another problem in opting for one alternative to the exclusion of the other is clearly evident in recent works which attempt a wholly epistemological interpretation, which see the *Critique* as demonstrating the limits on any *concept* of empirical knowledge that we could make intelligible to ourselves, and which encourage us to jettison the "metaphysics of transcendental idealism." Such works must, quite self-consciously, abandon one of Kant's most cherished goals — defending the *synthetic* nature of the a priori results of his analysis. Viewing transcendental philosophy as an extended analysis of the concept of experience (instead of as a more direct investigation of the possibility of experience itself) results instead, as is freely admitted, in "complexly" analytic propositions.[26] Regardless of the advantages of such a reconstruction of Kant, it is at least clear that we have thereby seriously altered what he meant by transcendental philosophy, and are not thereby much closer to understanding what it is supposed to be.[27]

More seriously, it is also not clear how much of the rest of Kant's

---

can be found in Richard Kroner, *Von Kant bis Hegel* (Tübingen: J. C. B. Mohr, 1961). Kroner's overall emphasis is, appropriately, on reactions to problems in Kant's practical philosophy, but the "speculative" interpretation of Kantianism is clear throughout.

26. The phrase is Jonathan Bennett's, in *Kant's Analytic* (Cambridge: Cambridge University Press, 1966), p. 14. In general, as must be the case in any limited interpretation, I shall not be discussing a number of important critical themes in the following, including the analytic-synthetic distinction. My own view of the unlikelihood of any reductionist approach to Kant's doctrine of the synthetic a priori would follow L. W. Beck's lead in "Can Kant's Synthetic Judgments Be Made Analytic?" in *Kant, A Collection of Critical Essays*, ed. R. P. Wolff (Garden City: Doubleday Anchor, 1967), pp. 3–22; as well as Kant's own remarks in his response to Eberhard. Cf. *The Kant-Eberhard Controversy*, trans. Henry Allison (Baltimore: The Johns Hopkins University Press, 1974), pp. 139–56.

27. Of course, there is always a tension, in any philosophic commentary, between historical accuracy and what some call a "rational reconstruction." All that I can say about that issue is that a great deal can be gained from going as far as possible in attempting to state Kant's case in his terms; that, especially, the "problems" that emerge will look less like Kant's "mistakes" and more like general difficulties with his project if one keeps in mind his own understanding of the context of various problems. But such a claim can only be defended *in concreto* in the following.

project can be defended when such a severe epistemological limitation is placed on it. For example, Kant clearly insists that he wishes to set, once and for all, the "limits" of human knowledge, those limits beyond which speculation is a "Herumtappen," a kind of whistling in the dark.[28] Such cannot, though, be done ad hoc merely by showing that this or that attempt to answer this or that question runs aground, or has no real standards by which to direct its enquiry. Kant's own simile is helpful in stressing this point.

> Our reason is not like a plane indefinitely far extended, whose limits are known only generally, but must rather be compared to a sphere, the radius of which can be determined from the curvature of the arc of its surface (from the nature of synthetic a priori propositions), whereby its contents and limits can be specified with the same certainty. (B791 = A762)

To do this, Kant must have transcendental philosophy actually establish what those limits are, formally, and not simply analyze the concept of experience as we are able, at our present level of conceptual clarity, to understand it. *That* kind of a "material" base or ground for analysis he would clearly regard as far too contingent, incapable of fully providing the answer to the *quid iuris* about pure knowledge that will refute the skeptic. Instead, he says he wants to establish the conditions for experience itself, an attempt that one does not have to regard as transcendental psychology to see as something more than a complex analysis of the concept of experience we happen to possess. In sum, Kant quite clearly did intend to establish in this transcendental philosophy an "a priori relation to objects." Such indeed is the very difference between a general or wholly "formal" logic and a "transcendental logic."

Nevertheless, such a logic was also clearly meant to be, in some sense, formal, and that is what, from a Kantian perspective, is often lost in metaphysical interpretations of a nonphenomenalist variety. The idealists who followed Kant certainly wanted to make more of the "first principle" than he did, but, again with respect to Kant's intentions, they too had to abandon many central Kantian restrictions, in this case that the "unity of apperception" was exclusively a *formal,* and in no way a substantive, principle. In fact, they had to abandon (as did Husserl, for different reasons, later)[29] the important Kantian claim that all a priori knowledge

28. On the determinateness, or "once and for all" character, of these limits, see discussion in the *Prolegomena* of "Grenzen" and "Schranken," section 57, *Gesammelte Schriften,* vol. 4, pp. 350–54. This difference also accounts for a difference between a *Kritik* and what he calls a *Zensur,* and helps clarify his own view of his relation to Hume. A good discussion of this topic can be found in Krüger, *Philosophie und Moral,* section 24. He makes use of the distinction to help establish his case that, for Kant, a true self-*criticism* by reason is a practical (or moral) task for reason.

29. The clearest phenomenological discussion of the difference between a "formal" and a

was exclusively formal, and not directly about any object of knowledge. Once this departure is made, though, and Kant's principle of apperception is interpreted so metaphysically, many of the dangers Kant obviously worried about are quickly evident. Most significant, it is hard to determine the precise status of such a metaphysical subject, the nature of our access to it, the kind of knowledge we have about it, and the relation between such a priori and a posteriori knowledge.[30] It also goes without saying that such an absolutizing of Kant's enterprise must eliminate as well his doctrine of the "thing in itself," and many of the restrictions he placed on his results by means of that doctrine. Indeed, one could say that the doctrine of things in themselves is as unpleasant a reminder of how much such views have departed from Kant in this view as is the doctrine of synthetic a priori judgments in the former interpretation.

One lesson one could draw from such a preliminary look at various different emphases in the literature is that perhaps no overall consistent interpretation of Kant can be formulated. Something will simply have to be given up somewhere. Another might be that this opposition between metaphysical and epistemological views is a false one, that no philosopher can say everything at once, that of course there are various tendencies present in the *Critique,* but there is nothing that strange in presenting an analysis of human knowledge and then trying to draw some substantive conclusions from it. Both such responses seem to me reasonable at this stage, but I think a more concrete lesson emerges from this brief overview. Namely, what emerges from this look at various ways of interpreting what transcendental philosophy is, is that the single most important issue in coming to a decision about that problem lies in deciding what transcendental philosophy is *about,* what this special object it has — "our mode of knowledge" — really amounts to. As I shall try to show, coming to a decision about that, and looking at the difficulties involved in Kant's own formulations of this object, will not only help in understanding the transcendental turn, but will also, I hope, raise general issues involved in any attempt to turn philosophy to an exclusive, foundational concern with our "mode of knowledge." Further, as I think will

---

"material" a priori occurs in Scheler, *Der Formalismus in der Ethik.* Also important in such a discussion would be Nicholai Hartmann, "Diesseits von Idealismus und Realismus," *Kant-Studien* 29 (1924): 160–206; and Adolph Reinach, *Gesammelte Schriften* (Halle, 1921), pp. 6, 171, 397. Reinach insists on what he calls a "phenomenological a priori," which as a property of *Sachverhalte* is not an epistemological category.

30. I am thinking here of the "Young Hegelian" attempt to preserve Kant's idealism, but to substitute an empirical and historical subject for Kant's transcendental subject. A clear manifestation of this sort of strategy in a more contemporary thinker: Max Horkheimer, "Traditional and Critical Theory," in *Critical Theory* (New York: Seabury Press, 1972), p. 188 ff.

become clear in the following, it is just the unusual features of this type of inquiry that make it so very dificult to place the *Critique* within the traditional boundaries of epistemology or metaphysics. Indeed, some of the ambiguities in Kant's project may make questionable those very boundaries themselves.

4. Some Limitations

The above discussion might seem to call for quite an exhaustive commentary on virtually all the important passages of the *Critique of Pure Reason*. After all, one very general way of restating the above question is to ask how Kant thinks transcendental philosophy itself, as an a priori enterprise with synthetic results, is possible; and that question simply seems to take in everything.

However, the following is in no sense a commentary on the whole of the *Critique*. First of all, while introducing material from other passages where required, I have focused attention on those sections Kant himself admits are foundational for everything else he wants to say — the Transcendental Aesthetic and the Transcendental Analytic. It is also in these sections that Kant presents his case for the positive results of his critical philosophy, the substantive, even if still somehow formal, claims about experience he wants to defend. Second, even within these sections, I shall not discuss a number of important themes, argued for at length by Kant. My interest is restricted more to those topics I think directly illuminate the strengths and weaknesses of the transcendental turn itself and its formality, and so is, if you will, more a kind of meta-level interest. I shall be interested in such things as *how* Kant intends to establish many of the claims mentioned earlier as so controversial in the literature: that sensations are only "material" elements in knowledge, that pure intuitions are "formal"; that concepts, both pure and empirical, are "rules" for synthesis, and so are only "forms of the thought of an object"; that a "schematism" for such concepts is required; that the "supreme" condition for all experience, the "transcendental unity of apperception," must be understood as only a formal principle; or that the main result of transcendental philosophy is the knowledge that all human knowledge is only of "appearances." That is, there is simply a difference in Kant between the synthetic a priori judgments explicitly defended as necessary conditions for the possibility of experience (substance, causality, etc.) and the "transcendental" a priori claims he makes *in support* of such assertions.[31] It is these latter kinds of questions, I am suggesting, which pose the greatest difficulty for Kant's transcendentalism, that I want to concentrate

---

31. This is put well by L. W. Beck in "Towards a Meta-Critique of Pure Reason," republished in *Essays on Kant and Hume* (New Haven: Yale University Press, 1978), p. 25.

on in the following, and that I think are illuminated in common by the general problem of form. In other words, cut off from an empirical or rationalist view of mind, *and* from concepts and scientific theories simply there "to-be-analyzed," one can ask: Is transcendental philosophy "suspended from nothing in heaven and supported by nothing on earth"?[32]

Finally, I shall be especially concerned with a problem that arises once some of Kant's most important presuppositions are accepted. Kant's analysis of the forms of experience, however interpreted, commits him to some account of the relation between these pure forms and the "material" of experience. Kant was quite proud that his transcendental idealism was only a *formal* idealism, that the "material" of knowledge is supplied "from without," empirically, by contact with the external world. If that formal idealism is to be successful, we must be able to understand its connection with this "material" or empirical *realism,* and this question will require discussion of numerous features of that realism not often analyzed, features indeed often left undeveloped by Kant himself.[33]

To begin to answer such questions, I turn first to the initial presentation of his theory of "matter and form," his theory of sensations and intuitions.

---

32. Ibid., p. 30. Further, I agree with Henry Allison's statement of the problem in "Kant's Transcendental Humanism," *The Monist* 55, no. 2 (April 1971): 194, 199. I am, however, not sure that Kant can do what Allison there claims he must do, if his transcendental philosophy is to be a success. At least in this article, Allison himself must import the language of transcendental phenomenology for help (204).

33. Even though there is much to be gained by examining the history of Kant's use of the notion of form, I haven't the space for such a discussion here. Graubner has some interesting things to say about that background in the first part of *Form und Wesen* (pp. 37–92). I am interested in the use of the term in the so-called critical period; after Kant's 1770 *Dissertation, On the Form and Principles of the Sensible and Intelligible World, Gesammelte Schriften,* vol. 2. A number of important "critical" characterizations of form are already prominent there, among many: the importance of the forms of intuition for distinguishing a priori between logical and real possibility (pp. 388–89); form as a principle of "*Beiordnung*" or unification (p. 390); form as a "law of the mind" (*Gesetz des Gemüts*) (p. 393), and especially p. 398: "Insofar as one considers the world as phenomenon, that is in relation to the sensibility of the human power of knowledge, one does not recognize any other ground of form than a subjective one."

2
Sensations

That in appearance which corresponds to sensation I name its matter, but that which determines that the manifold of appearances can be ordered in certain relations, I name the form of appearances. (B34 = A20)

Space and time are its (our mode of perceiving objects) pure forms, and sensation in general its matter. (B60 = A42)

The form of intuition (as a subjective property of sensibility) is prior to all matter (sensations). (B323 = A267)

1. Kant's Problem

The problem of explaining knowledge gained by means of sensation is obviously of fundamental importance for any theory which ultimately claims that *all* cognition is based on, derived from, or reducible to such sensory knowledge. Conversely, one might expect that a theory like Kant's, so famous for its critique of empiricism and so insistent on the subjective status of forms which "legislate" unity to all experience, would be much less concerned with the details of sensory apprehension. Such problems might appear to sink below the bottom line of what is transcendentally interesting.[1] To an extent, that would be a correct expectation. We certainly do not find Kant engaged in any detailed investigation of the nature of "impressions" or in an "impression hunt" when concerned about some epistemic claim, and we find little discussion of missing shades of color, primary and secondary qualities, and the like. But it would be most inaccurate to remain content with this sense of Kant's idealist indifference to such traditionally empiricist problems. For one thing, Kant intends, at least, to beg no questions concerning his argument about the necessity and constitutive role of such ideal forms of experience.[2] That is, as part of that case he must show that sensory awareness cannot do by itself what the empiricists said it could. That negative case

1. In his *Anthropologie in pragmatischer Hinsicht,* Kant remarks that sensation has acquired a "bad reputation," and even that it is mere "rabble" (*Pöbel*); *Gesammelte Schriften,* vol. 7, pp. 143 and 144.
2. There is a long history of discussion about this issue of begging the question by already assuming a conception of experience which will yield what Kant wants. Probably the

alone commits him to *some* views about sensation, and already indicates that those views will be important in the overall case for his idealism. Indeed, we shall find that Kant was quite interested in denying a number of alternate accounts of sensation; he is after so-called "classical" realism, the "unclear representation" theories of the rationalists as well as the "processing" or "inferring" models of the phenomenalists. If all these denials are to count as contrasts with his own position, obviously there must be such a position, and that position must be supported independently, not by appeal to later arguments which often already presuppose it. For another thing, Kant was quite proud of what he termed his "empirical realism," and that too would not be intelligible without some position on sensation. Roughly, that position is that sensory awareness is not in any sense a mode of (even very unclear) knowledge, that it is only the mere "material" of experience. This is admittedly not an altogether pellucid metaphor, and I want to investigate what Kant means by it, how he supports the claim, and what role the thesis plays in his overall defense of formal idealism.

It might be best to begin, though, by noting one context in which a "theory of sensation" is indeed a topic of little interest for Kant, and another in which the issue is so deeply connected with his whole project that it cannot fruitfully be discussed separately. In the former case, Kant is relatively uninterested in the empirical or, as he might say, "physiological" details of sensation. In that context, "how the senses work" is an empirical question like any other about the phenomenal world, and has no direct role to play in a transcendental analysis. Like all empirical knowledge, it presupposes a transcendental justification of knowledge itself. There is little to be gained, then, for epistemology, by direct experimental attention to the details of our sensory contact with the world, prior to an independent justification of this and all other forms of knowledge. (Or, to put the point in more contemporary language, for Kant, any so-called naturalized epistemology begs the important question, since it needs to presuppose a legitimate knowledge of "nature" just in order to naturalize epistemology.) Moreover, Kant also implies that it is misguided to *begin* any theory of knowledge with doubts about the "untrustworthiness" of the senses.[3] For him, such questions about sen-

---

best-known formulation of the charge is C. I. Lewis's in *An Analysis of Knowledge and Valuation* (La Salle, Ill.: Open Court, 1946), pp. 161–62, made with respect to the Second Analogy. Cf. L. W. Beck's discussion of the issue in "Can Kant's Synthetic Judgments be Made Analytic?" in R. P. Wolff (ed.), *Kant, A Collection of Critical Essays* (New York: Doubleday Anchor, 1967), p. 13. The issue is also important to the whole "transcendental arguments" controversy, which I discuss in more detail in chapter 6. Cf. also Richard Aquila, "Two Kinds of Transcendental Arguments in Kant," *Kant-Studien* 67 (1976): 1–19.

3. Cf. his discussion in the *Anthropologie* on the issue of the dubitability of the senses, p. 146.

sation are also empirical. They presuppose a criterion of trustworthiness or knowledge and, with respect to the most famous such doubt, there is no reason to attempt to understand such principles by a methodological decision to adopt the criterion of mathematical certainty. In both contexts, then, the issue of *Empfindung* is an empirical one, either as a question concerning the physiological structure of the human sensory apparatus or as regards some specific issue concerning the reliability of an individual epistemic claim based on sensory information, an issue to be decided on the basis of evidence, given a successful, transcendental account of knowledge itself.

In another way, though, the issue of sensation can be viewed as crucial to, but almost inseparable from, the core of Kant's overall project. As indicated above, he must be careful not to beg any questions in his appeal to the necessary conditions for any experience. Avoiding this charge, however, involves him in a complex, multilevel defense of one of the basic principles of his whole epistemology: his critique of intellectual intuition, and the "discursive" theory of the understanding central to that critique. That is, if we are looking for some justification of Kant's claim that sensory awareness is not, considered by itself, a mode of knowledge, but only the material of knowledge, a very broad answer to such a query surely must involve his theory of the necessity of synthesis in *all* knowledge.[4] Kant will argue in great detail that there *cannot* be a determinate awareness of "unity" in sensation, that there must be judgment or synthesis in order for such awareness to occur, and finally that there must be, a priori, rules for such judgments. All of this is established by appeal to the "highest" condition for any experience, the "synthetic unity of apperception," and can only be fairly assessed by attention to the details of the Transcendental Deduction. However, it would be unfair to Kant, and to the issue itself, to consider the argument there the sole justification of Kant's views on sensation. For one thing, it is not always possible to disentangle what Kant assumes in such an argument from what he considers part of his conclusion. The direct task of the Deduction is to prove that the categories have objective validity, and is not explicitly involved in any clearly announced, independent proof either that the understanding is discursive, that it can give itself no content but can only organize and discriminate what comes from without, or that "no unity comes to us from the senses." Although I think such claims are part of what Kant is demonstrating in the Deduction and Schematism, and shall

4. This kind of argument is made persuasively by Dieter Henrich in *Identität und Objecktivität* (Heidelberg: Carl Winter, 1976), section 2, "Objeckt und Urteil," pp. 16–53. I discuss Henrich's interpretation in more detail in chapter 6, and return there to some of the problems which arise here.

deal with them again in chapters 5 and 6, Kant's larger interests (in the possibility of synthetic a priori knowledge) so cloud the issue there that it is prudent to investigate any independent reasons he may have had for construing sensation as the "material" of knowledge. This is especially important since this account of sensation as "matter" is a crucial element in Kant's criticism of any empiricist "foundationalism." It is, after all, his critique of "the myth of the given," and can, I believe, be at least partly isolated from his larger concerns.

Said another way, Kant's views on the relation between the doctrines of the Analytic and his account of sensation can be put as follows. Kant will indeed argue that synthesis is necessary in any determinate, empirical awareness. Representations are never simply objects seen in the mind's eye, but judgments *that* this is a such and such, and so forth. But this thesis alone does not logically presuppose, and it certainly is not logically equivalent to, Kant's thesis that sensation is the "matter" of knowledge. Neither is true because the discursivity thesis does not establish by itself what is united by the understanding in judgment, where that content comes from, or how we determine in empirical knowledge what belongs together with what. Without more ado, the discursivity thesis is compatible with claims that the content of thought is recollected from a former life, invented by the imagination, or supplied by God.[5] Morever, Kant himself does not directly attempt to establish his views on sensation by appeal to these larger claims. He appears to have simply held various views on sensation independently, to have believed in what some have called an "atomistic" theory — that there was no complex unity within or among sensations, that they were "absolute unities."

However, even when the problem of sensation is thus isolated and circumscribed, one still faces a well-known ambiguity in his account, one that will have to be addressed in what follows. Put quite simply at the outset, that ambiguity turns on the dual characterization Kant gives of the sensory manifold. On the one hand such a manifold is exclusively to be understood as the "material" of experience, and that means, for Kant, that it is undifferentiated and indeterminate. As we have seen, this means that the mere possession of sense impressions is in no sense to be taken as having knowledge of any kind, even inferior. On the other hand, Kant's often repeated description of the distinction between his own and other "idealisms" is his insistence that sensory receptivity plays a decisive role in his epistemology, that the human intellectual faculty can provide itself with no content, but must be given such a content from without, and

---

5. Said another way, the intellect may not be intuitive, but that by itself does not establish that sensibility is not (at least not in the classical sense of passive reception of form). Kant is aware of this distinction at B323 = A267 and B333 = A277.

must be guided by such received material in empirical knowledge. Thus sensations, considered by themselves, are "blind," and yet somehow decisively direct our empirical knowledge.

Such initial reflections on Kant's theory of sensation thus suggest the need for answers to two separate questions: (1) Aside from the general case for the role of synthesis in all knowledge, what independent arguments does Kant provide for his claim that sensory awareness considered by itself is "formless" and hence not a mode of and hardly a "foundation" for knowledge? and (2) How should we understand the results of this claim about sensory matter for Kant's empirical "realism"? Two brief arguments can be identified and isolated in answer to the first question (sections 2 and 3 below). I shall argue that they establish some but not all of what Kant claims, and in section 4 shall answer the second by examining a recent reconstruction of a plausible Kantian response to (2).

2. Sensations as Matter: Kant's Argument

It is often quite correctly remarked that anyone looking for Kant's clearest and most decisive break with both the rationalist and empiricist traditions would do well to consider carefully his claim that all of our knowledge involves two fundamentally different faculties working in unison, faculties usually named "sensibility" and "understanding."[6] On Kant's reading of the history of philosophy, the most serious problems experienced by his predecessors involved misinterpretations of the nature and relation of these faculties. The rationalist tradition, exemplified most clearly by Leibniz, mistakenly considered sensibility a less clear version of the faculty of intellectual representation, and so "intellectualized appearances"; on the other hand, the empiricists, especially Locke, "sensualized" all concepts of the understanding by considering such concepts "empirical or abstracted concepts of reflection," that is, reducible to sensible representations. Their common error lay in not realizing that these faculties were not at all part of a continuous mental capacity, but were rather "quite different sources of representation." Kant's best-known statement of his own view of the matter occurs at B74 = A52 ff.:

6. The scholar who has made this point most clearly and most astutely is Lewis White Beck, in "Kant's Strategy," reprinted in his *Essays on Kant and Hume* (New Haven: Yale University Press, 1978), pp. 3–19, and *Early German Philosophy* (Cambridge: Harvard University Press, 1969), p. 458. Walsh, in *Kant's Criticism of Metaphysics* (Edinburgh: Edinburgh University Press, 1975), also notes how important such a distinction is for Kant's criticism of metaphysics. To anticipate a bit, I agree with such claims about the foundational status of the distinction, but want to raise some doubts about the possibility of such a strong distinction, and about how Kant argues for it. The most direct, and ultimately most revealing, contrast with Kant's position would be Aristotle's in the *De Anima*; but that is certainly enough of an issue for a separate book.

Intuitions and concepts, constitute therefore the elements of all our knowledge. . . . Pure intuitions, therefore, contain only the form under which
something is intuited; the pure concept only the form of the thought of an
object in general. . . . These two powers or capacities cannot exchange their
functions. The understanding can intuit nothing, the senses can think nothing.
Only through their union can knowledge arise. But that is no reason for
confounding the contribution of either with that of the other. We therefore
distinguish the science of the rules of sensibility in general, that is aesthetic,
from the science of the rules of the understanding in general, that is, logic.

This justly famous passage already contains the essence of Kant's
reaction to virtually all prior philosophy, and it is worth noting how much
is compressed into his assertion that "the understanding can intuit nothing, the senses can think nothing." To say in this way that the understanding is wholly discursive and not intuitive means that the human
intellect considered *by itself* has no special access — indeed, no access at
all — to the way things are. Moreover, it is to imply, as Kant will
frequently point out, that all that the intellect can know a priori is *itself*,
its own "rules" for the unification and discrimination of material provided
by sensible contact with the world. This, in a nutshell, *is* Kantian
formalism, and clearly marks his break with rationalism from Parmenides
to Leibniz.

Further, although not tied logically to this discursivity thesis, Kant's
account of sensation is quite a reasonable complement to it. It accounts
for how we *do* obtain the material of cognition, and it too has a large
consequence for Kant's whole position. For, if sensation is not an unclear
mode of representation, indeed not a mode of representation at all, then
what it is that I know by means of sensation cannot be said to be "reality
as it is in itself" (obscurely but directly conveyed by the senses). That
content is known only as a *result* of this affection, as represent*ed*, or as
subject to (and only as subject to) the distinctly human powers of
representing. As we shall see, this all doesn't amount to a "two worlds"
theory or a "veil or perception" phenomenalism, but it is a central
element in Kant's attack on all "transcendental realism."

However important this distinction is, though, most of the famous
statements about it are hardly clear-cut explanations of what it really
amounts to. For example, in the above quotation, while intuitions and
concepts appear indeed to be "quite different," they are nonetheless also
clearly associated as "pure forms," and therefore, as we have already
seen, both "subjective" and capable of being known a priori. This
assimilation seems to mean here that we should consider *both* intuitions
and concepts as "*powers* or *capacities* of the mind." Further, in a way that
will have to be dealt with in the next chapter, Kant seems intent on
making out some theoretical difference between "sensations," always

called the "matter" of experience, and intuitions, especially the pure forms of intuitions, space and time. However, in the above passage, in trying to contrast intuitions and concepts, he says only that "the senses can think nothing, the understanding can intuit nothing," apparently identifying sensation and intuition. The whole issue is made even more complicated by the fact that Kant, even though maintaining this theory of intuition as a power or capacity (*Vermögen, Fähigkeiten*) generally contrasts "intuition" and "understanding" as a contrast between "receptivity" and "spontaneity." It seems to be stretching the senses of *Vermögen* and *Fähigkeiten* quite thin to say that receiving impressions is something we have the ability to *do*.[7]

Naturally, nothing is easier, especially with a writer like Kant, than to collect random passages which, in different contexts, seem to say quite different, even contradictory things. However, this present problem of precisely distinguishing what Kant means by "sensation," "intuition," "pure intuition," "form of intuition," "form of sensibility," and other related terms does not arise only from carelessness on Kant's part. This distinction between the respective roles played by whatever it is that results from the impingement of the physical world on our senses, and what we say, or think about, or "do" with the results of such impingement, is indeed at the heart of Kant's enterprise, most important for the clarification of his own form of idealism, and his relation to philosophers before and after him. That fact, though, and the fact that Kant thought his ability to make this distinction allowed him to reconstruct finally his balanced synthesis between transcendental idealism and empirical realism, do not alone mean that the distinction *can* be drawn given the requirements Kant has set for transcendental philosophy.

His first try at defining these terms occurs at the beginning of the Transcendental Aesthetic. In fact, he begins with a flurry of definitions (B33 = A19 ff.). Three terms are especially important: sensation (*Empfindung*), intuition (*Anschauung*), and appearance (*Erscheinung*).

"The effect of an object upon the faculty of representation so far as we are affected by it, is sensation." Kant had, just prior to this official definition, remarked that it was "by means of sensibility" (*vermittelst der Sinnlichkeit*) that objects were given to us, and that, as an apparently independent element in this analysis of our immediate relation to objects, these sensations then "yield" or provide us with (*liefert uns*) intuitions (*Anschauungen*). Intuitions related to objects *through* sensation are said

7. More has to be said about the issue of the separation of various topics in Kant's theory, and I do so in chapter 3. Klaus Reich has some interesting, though highly speculative, things to say about the general order of presentation in the Aesthetic in his *Die Vollständigkeit der kantischen Urteilstafel* (Berlin: Diss. Rostock, 1932). Cf. especially his remarks on the philosophical significance of these "meta-critical" considerations, p. 60 ff.

to be empirical and the "undetermined object of an empirical intuition is called an appearance [*Erscheinung*]."[8] These definitions alone give rise immediately to one of the most important points of possible dispute: what Kant says directly *about* this manifold of sense impressions, and the role it can and cannot play in empirical knowledge. As we have already seen, the most important aspect of that description is Kant's claim that, considered as such a manifold, sensations cannot in any sense be considered a mode of knowledge, or determinate representations at all.[9] Relation to an object is something that must always be *established* by the understanding in judgment, and it must be established just because no immediate relation to objects is contained in sensation. He is also claiming, more generally, that sensory awareness cannot be considered an awareness of anything complex or determinate at all. A manifold is so determinate only when "thought" in a determinate way, whether we only notice the subjective contents of inner sense, or intend some relation to an outer object. Such, at any rate, appears to be the force of his constant characterization of sensation as only the "manner in which we are affected by objects," and his claim that it provides the mere *matter* of experience.

In one (fairly loose) sense, such a result should not be surprising at this point. Considered apart from any description, any discrimination on the part of the subject, or any "conceptualizing," such a theoretically isolated manifold turns out to *be* undiscriminated, a "blank" state for which no conceptual description, however minimalist, would be appropriate. Just by definition so far, even "whiffs," "patches," and "hues" are of no help in understanding this purely given manifold. Such descriptions of the "contents of inner sense" count as much as "outer sense" object language as a mediated knowledge of objects, only here inner objects.

Great care, though, needs to be exercised in so construing this descrip-

---

8. The very notion of an undetermined *object* of intuition poses problems in itself. The most exhaustive analysis of these problems is Gerold Prauss's in *Erscheinung bei Kant* (Berlin: de Gruyter, 1971). I discuss Prauss's whole interpretation in chapters 6 and 7. Ingeborg Heidemann, in her rather dense *Spontaneität und Zeitlichkeit* (Köln: Kölner Universität Verlag, 1958), points out how Kant's statement of the problem changes the question of *das Gegebene* from a "*woher*" to a "*wofür*" question, p. 33 ff.

9. Kant is often (though not always) careful to point out that we do not "represent" by sensing, but through (*durch*) sensation (B147), or, as in the passage quoted above, "by means of" sensation. Cf. also his parenthetical explanation of *Wahrnehmung* as "*mit Empfindung begleitete Vorstellungen*" (B147). Perceptions are perceptual judgments (not to be confused with "judgments of perception") and only thereby representations, within which representing sensations are only a component. There is a monograph devoted solely to the topic of *Vorstellung*, Theodor Ballauf's *Über den Vorstellungsbegriff bei Kant* (Berlin: Verlag für Staatswissenschaft und Geschichte, 1938), but it is more concerned with

tion of receptivity. Kant is not claiming that "we can only experience sensations," or that they are the immediate objects of consciousness to which object statements can and must be reduced.[10] Far from it; so far the talk is not about what is *experienced* by itself at all. Again the point is to consider theoretically that element in our experience contributed by affection independently of conceptualizing *or* "intuiting." What is now under discussion, according to Kant's language in the Amphibolies, is a transcendental reflection, assigning various elements in knowledge their rightful place in the intellectual landscape (Kant even calls it a "geography") in order to avoid dangerous confusions. The argument here is that when considered apart from any discriminations or interpretations made by a subject actively sorting out and describing, these immediate determinations of sensibility turn out to be a theoretically necessary foundation for such empirical discrimination, but taken by themselves, the mere formless stuff or matter of experience.

There is clearly a very deep premise, though, in even this purely methodological or reflective consideration of Kant's doctrine of sensibility. Namely, the above characterization assumes what Kant later is everywhere only too eager to point out: that the experience of discriminateness is always the result of our describing; that there *is* no immediate unity in this given matter. As above, all this proceeds on the assumption that Kant is theoretically considering our sensory experience apart from any of the articulations of that experience we make in sorting out the given. But even his theoretical isolation of the sensible manifold still presupposes that these articulations or any determinate unity cannot be immediately experienced as present in the manifold as such, that, even apart from a full-fledged relation to objects, there cannot be *any* determinate unity in the manifold apart from what, to use his language, *we* put there. Now Kant may well be able to prove later that no experience is possible except as somehow subject to our powers of discriminating. But he also clearly does not claim that our experience has the particular characteristics it has solely by virtue of these conditions. "Sensations" play the decisive guiding role in Kant's mixed version of idealism and empiricism. So far, though, when we try to explain those features of

---

Reinhold's *Satz des Bewusstseins* as a solution to various Kantian paradoxes than it is with Kant.

10. Graham Bird's *Kant's Theory of Knowledge* (New York: Humanities Press, 1974) and Prauss's *Erscheinung bei Kant* are both convincing refutations of the phenomenalist interpretation, an interpretation not easy to counter, given the long-standing influence of the interpretations of Vaihinger and Kemp Smith. For an inaccurate characterization of Kant's position, see J. Bennett, *Kant's Analytic* (Cambridge: Cambridge University Press, 1966), p. 22. Perhaps the worst offender is H. A. Prichard in *Kant's Theory of Knowledge* (Oxford: Oxford University Press, 1909).

sensations which could explain or account for that guidance, we are left with only negative characteristics — formless, disunified, indeterminate.

Such a consideration forces us to ask this theory the question suggested earlier. Thus far it has emerged that the basic claim in Kant's theory of sensation is that "no unity comes to us through the senses." But why not? Even if we admit that awareness of a sensory manifold is not equivalent to an awareness of an object as sensed, why shouldn't we describe the relation between sensations and the concepts used to describe them in terms of some "awareness"[11] of received determinate impressions, instead of in terms of the subjective activity, synthesizing and judging Kant will later use? What is his basic argument against the classical and rationalist conception of a passive intuition of sensible form, Plato's *noesis,* Aristotle's *nous pathetikos,* or Leibniz's *petites perceptions?*

Even admitting in a general sense, for the sake of argument, that sensation plays a decisive "mediating" function in our knowledge of the world (a claim, for example, that Aristotle would not deny), why not allow that such a sensory manifold, just as attended to, is in itself immediately determinate? In broad, metaphorical terms, what convinced Kant, aside from the decisive historical influence of Leibniz, that the classical model of consciousness itself as "awakeness" should be replaced by his conceptualizing *Verstand,* a kind of "empty grasping"?

To be sure, such questions cannot be *fully* answered without attention to what Kant says about space and time, and what he says about the understanding, but even at this point we can anticipate that those claims, the ideality of space and time, and the necessity of synthesis, need not necessarily imply that no complex of sensations can be a sensation of complexity. The result of the deduction, for example, could just establish that all of the basic categories in our conceptual scheme are a priori applicable to all objects of experience, and not that they are, even in some nonsimplistic way, a priori *responsible* for the unity of all objects of experience. In short, there is all the difference in the world between claiming that we do not seem to be able to make intelligible to ourselves a conception of experience wherein some item is not experienced under some description ("intuitions without concepts are blind"), and claiming

11. I quote "awareness" because of the difficulty in deciding how such a notion is to be interpreted in Kant's theory. As indicated in the first chapter, Kant interpretations divide along numerous lines, but perhaps none is more clear-cut than between those who think that the proper task of a transcendental justification of a priori knowledge resides in a demonstration of a complicated, essentially deductive relation between propositions (some of which seem to have a privileged kind of undeniability), and those who think that Kant's account of the necessary conditions of human experience requires that his troublesome metaphor of a "mind imposed" unity be taken seriously and interpreted or reconstructed in

that the describing constitutes the item's being experienced ("the combination of the manifold in general can never come to us through the senses"). The former interpretation is compatible with the description of the way sensibly apprehended unities are experienced (or described) within the conceptual scheme we have; the latter ties any experience of unity (or determinacy or complexity) much more closely to those describing capabilities. Thus, the question to raise is why *this* use of the matter-form dichotomy; this claim that sensations comprise only the undifferentiated material of experience, and that *all* formal unity or determinacy is a result of taking up the manifold and unifying it?

Now, one could start to approach such issues modestly, and look to the features of the transcendental turn for help. The role of sensations in knowledge, it could be argued, is now being considered only in terms of its role in any knowledge we could universally explain. In such a context, the only elements of an immediate sensory manifold relevant are those which can be formally described in such an experience — in particular the immediate conditions of any such awareness, space and time. To ask any further question about a material of sense is to miss the point that it is just that — the *material* of sense. The question of what accounts for the particular determinacy of an experience can be answered in the empirical manner suggested at the outset of this chapter by examining that particular experience, noting its formal conditions, and the empirical "rules" for responding to sensory stimuli, empirical concepts, learned by any subject (or language user) as appropriate to stimuli of this kind. In a transcendental context, all we are interested in is the role of sensation as that-passively-received, as that element in knowledge over which we exercise no active control. To ask any other question about the manifold of sense is either to ask a specific question about whether our empirical concepts correctly discriminate items in our experience (a question that itself can only be answered empirically), or it is to ask some particular scientific question about the nature of our sensory apparatus (a question that can be answered by physiology or psychology), or it is to misunderstand the limits and interests of Kant's enterprise.

Such a defense, though, would miss the point of the questions asked above. The point is not that Kant must somehow describe what must be happening in our minds below the level of conscious awareness, such that we respond to sensations with the correct concepts. The questions at issue are about the transcendental, not empirical, characterizations of sensibility offered by Kant. In particular, the issue involved in Kant's discussion of sensation is not so much his characterization of it as the immediate

---

some way. The account of *Empfindungen* is an appropriate place to begin to test the possibilities for such a latter interpretation, however hard that doctrine is to isolate.

content of receptivity, but his denial that such sensation is in any way complex. The idea is not to ask Kant what sensations "look like"; that would be a nontranscendental, material question. It is rather to search for his strongest defense of this very close association of the concept of "givenness" in experience with the concept of indiscriminateness, or lack of unity.[12]

So, while this question does seem to me an appropriate one — one indeed that is foundational for much of what Kant wants to say later — there is not much of a direct argument in support of this characterization of sensation in the *Critique*. There are, however, two important, though undeveloped, arguments in support of his position. They both appear briefly at the conclusion of the Transcendental Aesthetic (at B61 = A43 ff., and at B66 ff.) and can be noted elsewhere, especially in the Amphibolies and the *Prolegomena*.

A trace of the first is also evident at B359 = A293. Kant writes, "It is therefore correct to say that the senses do not err — not because they always judge rightly, but because they do not judge at all." Since a necessary feature of all modes of knowledge is that they be capable of being true or false, this claim, if supportable, would be an excellent reason for never regarding the senses, taken by themselves, as being modes of knowledge, and in that sense, never "on their own," being representations of complexity. If the senses never are capable of representing something either truly *or* falsely, then they cannot in any way count as knowledge.

This is, in fact, just the argument Kant uses in the *Prolegomena*, a book which, as Prauss has pointed out in great detail,[13] often reveals how much Kant realized he still had to say about these foundational claims. In the third Remark to Section One, he states clearly what he considers himself to have done. "We proved that sensibility consists, not in this logical distinction of clearness and obscurity, but in the genetic origin of knowledge itself."[14] He goes on to insist that he has proved that the senses cannot do more than offer material to the understanding for reflection, and that they thus cannot in any way represent, however unclearly, things in themselves. His defense of that claim turns again on

---

12. Strictly speaking, there is no reason why the fact that sensations play no direct cognitive role in perception means they should not play some conceptual role (just as there is no reason to believe that the dependence of perception on sensation implies that the relation between the two is one of "causal triggering.") For a denial of the thesis that sensations are nonconceptual, see Romane Clark, "Sensuous Judgments," *Nous* 7 (March 1973), pp. 45–46.

13. See especially chapter 1, paragraph 2 of *Erscheinung bei Kant,* and his article, "Zum Wahrheitsproblem bei Kant," in G. Prauss, *Kant* (Köln: Kiepenhauer und Witsch, 1973).

14. Kant, *Prolegomena, Gesammelte Schriften,* vol. 4, p. 290.

the question of truth and falsity. Simply put, any claim for the representative function of sensation alone will founder hopelessly on the question of
false representations. Considered as a mode of knowledge, such purely
sensory representations must be capable of turning out to be false;
however, if still considered as representations, they turn out then to
represent false *objects,* or negative things. And from the very beginnings
of philosophy with the Eleatics, postulating such negative entities has
never promised to get one very far. If it is the *senses* which represent X to
me, and if X was not in fact the object sensed, how am I to explain what
happened? If the senses represent things in themselves unclearly, and it
turns out that the object represented was not the object the senses
purported to represent, I seem to be faced with either the alternative of
saying it represented what was not, or saying that in such cases the senses
do not represent at all. The first has never been successfully explained,
and it is not open to us to argue that the senses only represent when they
represent truthfully. (Of course, if I claim that the senses represented
obscurely, and that I misconstrued that representation, Kant would claim
that this concedes his whole point. He would claim that this admits that
the senses do not represent but merely provide the material which the
understanding must discriminate.) The solution must be that the senses
do not represent at all, but only contain the results of the affection by
objects on our senses (appearances) and are construed as representing
only when so interpreted by the spontaneity Kant calls the understanding.
In the latter case, if my claim to know turns out to be false, it will only
mean that I have discriminated and judged by means of sensations
incorrectly, not that I have pictured some *Unding.* As is clearer in the
Deduction, "representation of an object" can be said to occur when some
sensed manifold is thought together according to a rule, not when a
representative sensation is more clearly thought. As stated in the *Prolegomena*:

> The appearance depends upon the senses, but the judgment upon the under-
> standing. . . . The difference between truth and dreaming is not ascertained by
> the nature of the representations which are referred to objects (for they are
> the same in both cases) but by their connection according to those rules which
> determine the coherence of the representations in the concept of an object and
> by ascertaining whether they can subsist together in an object or not.[15]

Thus we have a clear-cut argument by Kant which, although it appeals
to later results of the Deduction, can stand on its own as an independent
reason for his consideration of sensation as in no sense a mode of
knowledge. The senses cannot represent the world as it is in itself, but

15. Ibid.

can only produce undifferentiated subjective affects, which together are called "appearance" ("The *undetermined* object of an empirical intuition is called appearance.")

As a claim about possible candidates for any mental content, this argument's implications are also quite far-reaching, denying at once central, although differently expressed, claims in Plato, Aristotle, Descartes, Locke, and Hume. The broad results of such an argument are worth stressing. Kant has denied that "having a sensation" amounts to "knowing" anything. As his later claims in the *Prolegomena* make clear, however, he also takes this to mean that having a sensation does not amount to a "determinate" experience at all. A result of this argument is to introduce "judgment" as the central feature of knowledge, as both the bearer of possible truth and falsity and the key to understanding determinate awareness. Apart from judging, discriminating according to concepts, the manifold of sense cannot count as an awareness *of* anything. Awareness of both "outer" *and* "inner" objects requires a judgment, even if "judgments" that we are having such and such a sensation are of a special kind ("judgments of perception"), which require a special interpretation.

Now this argument does seem effective in proving that our immediate awareness cannot itself count as either true or false, and so must be "judged about" to play any epistemic role. However, it is hard to see how the extension of this argument can be so all encompassing. Put briefly (and in a way that must be expanded later), it may be that we need to conceptualize a sensory manifold in order to become aware of it as this or that manifold; but it seems equally the case that we must have *some* cognitive grasp of the manifold as itself this or that in order to know which concepts to apply.[16] The above quotation from the *Prolegomena* asserts that the difference between truth and dreaming can be ascertained not "by the nature of the representations" but "by their connection according to . . . rules." So far it seems equally open to assert that we only know which rules to apply in order to connect these representations because of something apprehended "in the nature of the representations."

However, before raising such questions explicitly, we should also consider another argument, again offered independently of Kant's synthesis doctrine. This second consideration in support of the indeterminateness of the given depends on Kant's account of unity, relations, and ideality.

16. This way of posing the problem again raises a separate issue — the problem of "judgment" and again requires a promissory note. See chapter 5, p. 143 ff.

3. The Ideality of Relations

At the end of his polemical response to the Wolffian philosopher Johann August Eberhard, Kant makes the surprising, somewhat ironic, but not wholly disingenuous, claim that "the *Critique of Pure Reason* can thus be seen as the genuine apology for Leibniz."[17] Obviously, Kant was being a bit playful here with a Leibnizian opponent whom he regarded with barely disguised contempt. But apart from the criticisms of Leibniz in the Transcendental Aesthetic and Amphiboly of Concepts of Reflection, there are indeed certain contexts where the kind of debt suggested in this passage is apparent. Certain features of his treatment of sensations and their possible unity demonstrate such Leibnizian background assumptions and constitute another reason for Kant's claim that sensation is only the matter of experience.

To be sure, there is no direct borrowing from Leibniz's own account of sensation. Kant strongly criticizes Leibniz for leaving "to the senses nothing but the despicable task of confusing and distorting the representations of the [understanding]" (B332 = A276). But aspects of his agreement with Leibniz concerning other matters of importance for the *Empfindungstheorie* are evident in a long paragraph added in the second edition of the Aesthetic (B66 ff.) To understand that connection, one need only consider that Kant's atomistic account of sense impressions treats such data very much like discrete "monads," internally noncomplex and "windowless" with respect to other such impressions (i.e., there are no real relations among sensations). Obviously, Kant's transcendental context is quite different from Leibniz's metaphysical one, but many of the same motivations for this atomicity thesis are present, and many of the same consequences follow. There is certainly a Leibnizian flavor to Kant's claim at A99 that each sensory representation (using the latter term to refer to a mere content of consciousness) "insofar as it is contained in a single moment, can never be anything but *absolute* unity [my emphasis].[18] The same point is made later, in the Anticipations of Perception, when Kant claims that *since* "sensation is not in itself an objective representation . . . its magnitude is not extensive but intensive" (B208 = A166). Such atomistic characterizations of sense impressions make quite plausible the Leibnizian tactic Kant adopts in discussing any possible "unity" among such representations. That is, Kant takes it as

17. Kant, "Über eine Entdeckung . . . ," *Gesammelte Schriften*, vol. 8, p. 251.

18. One of the most involved interpretations of Kant's scattered remarks on *Augenblicke* is by Gerhard Krüger in "Über Kants Lehre von der Zeit," in *Philosophie und Moral in der Kantischen Kritik*, pp. 269–94. I agree with Dieter Henrich's statement of the limitations of Krüger's interpretation in his "Zur theoretische Philosophie Kants," *Philosophische Rundschau*, 1: 4 (1953).

undeniable that all knowledge or empirical awareness of all kinds involves awareness of *some* unity or connection of content. A mere "this" with no properties or relations with other objects is ineffable and cannot be a content of consciousness. Even to respond to this with a name, if that is to be more than the stimulated utterance of a sound (as it surely is in Kant), is to treat something as a thing, a unit, and that presupposes some internal complexity by virtue of which this has been distinguished from that. The whole question at issue for sensations is, to speak loosely, whether this unity or connection *can* be said to "come to us" in receptivity itself, whether it can be directly given and passively perceived. We know that Kant's position is that it cannot, and what I've called his Leibnizian argument for why that is so amounts to the claim that the only unity possible in sensory complexity is relational, and, as Leibniz insisted, all relations are ideal, *entia rationis,* supplied by the intellect not given. Thus Kant argues,

> everything in our knowledge which belongs to intuitions . . . contains nothing but mere relations. . . . Now that which, as representation, can be antecedent to any and every act of thinking anything, is intuition; and if it contains nothing but relations, it is *the form of intuitions.* Since this form does not represent anything save in so far as something is posited in the mind, it can be nothing but the mode in which the mind is affected through its own activity (namely, through the positing of its representations), and so is affected by itself. (B67–68)

Or, in sum, relations between monadic sensations must be the "form" not the "matter" of empirical intuition *because* all relations are "posited in the mind." Such claims put one in mind immediately of Leibniz's famous and, to judge by recent discussions, ambiguous "Relationem . . . esse rem mere mentalem."[19] Admittedly, if one were to ask why Leibniz believed that all substances were monadic, in no real relation to each other, and that thus relations were ideal, the answer would take us very far into his metaphysics and perhaps his logic. But the results of his analysis are clearly visible in Kant's argument about the unity of sensory "atoms."

In the context of this passage from the Aesthetic, it is clear that the relations among sensations Kant is thinking of, the minimal relations necessary for there to be any perceived unity among sensations, are temporal relations; i.e., succession, coexistence, and duration. This is an argument to which he will return, in much greater detail, in the Deduction, and especially in the Analogies. But he also indicates that relations

19. G. W. Leibniz, *Die philosophischen Schriften,* ed. C. J. Gerhardt (Hildesheim: Georg Ohms, 1960), vol. 2, p. 486.

among the contents of outer sense, relevant when we perceive an extended, changing, or moving body, must also be "posited" and cannot be
immediately perceived. To be sure, Kant will later attempt to establish that
we can also discover an a priori condition of sensory awareness, an "anticipation of perception"; that sensations must have an "intensive magnitude," a degree of intensity. However, aside from a strained relevance to
the debate in natural philosophy over whether "empty space" is necessary
to explain various attractive and resistant forces, much of Kant's argument
there comes down to the uninteresting assertion that in order to have
sensations we must in fact *have* a sensation (i.e., the "intensity" is > 0).[20] It
is the argument about the necessarily ideal nature of all relations among
sensations (and, of course, of the relation between a sensation and a
subject) which represents one of his clearest transcendental grounds for
claiming what he does about the given.

Now all of this might seem just to open doors to all sorts of problems.
Just as it is unclear what exactly Leibniz meant by claiming that relations
were ideal, so Kant had to face the immediate impression that he meant
to assert, for example, that change, or even succession, was "illusory,"
since ideal. Kant tries to correct this impression in the next section of the
Aesthetic, pointing out that his doctrine of sensation and its ideal unity is
not meant to assert that determinate sensed objects do not really exist,
but rather that they can only be known *as* they affect our senses (B49),
and that the ideal forms of unity are necessary conditions of experience,
hardly fictitious or in some metaphysical sense "unreal" just because
"ideal." But it must be admitted that even these qualifications still *do*
leave a great deal unsaid that will have to be clarified, especially with
respect to the forms of intuition. But that is only appropriate at this very
early stage. One can, though, note at this point the "ideality of relations"
thesis as a motivation for Kant's *Empfindungstheorie,* and suggest some
general reasons for his holding *that* thesis.

For example, Gottfried Martin and others have associated Kant's
position on the ideal status of the unity of any manifold with the
traditional "transcendental" question of unity and being.[21] Martin even
tries to show that a continuous tradition on this issue exists, beginning
with Aristotle's association of unity with logos in *Metaphysics* 1003b22,
and extending through Aquinas, Ockham, and Leibniz and ending in
Kant, whose position is that not only must the unity of relations involve
ratio, but is "wholly grounded in *ratio.*"[22] The details provided in this

20. Bennett points out well the numerous weak spots in Kant's argument. See *Kant's
Analytic,* pp. 170–76.
21. G. Martin, *Immanuel Kant* (Berlin: de Gruyter, 1969), pp. 115–48.
22. Ibid., p. 142.

interpretation are helpful, but aside from occasional summaries of the problem of numerical unity, he does not ask if Kant was entitled to such views, or whether they led to any problematic consequences. To be sure, in the passages examined above, Kant does indeed seem just to be relying on an established position about the ideality of relational unity. But he also has in mind the arguments developed in the Aesthetic concerning the ideal status of space and time, arguments which are obviously indebted to Leibniz, but which just as clearly strike out in a new direction. Those are the arguments behind his claim for the ideality of relations, and if they can be established, we shall have a much clearer, more unified case for the material nature of the sensory manifold.

Again, though, some of what Kant has said already provides some good reason for concluding what he does. Note, for example, the initial superiority of his position over the empiricist position of Hume.

As I've indicated, Kant criticizes the general "continuity thesis" he believes is held by both rationalists and empiricists. Against the rationalists he has argued that their sensory representations could not deal with false representations. Against the empiricists he has argued that sense impressions cannot cause or provide the foundation for ideas or knowledge in general because impressions, considered on their own, are atomistic and cannot be said simply to "be" in relation to other impressions. They are indeterminate because the unity required to discriminate them must be ideal. Against Hume, for example, this latter claim would mean that Hume must show how some determinate thought or "idea" can indeed be caused or grounded in some determinate impression. Without being able to give a clear account of this connection, Hume will be unable to defend the heart of his epistemology and theory of mind, that " 'tis impossible perfectly to understand any idea, without tracing it up to its origin, and examining that primary impression, from which it arises."[23] Now Hume cannot hold that all ideas are caused by a corresponding impression. He admits, or seems to admit, that my idea of an apple, for example, cannot be said to be caused by any *one* impression. It is, rather, a complex idea, which can be analyzed into several constituent simple ideas; perhaps its "color, taste, and smell."[24] These simple ideas, in turn, can be said to be caused, with a one-to-one correspondence, by a simple impression. But at this point, Kant wants to know Hume's criterion for a simple, yet determinate, impression, all because Kant's charge is that any sufficient criterion of simplicity will make it impossible to claim that the mind does have anything determinate before it in having an impression.

23. D. Hume, *A Treatise of Human Nature,* ed. L. A. Selby-Bigge (Oxford: Clarendon Press, 1967), pp. 74–75.
24. Ibid., p. 2.

An impression of a color is itself still complex, analyzable into its hue and intensity.[25] Thus, according to Kant, the more rigorous Hume is with his criterion of simplicity, the more his account of impressions turns into the Kantian account of the mere *un*differentiated material of experience, and the less Hume is able to claim that knowledge can be explained by grounding it in impressions. That is, without *some* "taking up and running through" by the mind, one cannot say that there is anything determinate before the mind at all.

Moreover, Kant would consider it question-begging to argue that this connection between impressions can be accounted for by reference to any qualities the impressions possess, or to any "gentle force" they create in affecting the mind. Impressions simply occur and vanish, in an undifferentiated, formless way. To be perceived together, they must be thought together by the mind, and thus *every* aspect of their unity and determinacy, not just those defined by Hume's three principles of relation, is ideal and cannot be accounted for by the simple having of a sensation.

To summarize the results of these arguments, then, it would seem as if Kant does have some strong reasons for rejecting many traditional rationalist and empiricist accounts of sensation. Without a good deal of effort, it would indeed seem difficult to defend the claim that the senses represent unclearly, or that they establish the "given" foundation for all knowledge. But Kant seems to have been almost too successful in arguing that the senses do not represent, and are not immediately differentiated. His position on the purely material character of sensation is so abstract that it is difficult to know how even to begin to answer the second question posed at the beginning of this discussion: If Kant's claim is true, how do we then describe the fact that empirical knowledge about the external world seems to be directly guided by sensations, that our interpreting faculties are restrained in a way yet to be explained by some feature of our sensations that does seem directly connected with what we ultimately take to be a public, spatio-temporal world? If sensations do not provide any direct (i.e. representative) link with such a world, what kind of a link do they provide?[26]

25. Barry Stroud points this problem out clearly in *Hume* (London: Routledge & Kegan Paul, 1977), pp. 20–21.

26. There is an interesting discussion by Richard Aquila of the kind of account Kant would have to give in order to answer this question, in "The Relationship between Pure and Empirical Intuition in Kant," *Kant-Studien* 68 (1977): 275–89. Aquila's case comes down to showing that "our sensations have a certain structure" (p. 276) — indeed, a "nonspatial form" (p. 280). This issue is related to problems discussed in the next chapter, and to section (4) here, but briefly, Aquila's interpretation seems to me to depend on a notion of the role of the understanding which is hard to make out. Cf. p. 283, and his discussion of the "tasks" of the understanding: "The first is the task of providing for the necessary forms of our sensible affection by objects a semantical significance which converts these forms into

This issue is an especially important one for Kant to answer since a natural conclusion would be that there is no such link, at least none we could discover. If we followed that line we would soon end up with a familiar picture of Kant: the world in itself, on this view interpreted as the external world of physical objects, is inaccessible and unknowable by us; we are able to discover rules for the well-ordered coherence of a sensory manifold and thus the "objectivity" of empirical judgments, but the knowledge thus gained through sensation is wholly internal, and is especially not gained by a comparison between our sense impressions and actual states of affairs. The severing of the above-mentioned representative link means empirical knowledge, while demonstrably objective (contra Hume) is only "about" inner objects, states of the mind, and not at all about real objects, or more famously "noumena."

Such a view of Kant cannot be wholly wrong, given so many of his own statements about the implications of his answer to the above question about the nature of sensation. But it surely cannot be wholly correct either. For one thing, as Bird has quite persuasively shown,[27] precisely that view of the relation between the mind and the world is attacked frequently by Kant, most directly in the Fourth Paralogism and the Refutation of Idealism. Second, and more generally, nothing seems to have irritated him more than this "noumenalist" view, as Bird calls it, of the *Critique*'s *Restriktionslehre*. And finally, Kant is quite proud of being an "empirical realist," of having proved that, once we are careful about what we mean, we can indeed say that we know a good deal (directly, not by inference) about the external, independently existing world of material objects, *and* that sensations are the primary way we have to know that world.

To be sure, part of Kant's answer to this question is his theory of the categories. That is so because an indispensable element in explaining the final unity of some sensory material will turn out to be the general rules which, Kant will try to prove, determine what can *count* as an object of experience for us. Indeed, this is the heart of his transcendental, non-empirical explanation of knowledge. Put otherwise, Kant will try to prove that the rules which prescribe the relationship between the conceptual and the nonconceptual orders in knowledge cannot themselves be empirical rules (as in merely associative principles), since any such empirical

---

a means by which our sensory states become an awareness of objects. The second is to introduce into sensory states . . . further elements . . . which allow the conversion of 'purely intuitive' states into perceptions of objects in a stronger sense." I would claim that this talk of "conversion" suffers from the same problems as Sellars's notion of analogy. See pp. 50–53 below. Cf. also Paton's hints about a "sensible form," *Kant's Metaphysic of Experience* (New York: Macmillan, 1936), vol. 1, pp. 137–43.

27. Bird, *Kant's Theory of Knowledge,* pp. 18–35.

rule can be shown to presuppose and depend on a higher-order "pure" category. Thus, one way of answering a question about the principles by virtue of which our sense impressions can be discriminated and interpreted so as to yield objective knowledge of the physical world would be to point to the general rules which prescribe a priori what an object of experience in general *is*: the categories. But such an answer, while surely complicated enough to deserve treatment on its own, only goes part of the way toward explaining the present difficulty. It is clear that Kant meant only for the categories to be the necessary conditions of experience, that without which no experience would be possible for us, and not that they were the sufficient conditions of experience. He did not intend that our conceptual structure was a priori sufficiently complex to prescribe the "discrimination rules" by virtue of which any conceivable empirical manifold could be apprehended. Put more simply, Kant may be able to prove that we are warranted in looking for causes for any event in nature, and that such a warrant comes from a source far more authoritative than experience. However, such a justification itself is no guarantee that we will ever actually find such a causal connection. Kant never meant to deny that empirical knowledge remains contingent, always subject to later revisions. The categorical relation of cause and effect instructs us about what a cause is, and proves that nature must be in *some* causal relation, but which ones in particular hold are "derived from experience" and remain contingent. All of which raises again the question of what features of our experience are relevant to such contingent knowledge.

Here, of course, one is tempted to rely on Kant's doctrine of empirical concepts as specific rules for interpreting sensations objectively. And here again the topic is sufficiently complex to require separate treatment, but the inadequacies of such an answer to the present question are immediately obvious. An empirical concept is supposed to be derived from experience, and this again raises the question of what features of our immediate experience of the world of material objects are relevant for the correct formation of such concepts. Again something must be said directly about the role of sensations, considered independently of conceptual rules, and so far, even from spatial and temporal predicates, in directing our empirical knowledge.

4. Empirical Guidedness: An Attempted Reconstruction

This general issue, sometimes called the problem of the *Angewiesenheit* or guidedness of empirical knowledge, has often been discussed together with an even thornier problem supposedly created by the *Critique*'s account of sensibility — the problem of "affection." Most famously that issue involves the "theory of double affection," an attempt to resolve a dilemma that is said to arise when we attempt to specify what it is that affects our sensibility, spatio-temoral objects or things in themselves.[28] However, that problem can be ignored here. For one thing, that dispute involves the issue of the *cause* of sensation, and the present problem calls for an account only of the nature of the effects of such interaction, and their role in empirical knowledge, whatever the original cause. For another thing, such a problem immediately involves a full interpretation of Kant's distinction between phenomena and things-in-themselves, and that is at this point a separate issue that requires its own discussion (chapter 7). Finally, several recent studies have argued quite effectively that the whole "double affection" approach is seriously misguided, and their results do not need to be repeated here.[29]

However, the separate issue of the nature of sensory information in Kant is quite difficult to address by attention to any series of passages from his text. There is, however, one extended attempt to reconstruct a possible Kantian position on the issue, Wilfrid Sellars's in *Science and Metaphysics*,[30] and I think something can be gained by considering it in detail.

That case occurs in the first chapter of *Science and Metaphysics* and rests on the following claims. (1) There is a distinction in Kant between "intuitions which do and intuitions which do not involve something over and above pure receptivity." Such intuitions which do not involve anything other than receptivity are a "radically different kind of representation of an individual": in fact they are sense impressions. (2) Intuition itself must be considered conceptual, although conceptual in a nonjudgmental, special sense (the sense in which representing "this-cube" is conceptual but differently so than "this is a cube"). (3) Since conceptualizing is an indispensable element in all apperception, we must be able to describe "broad classes of states of consciousness *none* of the members of which are apperceived." This requirement means that we must find a special way to explain the guidedness of empirical knowledge, dependent as it now is on nonapperceived (wholly nonconceptual) states of con-

28. The classic statement of this wholly unintelligible interpretation is E. Adickes, *Kants Lehre von doppelten Affektion unseres Ich als Schlüssel zu seiner Erkanntnistheorie* (Tübingen: J. C. B. Mohr, 1929), although Vaihinger must take most of the blame. It has also been taken seriously, in one form or another, by Busse, Drexler, Kowalewsky, de Vleeschauwer, Kemp Smith, R. P. Wolff, and, apparently, Sellars. For a review of the extensive literature, see T. Herring, *Das Problem der Affektion bei Kant* (Köln: Kölner Universitäts-Verlag, 1953).

29. Cf., inter alia, G. Prauss, *Kant und das Problem der Dinge an sich* (Bonn: Bouvier, 1974), p. 192 ff.; B. Roussett, *La Doctrine kantienne de l'objectivité* (Paris: Vrin, 1968), pp. 178–98; and M. Gram, "The Myth of Double Affection," in *Reflections on Kant's Philosophy*, ed. W. H. Werkmeister (Gainesville: University of Florida Press, 1975).

30. All quotations in the following section are, unless otherwise indicated, taken from pp. 1–30 of *Science and Metaphysics*.

sciousness which are in no sense, however minimally, conceptually (but only physically) describable. Such a way of describing their role in explaining "Why does the perceiver conceptually represent a red (blue, etc.), rectangular (circular, etc.) object in the presence of an object having these qualities?" is to claim they only guide "from without," strongly distinguished from any conceptual discrimination. ("From without" here means that while this manifold is a *state* of consciousness, it is not an *object* of consciousness.) (4) While it is true, for Kant, that an impression of a complex is a complex of impressions, and that all awareness of a complex is owing to the spontaneity of the understanding, he was not committed to denying that the manifold of external sense *as such* is a relational structure. (5) The proper way to describe the relation between such nonapperceived, but in their own way complex, states of consciousness and even minimal conceptual (apperceived) consciousness is in terms of *analogy*. E.g., "Thus, these nonconceptual states must have characteristics which, without being colors, are sufficiently analogous to color to enable this state to play this guiding role."[31] A particularly useful example of the latter is the experience of a spatial relation (colored squares adjoining one another) which must be somehow "based" on sense impressions, which, while consisting of an impression of one colored square, and an impression of another colored square, must also consist of some other element which, while not itself the relation of "being next to," must be sufficiently analogous to that relation to allow us to experience such a relation correctly (sense impressions themselves, of course, are neither colored nor next to one another).[32] Finally, given his failure to make this distinction (1) clearly enough, "Kant reduces the concepts of receptivity and sensibility to empty abstractions."

Sellars has a good deal more to say about such issues throughout his book. For our purposes, the importance of this interpretation lies in how much the concept of "analogy" can be used to help explain the role of sensations in knowledge, once the distinction in (1) is admitted. Admittedly, there is a problem in Sellars's imputation of (3) to Kant. He admits what seems to be some uneasiness about that imputation when he asserts:

31. Of course, it is important for Sellars to deny an alternate interpretation of "an of-a-red-rectangle impression"; namely that such is "a nonconceptual state of the perceiver (mediating between the stimulus and the conceptual outcome) of *the kind which* has as its standard cause a real and rectangular physical object." He does offer a series of arguments against this construal (pp. 20–23), many pointing to the fact that the problematic singularity of the impression (it is tied to a particular triangle) should be explained in terms of a description of the *impression,* not by virtue of the object causing the impression. In other words, we must continue to try to explain the unique properties of the *impression,* and must not slide into a discussion of the properties of the physical object.

32. Once a claim like this is established, it becomes apparent that the same sort of

This was, in essence, the Kantian position, though he tends to restrict the term "consciousness" to apperceiving and to the apperceived as such.[33]

He certainly does, particularly in the second edition. But Sellars is also careful to point out that his postulation of this manifold is purely "theoretical," and he suggests his own criterion for what that means. At any rate, I shall interpret Sellars's reconstruction to claim that Kant should have had (3) if he was serious about the distinction in (1), even if Kant himself did not realize that he should have. And this, of course, is just the point at issue — to what extent Kant could have held (3) and thereby also held the implications Sellars draws from it, (4) and (5). The basic question, then, is whether Kant could admit this indirectly described unity or complexity in a manifold of sense, and if so, whether the concept of analogy can explain the relation between this nonperceived complexity and our awareness of complexity.

The former question seems easy to answer in Sellars's terms, first of all because this "purely" sensed manifold is theoretically postulated as independent of direct, conscious awareness. Speculations about what properties such a manifold must be assumed to have seem relatively unrestricted by many of the other things Kant says about the conditions for the possibility of *experience*. Instead, we try to assume what such a complex of impressions would have to be like, if Kant's general claims about the relation between the awareness of complexity and spontaneity, the thesis of empirical realism, and the unity of apperception are all assumed at once. As such an attempt, Sellars's interpretation should be seen as a way to avoid two equally unacceptable (to both Kant and Sellars) results.

On the one hand, we want to avoid saying that the "forms of the manifold of sense representations" should be taken *exclusively* to mean the form of represent*ing* the manifold. This would mean that any discrimination in what we perceive, at whatever level of conceptual complexity, is a result of the spontaneity of the subject (synthesis). In such a case the notion of any form of *outer* sense threatens to disappear. If the sensed manifold itself is to have any "say" in the outcome of our "taking it up" we must be able to describe (indirectly and theoretically) *its* form, the form of the represent*ed*. On the other hand, we do not thereby want to reintroduce the empiricist notion of some "given" direct awareness of sense impressions as our most reliable candidate for original knowledge (original in the sense of noninferred). For Kant, even such minimally conceptual awareness of sense impressions as such, precisely because

"counterpart" explanation has to be given for either of the colored square impressions themselves (neither impression is colored nor square).

33. Wilfrid Sellars, *Science and Metaphysics*, p. 11.

discriminable and discernible, must already involve the play of concepts and so cannot be simply "given."[34] Sellars has his own reasons for attacking the notion of self-presenting, noninferentially warranted states of affairs — the "myth" of the given.[35]

His point here is to walk between the Scylla of idealism (a self-determining conceptual, wholly "internal" model of experience) and the Charybdis of foundationalist epistemologies (with the postulation of "givens" that cannot do the work they are meant to perform). His answer to the first is this notion of a nonapperceived manifold "guiding from without," that is, from outside the conceptual order. His answer to the second is his claim that such a manifold is not a minimally conceptual "given," but is describable only in minimal *physical* terms, and is related to the awareness we do have (colors, shapes, etc.) only by way of analogy, not by being such a self-presenting, directly perceived state.

At this point, though, the second of the above two questions becomes relevant. The notion of analogy may serve well as a kind of "external," theoretical characterization of the relation between sensation and minimal conceptual awareness, but it is not clear it can also serve as an explanation "inside" an empirical judgment. That is, Kant might argue from his position that there are still too many traces of the "the senses represent but not clearly" model left in this account. To be sure, we now say, "The senses sort of represent, but only by way of analogy; for example in the way we might represent God's infinite knowledge only on analogy with our own." But for Kant, many of the same problems of any such vaguely representative model would reemerge. For one thing, we would have to ask about the "transition" from unapperceived sensory states to apperceived ones. That is, if such sense impressions guide "from without," it is not yet clear how they guide at all (as opposed to merely *determining* our response). Oddly, Sellars does not include an account of sensory *misapprehension,* an explanation that would have helped make clearer how it is that we do not simply respond with words to sensory stimuli, but make judgments about the objects we know sensorily. As it is, Kant might say that this "analogous counterparts" model of sense impressions either reintroduces too many of the representative model problems (false sensory judgments), or too much underplays the role of spontaneity in fashioning sensory judgments.

Along the latter lines, he would still claim that *we* determine the rules for construing sensations as having characteristics *taken* to be analogously

34. Cf. Sellars's own statement of the alternatives, *Science and Metaphysics,* paragraph 77.

35. Probably the best known of Sellars's arguments against the given occurs in "Empiricism and the Philosophy of Mind," section 7, in *Science, Perception and Reality* (New York: Humanities Press, 1963).

connected to physical objects. There is still no direct link between the nonapperceived possession of this Sellarsian manifold and our awareness of this sensed object. If Sellars's central question is: "Why does the perceiver conceptually represent a red (blue, etc.), rectangular (circular, etc.) object in the presence of an object having these qualities?" the answer cannot simply be, "Because the perceiver *has* sensations whose characteristics are analogously blue and rectangular." Much more crucial in such an answer must be *our* rules governing what Sellars elsewhere calls the "ought-to-be's," the normative, restraining limits within which our conceptual discriminations are to be evaluated. Nothing Sellars says about this manifold, as he himself stresses, can minimize Kant's "agnosticism" about the transcendentally real status of these limits. That is:

> Thus Kant is in a position to grant that empirical knowledge involves a uniformity of conceptual responses to extra-conceptual items and even that extra-conceptual items conform to general laws, without granting that the character of the items to which we conceptually respond, or the laws to which God knows them to conform, are accessible to finite minds.[36]

And this means that the whole issue of "guidedness" in Kant should be taken in his own special transcendental sense. We are so guided by our sensory experience only to the extent that we follow our own rules for what counts as guidedness. These rules may either be necessarily involved in any synthesis of the manifold (categories), or rules we construct further to discriminate experience as best we can (empirical concepts). What the notion cannot mean, after the transcendental turn, is the prima facie sense of guidedness, "from the (transcendentally real) world." The parenthetical qualification just expressed introduces important and difficult issues concerning the meaning of transcendental and empirical "guidedness" in Kant and must be discussed in more detail. But for now, in a strict transcendental sense, such a restraining function played by sensation is still itself a result of our conceptual activity, and the "immediate" characteristics of sensibility "restrain" our conceiving only to the extent that we follow our "rules" for what to regard as a restraint.

But this restriction on Sellars's "analogous counterparts" theory of the relation between the sensed manifold and our conceiving seems to leave us back where we started, with sensations described as the undifferentiated material of experience or as so indirectly related to our spontaneity as, in either case, to be unintelligible in any guiding role. Such is not quite the case, however. What Kant's brief remarks on sensation seem to have done is to have reinterpreted the only sense "guidedness" *could*

---

36. Wilfrid Sellars, "Some Remarks on Kant's Theory of Experience," *Journal of Philosophy* 64 (1967): 647.

have for finite creatures like us. One result of his emphasis on their material and so *"an sich"* undifferentiated status is to prohibit any attempt to construe sensations as so impinging on and guiding our conceptualizing *by virtue* of a direct link with external objects. They do have such a link, but it is not by virtue of that that they play some guiding role. Such guidance is, rather, determined by the complex conceptual rules for guidance specified by categories and empirical concepts. When we say that some in-itself-uncolored sensation must "have" some characteristic sufficiently analogous to color to explain this guidance, the claim is correctly understood only under the qualification that we determine the sense of such an analogy.[37]

The situation here is much the same as in theology. A comprehension of divine properties by way of analogy does not mean that we have "imperfectly" understood God, but that we have understood "God-insofar-as-he-is-knowable-by-us." Such a qualification is problematic, as was often pointed out in such debates, because it seems tantamount to admitting that we really don't know anything about *God*. The same problem will emerge for Kant once we get further into his empirical realism and try to understand better this reinterpreted notion of "guidance."

At this point, however, it is unclear just what one should conclude from this range of problems in Kant's theory of sensations. For one thing, his full doctrine of "sensibility" includes a complicated account of the forms of intuition, and that will have to be considered prior to any assessment. Perhaps at this point all one can say is that, while Sellars's reconstruction provides the most helpful way of thinking about this problem of *Angewiesenheit*, it also raises one of the most difficult problems. That problem comes down to the general characterization Kant seems to give of sensations. It still seems more a wholly "material" result of affection than a direct transfer of information; a kind of code which

37. In such a formulation it may be left undetermined what the physiologically appropriate properties of such impressions are, but, again, the importance of Kant's restriction of knowledge to phenomena must be kept in mind in evaluating the epistemological significance of such physiology. That is, Kant is denying a causal or phenomenalist theory of perception (or some combination of both). He is thus maintaining that we perceive the external world of physical objects in space directly, "by means of" sensation. But he is still, even in Sellars's reconstruction, not a "transcendental realist," that is, he maintains that no relation to such objects can occur except in terms of an a priori structure, or set of rules which define objectivity (for us). Whatever empirical or philosophic characterizations we give to the sensory manifold, the significance of those characterizations for human knowledge is thus necessarily determined by these a priori rules. Sellars is thus also correct in pointing out that unless the role of this manifold can be described somewhat more directly, the step from Kant to his successors in German Idealism is a small one indeed. Cf. paragraph 40.

can be "deciphered" as long as we mean by that deciphering arriving at a coherent, rule-governed, fully integrated result. We still need a further defense of the objectivity of this deciphering, particularly when confronted with a Humean-like skepticism about ever arriving at the "original" meaning of the code (the *Ding an sich*); and also a defense of *this* general manner of deciphering or judging as the *only* one available to humans. (Again, particularly important is how we could make such a claim while not making an empirical claim about human psychology.) I believe that proving both claims is just what the Transcendental Deduction is all about. But we are getting ahead of ourselves. We need first to examine Kant's theory of the "subjective" forms under which, and only under which, sensory information can be construed as telling us anything about singular objects, his theory of space and time as pure intuitions and pure forms of intuition.

3
Intuitions

The order of things which are next to one another is not space, but space is that which makes possible, according to determinate conditions, such an order, or better, coordination. *Reflexionen* 4673

That which so determines [*macht*] the manifold of appearances that it can be ordered in certain relations, I term the *form* of appearance. (B34 = A20)[1]

1. Stages in Kant's Argument

As admitted in the preceding chapter, it is difficult to sort out the different arguments at work in Kant's initial characterizations of the form and matter of experience. It was especially difficult to isolate why he believed what he did about the sensory matter of experience, although it was clear that much of his support for that position would ultimately have to depend on his first attempts to specify the forms of experience, and his case for their ideality. These forms, and only these forms, can supply the "immediate unity" of a sensed manifold. However, when we turn to that attempt in the Transcendental Aesthetic, it is again difficult to specify exactly what Kant is arguing for at various stages and how he supports his claim. For one thing, his introduction of the notion of a form "under which something is intuited" (B75 = A51) makes use of a number of different terms which he sometimes seems to use synonymously, sometimes appears interested in differentiating. Kant speaks freely of forms of appearances, forms of sensibility, forms of intuition, and forms of inner and outer sense, and also frequently calls space and time themselves "pure" or "formal" intuitions as well as forms.[2] It is also often hard to

1. The *Reflexion* is from *Gesammelte Schriften*, vol. 17, p. 369. Cf. also the definition of the form of phenomena as necessarily subjective and relational in the *Dissertation*, section 3, paragraph 13. The quotation from the *Critique* represents an important alteration in the second edition. Kant changed "that it is intuited ordered in certain relations" (*geordnet angeschauet wird*) to "that it can be ordered in . . ." (*geordnet werden kann*). The latter is more consistent with the *Reflexion* and obviously leaves room for the manifold to play some role in determining which order is apprehended.
2. H. J. Paton provides a useful discussion of the various differences among these terms. *Kant's Metaphysic of Experience* (New York: Macmillan, 1936), vol. 1, p. 101 ff.

determine what Kant thinks each of the arguments advanced in the text actually establishes. It is obvious that the central issue for him is the establishment that space and time are *ideal* forms of empirical intuition, and that thereby they do not apply to "things in themselves." However, it has never been clear to commentators just where he establishes that. Occasionally he writes as if he assumes that the arguments from the Metaphysical Expositions establish it; yet he seems to get around to the issue directly only in his concluding remarks. Occasionally he seems to assume confidently that by refuting his chief rivals on the issue (concerning space, particularly), Newton and Leibniz, he has *thereby* established the truth of the only alternative left, his. Finally, many contemporary commentators have confessed that they can find no clear argument about the ideality of these forms apart from one connected to Kant's views on geometry, and that those views, since refuted after Kant, will not bear the weight of the argument.[3]

In the face of all that, my central interpretive concern in the following will be to try to isolate the different claims Kant makes, and to try to assess which ones are important in establishing his central thesis: that there are ideal "forms" of sensibility. In doing so, of course, I hope to be able to say something about what a "form of sensibility" is. In order to simplify matters, because the case about time is deeply connected with so many other things Kant has to say about the issue in the Analytic, especially in the Analogies, I shall concentrate on the issue of space. My critical intention is to show that when the relation between Kant's arguments has been clarified, there is an argument apparent which attempts to demonstrate the ideality of space as a "form," and which does not directly depend on any views about geometry.[4] I shall attempt to show that significant difficulties develop in Kant's case, especially for his explanation concerning how the properties of space are determined in a "formal" intuition. I think that these problems are more than incidental difficulties in Kant's arguments, and that they bear on his general case for

3. Cf., for example, P. F. Strawson, *The Bounds of Sense* (London: Methuen, 1966), pp. 57–58.
4. I am, of course, not the first to claim that Kant's views on space are not directly and necessarily tied to his views about geometry. One of the clearest defenses of such a thesis about the separation of topics can be found in an important article by Ted Humphrey, "The Historical and Conceptual Relations between Kant's Metaphysics of Space and Philosophy of Geometry," *Journal of the History of Philosophy* 11 (1973): 483–512. Much the same point is made by R. P. Horstmann, "Space as Intuition and Geometry," *Ratio* 18 (1976): 17–30. Such a separation has also been defended in other ways by Gottfried Martin, *Immanuel Kant* (Berlin: de Gruyter, 1969), pp. 13–42, and D. P. Dryer, *Kant's Solution for Verification in Metaphysics* (London: Allen & Unwin, 1966), p. 155 ff. My own view of where to locate the ideality argument once such a thesis is accepted, and the problems it generates, are different from claims made by the above authors, however.

formalism in philosophy and for conclusions he draws from such formalism (that these forms are necessary conditions of any possible apprehension).

However, in the face of such putative problems, one can admit at the
outset that the general goal of Kant's enterprise in the Aesthetic is not
that hard to state. Empirical knowledge just means for Kant knowledge
of objects in space and time. This knowledge consists of judgments we
make about such objects. However, we obviously do not make such
judgments by first *judging* that such and such is a spatio-temporal object.
Space and time are the "immediate" conditions for there being anything
numerically identical to judge about. Objects are individual objects at all
(numerically) only by being in spatial and temporal relations, by being,
for example, "beside" or "outside" each other in some numerically
identical region of space, and by occurring "before" and "after" each
other in time. However, as we have also seen, Kant believes that our
immediate contact with objects results only in the "effect of an object
upon our sensibility," only in a formless material. While the information
gained "through" sensation (as he puts it) is obviously somehow relevant
to the specific empirical judgments we make about spatial or temporal
location, the spatiality and temporality of those objects themselves is not
a part of the information we gain from the senses and is certainly not the
source of our knowledge of those relations themselves. In Kant's language, in other words, he thinks he can establish (in arguments we shall
have to work through) that space is neither a concept nor "derived" from
the relations of empirically apprehended bodies. For him this means (by
virtue of an argument we shall have to find) that, therefore, "we"
contribute a priori the system of spatio-temporal relational possibilities
(the forms of intuition) by virtue of which awareness of spatio-temporal
particulars can occur. Knowledge is, thus, always judgment; empirical
knowledge is always judgment about spatio-temporal particulars; and the
spatio-temporality of these particulars, since explicable by appeal neither
to the application of concepts nor to the material of our receptivity,
requires another sort of explanation. For Kant, this explanation will
terminate in the claim that space is a pure form of outer sense.

As we shall see, there are a number of steps involved on the way to
that claim. All of these will have to be isolated and examined. Before
isolating these stages, though, we should note explicitly how much Kant
is committing himself to proving here. It is important to point this out,
because some of Kant's own formulations sometimes give the impression
that he could accomplish a great deal of what he needs without any
involved theory about formal ideality. For example, Kant greatly confuses any attempt to understand a distinctively "intuitive" form of experience by generally contrasting intuition and understanding *as* a contrast

between "receptivity" and "spontaneity." If one follows that contrast closely, one can conclude that forms of intuition should simply be regarded as a kind of passive form of receptivity. Looked at this way, intuitions would just be, as often stressed by Kant, the "immediate" elements in knowledge, that aspect of knowing by virtue of which we can be said to be in "immediate," passive contact with objects. Such a contact could still be called sensation, but now, we could simply go on to insist that such sensory awareness can only *be* of objects in time, some of which must also be in space. If we thus focus attention on what Kant calls empirical intuitions, the distinction between the understanding and intuitions should thus be taken to be a distinction between general concepts and the immediately encountered particular items which fall under such concepts.[5] Space and time would just be the forms of, or conditions for, this particularity; spatial and temporal determinations are just what constitutes the particularity of such items.

However, when he makes the contrast between intuitions and the understanding in this way, Kant is always thinking just of such "empirical" intuitions, or, speaking clumsily, of an intuitively enformed manifold (spatial and temporal particulars). Thus, while the contrast so expressed between intuition and understanding does help clarify the respective roles of this spatio-temporal manifold and a discriminating, classifying understanding in experience as a whole, the contrast itself does not illuminate how such a manifold "becomes" a manifold of particulars only as subject to "our" forms of sensibility, and often obscures the fact that such an explanation must include some reference to "pure intuitions" as conditions for this possibility. Kant himself clearly insists that "empirical intuition is only possible through pure intuition," and, in a very dense passage (as is often the case in his footnotes), that "the form of intuition gives a mere manifold, but the formal intuition *gives* the unity of representation" (B160n).

That is, one aspect of the form of "receptivity" seems to be this pure or formal intuition, a fact stressed when he claims, "This pure form of sensibility may also itself be called a pure intuition" (B35 = A20). This claim thus leads to a specification of our problem. If we want to

5. This is the interpretation advanced by Strawson, *Bounds of Sense,* p. 48 ff., and can be connected with modern accounts like that of descriptives and demonstratives (Austin). Space and time as "forms" of these particulars just means, for Strawson, that there is an "intimate connection" (p. 52) between the idea of particular instances and those of space and time. He then goes on to try to show that Kant offers no argument (apart from one based on a theory of geometry) to demonstrate that these "forms" could be construed as subjective, or in any way contributed by "us." We have already seen, though, that given Kant's theory of sensation, when he confronts the question of how we are aware of such spatio-temporality, no appeal to the sensory manifold is possible, and the introduction of the ideality thesis is inevitable.

understand what a form of sensibility is, we shall have to understand how such is *also* a "pure intuition."[6] In the terms used above, what this question comes down to is an explanation of the possibility of a nonempirical determination of the properties of space, *and* a "transcendental" proof of some variety that the relations determined in such pure intuitions are the relations we can apprehend in empirical spatial awareness.

We should also note that this separation of various topics in Kant is artificial in another sense. Although both empirical and pure intuitions are, in Kant's final account, independent elements in empirical and a priori knowledge, his procedure in discussing them separately should not create the impression of some phenomenological independence.[7] Empirical intuitions, or spatio-temporal particulars, are not experienced "first" and then synthesized according to the understanding, and neither are pure intuitions some sort of *independent* procedure for mathematical knowledge. There is no empirical awareness or pure constructing in mathematics without the "spontaneity" of the understanding, and its rules, or concepts. Intuitions have a role to play in such judgments, but *only in* such judgments. It is possible transcendentally to say a great deal about that role, but again that separate discussion is a theoretical, not a phenomenological, separation. In sum, then, it should be noted that Kant insists that his doctrine of "receptivity" as a whole (or "sensibility") can and must be broken down into *its* formal and material elements, and that the account as a whole is only a preliminary step in a final theory of pure and empirical knowledge.[8]

6. One of the most complicated, misleading, and influential versions of this problem is that propounded by Norman Kemp Smith, *A Commentary to Kant's Critique of Pure Reason* (London: Macmillan, 1923), pp. 88–98 ("Kant's Conflicting Views of Space"). Confronted by the fact that Kant calls space both a pure form of intuition and a pure intuition, Kemp Smith reasons — as he almost always does when confronted by such problems — that Kant just held two conflicting views of space, that he believed both that space was a mental "disposition" and that a "conscious" awareness *of* a pure manifold "precedes" any empirical apprehension of space. This conflict then leads to others in understanding the respective roles of concepts and intuitions in spatial awareness. I shall try to show that this interpretation is based on a mistaken view of "pure intuition," and that, when properly understood, Kant's dual characterization of space is a classic example of the intentions of the entire "transcendental enterprise." An extensive version of Kemp Smith's interpretation can be found in Christopher Garnett's *The Kantian Philosophy of Space* (New York: Columbia University Press, 1939), chap. 8. A clear refutation of some aspects of Kemp Smith's interpretation can be found in Arthur Melnick, *Kant's Analogies of Experience* (Chicago: University of Chicago Press, 1973). I discuss some aspects of Melnick's interpretation in chap. 3, section 2.

7. Buchdahl makes some useful points about the dangers of a phenomenological reading of Kant's ideality thesis; *Metaphysics and the Philosophy of Science* (Cambridge: M.I.T. Press, 1969), p. 590 ff.

8. Kant himself indicates how this separation is to be understood, at B36 = A22. *After* isolating sensibility from the understanding, he says, we can then separate (*abtrennen*) that

It will become clear, I hope, as we move through Kant's text, that it is the argument that space is a "pure intuition," once properly understood, that alone is intended to establish that space is a pure form of empirical intuition, and is thus both transcendentally ideal and empirically real. However ultimately problematic, I think there is a good deal more to his elusive argument than Kant has been given credit for. But, as mentioned, it takes him a while to get to such claims. Before he does, he has to establish independently the following (none of which, by itself or collectively, establishes that ideality claim): (1) space is not known by abstraction from the relations of bodies, nor by empirical investigation of any kind; (2) any empirical apprehension of space depends on such spaces being already located in space as a whole (which space need not itself, though, he apprehended as a whole); (3) space is a pure intuition. Initially (3) will only mean that space can only be represented as a *singular* whole, that there is only one, infinite space, whose parts, and the properties of whose parts, can be known without appeal to experience. Finally, I shall argue that it is by attention to how this last claim *could* be fully justified, how the whole, single system of spatial relations could be known a priori as an "intuition," that Kant tries to establish that space must be an ideal form of outer sense. I shall discuss (1)–(3), or Kant's Metaphysical Expositions, in the following section and his claims about ideality in section 3.

2. Space as a Pure Intuition

Kant suggests very early in the Aesthetic what his favored alternative will be among all competitors concerning space and time, that they are such that "they belong only to the form of intuition, and therefore to the subjective constitution of our mind, apart from which they could not be ascribed to anything whatsoever" (B37–38 = A23). However, as indicated above, much of the analysis he then offers seems oddly to establish other claims. He appears to offer a direct argument for this thesis of formal ideality only in one sentence in the Transcendental Exposition added in the second edition (B41). But he begins his Conclusions by confidently restating the ideality thesis as the conclusion of the whole section. He then goes on to try to dispel possible psychologistic and erroneously idealistic interpretations of what he means. However, even though there appears to be a large gap between what Kant announces he will conclude and what his arguments entitle him to say, there is a rather straightforward if somewhat hidden argument at work. Briefly, his Metaphysical Expositions establish certain things undeniably true of our

---

in empirical intuition which belongs to sensation so that "nothing but pure intuition and the mere form of appearances remains."

representation of space. This representation, he argues, *cannot* be known empirically, and such an a priori representation of space *must* "underlie" all empirical representations of space. He then establishes that this representation must be a particular kind of representation, an intuition. These claims alone do not allow Kant to claim that space is therefore a subjective form, but they are necessary premises in that argument. For, in a move visible in the *Critique* (B41) and much clearer in the *Prolegomena,* Kant simply argues that neither of these two undeniable features of our representation of space could be true unless space were a pure form of sensibility.[9] The core of his method for establishing the formal ideality of space is thus to argue that no other alternative can explain what the Metaphysical Expositions establish. Obviously, in assessing this argument, we must be concerned both with whether the Expositions do establish the twin claims mentioned above, and with whether Kant is entitled to draw the conclusion he does.

The four Metaphysical Expositions of the representation of space have long been a source of great controversy. Indeed, considering their importance, they are extraordinarily brief, but I believe the general theses established can be successfully defended if we keep in mind the transcendental nature of Kant's analysis, and the limited focus of his argument. I mean by this that the arguments are best viewed as establishing what must be the case if we are to be able to represent *numerically distinct* objects or regions of space.

To make the force of these arguments clearer, however, we should also briefly note and keep in mind that Kant viewed his investigation as a search for an alternative to two competing and, to him, unsuccessful accounts of space (although he obviously also tried, in a manner typical of his philosophy, to find a way to preserve what he regarded as valuable in both).

On the one hand, there is the Newtonian option that space is absolute, an entity existing independently of objects in space. There were a variety of different reasons for Newton's defense of this view, but many of the most convincing for him appeared to be those drawn directly from reflections about the necessary assumptions (or even "conditions") for his

9. It should be stressed that Kant is using the notion of "representation" in quite a general sense here, not one that is tied to any claim about imaginability or empirical apprehension. Thus, arguments about "how space must be represented" could be said to be analogous to arguments about "how God must be represented" if God is to be God, or "how substance must be represented" if it is to be substance. On this last point, see J. Ebbinghaus's comparison of Kant with Spinoza in his "Kants Lehre von der Anschauung a priori," reprinted in *Kant: Zur Deutung seiner Theorie von Erkennen und Handeln,* ed. G. Prauss (Köln: Kiepenhauer und Witsch, 1973), p. 49. I shall return to this analogy below.

There is a good brief statement of Kant's strategy in Dryer, *Kant's Solution,* p. 173.

own science. For example, with respect to his axioms of motion, Newton realized that some frame of spatial reference must first be stipulated before the axioms could be employed to explain the motions of bodies. Even though he also realized that, for most practical purposes, this frame of reference could be relative, he went on to argue that it must finally be an absolute frame of reference, given, especially, the general noninvariance of the equations of motion under transformations to arbitrary reference frames. Without an absolute frame of reference (which, of course, Newton went on to interpret metaphysically, as absolute space or God's sensorium) he argued that this variation could only be unsatisfactorily explained in terms of ad hoc "deflecting," or "impeding" forces, and so forth.[10]

For a good deal of his adult life, Kant did not find such arguments convincing, and defended instead a modified Leibnizian theory of the "ideality" of space; a denial that there is such a thing (*wirkliches Wesen*) as absolute space, and a claim that spatial relations and properties are determined by the position and dynamical relation of individual bodies. However, as is well documented, around 1767 his views on this question began to undergo drastic alterations, particularly under the influence of Euler's research, and the so-called argument of incongruous counterparts.[11] Kant became convinced that a wholly relational view of space could not be defended, and, while for a time appearing to resort to some more Newtonian view, began his own search for a satisfactory solution short of the postulation of a metaphysical *Unding* like absolute space. The results of that search first appeared in their new critical form in his 1770 *Dissertation,* and a great deal of the case made there is preserved in the *Critique.* The assumption of an absolute frame of reference (or space as a singular whole) seemed to him unavoidable, even though there is, literally, no such thing as space; there are just individual bodies. It simply had to be the case that space could not be said to be derived from or in

10. Cf. the account of Newton's position on this issue given by E. Nagel, *The Structure of Science* (New York: Harcourt, Brace & World, 1961), p. 207 ff., Ivor Leclerc's account in "The Meaning of 'Space' in Kant," and Robert Palter, "Absolute Space and Absolute Motion in Kant's Critical Philosophy," the latter two in *Kant's Theory of Knowledge,* ed. L. W. Beck (Boston: Reidel, 1974), pp. 87–94, 95–110.

11. Kemp Smith has pointed out (*A Commentary,* pp. 161–66) how difficult it is to decide what exactly Kant thought this argument established. However it may have influenced his own views of space, all we need note here is how crucial it was in turning him away from the Leibnizian view once and for all. For further discussion, see John Earman, "Kant, Incongruous Counterparts, and the Nature of Space and Space-Time," *Ratio* 13 (1971): 1–18, and David Pears, "The Incongruity of Counterparts," *Philosophy of Science* 25 (1958): 109–15. A fine discussion of the argument and an excellent overview of the historical development of Kant's theory of space can be found in Buchdahl, *Metaphysics and the Philosophy of Science,* p. 598 ff.

any way dependent on individual bodies. Indeed, contrary to Leibniz's principle of identity, such bodies *were* individual bodies at all only by their already being spatially located.[12]

It is this last claim which is so clearly at work in the first two Metaphysical Expositions. In the First, he argues:

> Space is not an empirical concept which has been derived from outer experience. For in order that certain sensations be referred to something outside me (that is, to something in another region of space from that in which I find myself), and similarly, in order that I may be able to represent them as outside and alongside one another, and *accordingly not only as different but as in different places,* the representation of space must be presupposed. (B38 = A23) [my emphasis]

If we pay attention to the phrase in italics, it seems to me that this argument is not subject to some of the objections which have been raised against it. Kant is not trading on a tautologous and, in this context, trivial use of the concept "outside me" (i.e., that it is simply analytically true that our representation of space cannot be derived, since all derivation already presupposes things "outside me"), and his position cannot allow the sometimes suggested alternative that the representation of empirical spaces and the representation of space as a whole can be said to condition each other reciprocally.[13] He is claiming that no region of space, nor any particular object in some region, could be identified as outside, or beside or *indeed at all different numerically from* any other unless it were so differentiated by reference to an underlying, always presupposed representation of space as a whole. The location or position of two qualitatively identical objects cannot be in any way derived from the perception of these bodies, since such spatial identification is presupposed in being able to perceive them as distinct in the first place.

As Arthur Melnick has recently shown, this argument has nothing whatsoever to do with the ("absurd") claim that I must somehow empirically apprehend space as a whole in order to locate bodies within it.[14] There is no such direct representation for Kant. All representations of space simply *always already* occur against the "background" of space as a whole. More precisely, "we perceive space under the preconception (or better, under the 'pre-intuition') that the bounded spatial extents we do

---

12. Such a claim is already apparent in the *Dissertation,* paragraph 10.

13. Paton, *Kant's Metaphysic of Experience,* p. 112, suggests that this is left open by the first Exposition. The issue will come up again in the Second Exposition, below.

14. Melnick, *Kant's Analogies of Experience,* pp. 7–22. For direct confirmation of the interpretation that a representation can be said to "underlie" another (be presupposed in the latter) without being either consciously apprehended, or being an *ens rationis,* see H. E. Allison, *The Kant-Eberhard Controversy* (Baltimore: The Johns Hopkins University Press, 1974), p. 122.

perceive are parts of a limitless or unbounded space."[15] Or, "our ultimate distinction between numerical and qualitative identity rests upon our intuition that all spaces and all times are but parts of one space and one time."[16] It is especially clear in a passage from the Amphibolies that Kant regarded this argument as the core of his defense for the nonderived nature of our representation of space (B319–20 = A263–64).

Thus far, this argument is strictly transcendental. That is, it does not establish anything about the nature of space, just that our representation of space cannot be derived. The second exposition then goes on, as commentators have noted, to restate this point in a more positive, slightly stronger way. The argument again turns, though, on what must be the case if empirical spaces, and/or objects in those regions, are to be apprehensible as numerically distinct from each other, even if qualitatively identical, and again says nothing about the nature of space itself.

The Second Exposition goes further, however, in pointing out that an a priori representation of space is possible "empty of objects," and it is this representation which "underlies outer appearances." Again this does not mean that some empirical apprehension of space as a whole is possible and somehow involved (or even "temporally prior to")[17] our awareness of determinate spaces. Kant's point is, again, theoretical, not phenomenological. Individual spaces are apprehended against an always presupposed background of space itself. But, Kant is now trying to stress, this does *not* mean that space itself should be construed to depend on the position and relations of bodies in order to be present in such representations. If there must be a single space by reference to which (and only by reference to which) parts are identifiable, that space itself cannot be codetermined *by* those parts without gross circularity. Kant makes this point in a way that sounds psychologistic, thus leading some to think that his argument here depends on a dubious thought-experiment (e.g., what we can and cannot "imagine"). But when he says space can be represented without objects in it, but objects cannot be represented as not in space, he is not challenging us to refute him by stretching the powers of our imagination. He is making, in a stronger way, the point made in the First Exposition: that any representation of a region of space or body in space has always already presupposed an "underlying" reference to a representation of space as a whole, just in order that it be an individual region or object. This space itself is never directly or phenomenologically "given" (for one thing, as we shall see, because it is infinite), but must be always assumed.[18]

15. Melnick, *Kant's Analogies of Experience*, p. 11.

16. Ibid., p. 13.

17. Garnett, *Kantian Philosophy of Space* creates some wholly irrelevant problems concerning "temporal" priority. See note 6, this chapter.

18. Kant does speak of "an infinite given magnitude" at B39, but this again does not refer

Now, while these arguments still do not tell us anything about the ontological status of space, but only about what is required for any representation of space, at this point we are obviously entitled at least to ask about the nature of this a priori, underlying representation. Kant proceeds to that topic in the Third and Fourth Expositions, and argues that such a representation must be a pure intuition. "Space is not a discursive, or, as we say, general concept of relations of things in general but a pure intuition (*reine Auschauung*)" (B39 = A24–25). As we shall see, there is a great deal more involved in this claim than this brief Exposition reveals, and Kant defends the view in more ways than appear here. In this paragraph, Kant's *chief* intention is clear. Since there can be only one space, its representation must be that kind of representation by which a singular item is represented, an intuition. (Kant stipulates two criteria for intuitions at B317 = A320; intuitions are "singular" representations standing in "immediate" relation to objects. I shall discuss the immediacy criterion in a moment.) This means that the "diverse" spaces apprehended empirically cannot be considered instances of a common or general concept, but as all "parts," "limitations" of this one space. Actually, Kant's argument has three separate components to it here. He argues that the relations between individual spaces and space cannot be that of "instances" of a concept to a concept, but must be "parts." (Space is not a "general concept.") Then he notes that these parts do not precede the representation of such a whole, as if the whole were arrived at by adding up the parts. (Space is thus not an empirical concept.) Third, Kant gratuitously adds a remark about the possibility of geometrical judgments which obviously belongs in the Transcendental Expositions. But again, his main point is clear: since space can only be represented as singular, its representation must be an intuition, not a concept, and diverse spaces must be parts, not instances.

Later, in the *Critique,* Kant will add some important details to this characterization, and we should note them before examining the above argument in greater detail. As the geometry claim briefly indicates, one of Kant's other reasons for thinking that intuitions should not be confused with concepts is his thesis that pure intuitions make possible the "construction" of concepts in mathematics. Thus, while it is correct, I believe, to claim that Kant's argument for the formal ideality of space can be made out independent of any theory about mathematics, it will certainly be important to examine the role of pure intuition in mathematics, if we want to know more precisely what a pure intuition, also called a

---

to the perception of an infinite whole. Rather, Kant means that, insofar as space is presupposed in any representation of particular spaces, *that* presupposed space must be represented as infinite.

"formal intuition," is. Moreover, as will become clear when we examine what I shall identify as the "idealistic turn" in Kant's argument, another reason for Kant's claim about the intuitive nature of our representation of space is his invoking of the so-called "immediacy criterion" as definitive of intuitions. That is, because a presupposed "background" (to use Melnick's term) of space as a whole is *immediately* (noninferentially and nonjudgmentally) involved in *any* direct apprehension of objects it should be considered that kind of representation possible immediately for humans — an intuition. Indeed, this claim, when expanded, will function significantly in Kant's argument that space is not just a condition of apprehension generally, but a form of *sensibility,* of that faculty whereby (and only whereby) humans can be in immediate contact with objects.

But these two defenses of space as a pure intuition come later and are involved with the ideality arguments. For now, the point at issue is the singularity criterion. Kant's point itself is straightforward, although its force obviously depends on the "priority" arguments already developed in the first two Expositions. He is claiming here that the space, say, bounded by the walls of this room is not an instance of the concept, space, but a limited part of all space, whereas this particular dog, say, is not a limited part of dogness, just a member of a class. He puts this claim more explicitly, and with more transcendental flourishes, in a footnote at B136.

Space and time all their parts are intuitions and therefore, with the manifold which they contain within them, particular representations (see the *Transcendental Aesthetic*), and therefore not mere concepts through which one and the same consciousness is met with in many representations, but many representations are to be met with contained in one representation, and the consciousness of it, therefore as composite [*zusammengesetzt*]; therefore the unity of consciousness met with there is synthetic, but original.

As in the first two Expositions, it is the necessary priority of the whole of space which allows Kant to make these remarks. We do not *judge* (by means of a concept, space) that these objects are sufficiently like "something spatial" or "in spatial order" to be considered under such spatial concepts. All appearances of outer sense must be immediately *in* one space for them to be numerically distinct objects about which to judge.

Nothing said so far should preclude that we *can* consider and even analyze the "concept" of space, or, perhaps more properly, of spatiality. In fact, that is just what we are doing in these expositions, defined at B38 = A23 as giving the "clear, though not necessarily exhaustive representation of that which belongs to the concept." For example, if we were to try to prove that some of our experience must be spatial, we could try to prove that no *concept* of experience which we could make intelligible to ourselves could be so intelligible without including something like a *concept* of space (as in Strawson's "auditor" argument).[19] The point Kant wants to make here is that such a concept of space does not explain the original role of space *in experience itself.* (He will later add that spatial concepts in geometry cannot be derived from any such concept.) Thus we arrive at the somewhat confusing claim that, in analyzing the concept of space, we have to conclude that space is not originally a concept, but a "mode of representing," one whole singular mode (ultimately a single system of relations, determinable prior to experience).

As before, then, much of Kant's argument rests on an analysis of the possibility of numerical identity. In this paragraph, that tactic is evident when Kant explains what is required to speak of "diverse" or "many" spaces (*von vielen Räumen*). With respect to concepts, this requirement makes it impossible to speak of differentiated spaces as subconcepts of some general concepts. Or,

> If x and y are two cubic-foot regions of space then, qua falling under the general concept of a cubic foot region of space, x and y are indistinguishable. If we did not consider the instances of this concept as being different parts of one space, we could not distinguish *different* instances of the concept.[20]

And, again, the priority of this whole over its parts has nothing to do with the full conditions of empirical awareness. In this context, to use his language, space is a *totum,* not a *compositum,* although when we are trying to determine the extent of some empirical whole of space, then it is true that the parts precede the whole (B456 = A518). In other words, it is space as a whole, a pure intuition, that is always prior to any part (just for it to be an identifiable part), even though the apprehension of some determinate space (say a figure) may depend on a synthetic "construction," or even though an empirical apprehension of a particular region of space may involve the synthesis of parts into some determinate whole. (In the latter case, that whole *is* an empirical "collection" or "composition" but itself still depends, as does each part, on the background intuition of infinite space as a whole.)

Finally, essentially making use of the same "priority" strategy obvious in the first three Expositions, Kant again contrasts intuitions and concepts, this time, though, by making use of space's infinity. He begins the Fourth Exposition[21] by simply asserting that "space is represented as an infinite given magnitude" (B40). The question he wants to ask is whether we can explain this infinity by appeal to the logic of concepts. He argues

19. P. F. Strawson, *Individuals* (London: Methuen, 1959), chap. 2, pp. 59–86. For the relevance of the argument to Kantian themes, see J. Bennett, *Kant's Analytic* (Cambridge: Cambridge University Press, 1966), chap. 3, pp. 33–44.

20. Melnick, *Kant's Analogies,* p. 10.

21. I deal here only with the second-edition version of the Exposition.

that it cannot be. While it is true that every concept can have an infinite number of instances corresponding to it, no concept can *contain* an infinite number of representations "within it," i.e., as defining marks, as essentially involved in the *sense* of that concept. Such a concept would be impossible for a human mind to comprehend. But the infinity of space means that an infinite number of the parts of space are contained *within* that space. That is, *some* finite collection of subsidiary concepts must be used to define a concept if it is to be determinate at all. But we cannot consider the relation between "the distance between the earth and the moon," "the distance between New York and California" and "the distance between these four walls" in that way, as subconcepts of the concept, space. *Each* of these is numerically identifiable only as *already* part of one space, and the relation of these parts can be extended *indefinitely* (which is what Kant seems to mean by infinity here), and could never collectively constitute the concept of space, if space were only a concept.

Admittedly, much could still be said about each of these arguments,[22] but I believe the above gives a reasonably clear and defensible picture of what Kant wants to say and how he wants to defend it. He has specified what he believes to be two essential requirements for the representation of space — that it is a priori, not derived from but underlying all empirical apprehension, and that it is an intuitive representation, that space can only be represented as one space. The idealistic turn in his argument begins when he asks an archetypically transcendental question — What must *space* be like such that its representation has these characteristics? More precisely, Kant asks: What must *space* be such that we could represent it intuitively (not conceptually) and a priori? It is his answer to this question which clearly shows, I believe, a continually repeated mode of argument (Kant's "methodology," if you will), in his case for the formal results of his enterprise, and for the foundationalist status of these results.

First, though, we should stress the importance of being able to defend the thesis that there is here and must be an argument, and one that doesn't beg the question. Some commentators are content just to point

22. This is especially true of the last argument about infinity. See especially Charles Parsons, "Infinity and Kant's Conception of the 'Possibility of Experience'," in R. P. Wolff (ed.), *Kant: A Collection of Critical Essays* (New York: Doubleday Anchor, 1967), pp. 37–53. Parsons argues that there is a lack of fit between Kant's own views concerning the mathematical infinite and the notion of the possibility of experience. While I believe that some of Parsons's criticisms are based on too psychological an interpretation of the latter notion, he does raise an extremely important general question in the article: To what extent can we regard the appeal to a form of sensibility as an *explanation* of some basic

out here the connection that supposedly exists in Kant as an unquestionable presupposition between apriority and subjectivity.[23] However, even Paton, who occasionally appeals to this connection in this way, suggests an attempt at an argument by Kant. He writes that the idealistic argument is supported by two claims:

> (1) that we determine the nature of space and time through and through independently of experience; and (2) that in this way we can determine, independently of experience, the spatial and temporal conditions to which all objects of experience must conform.[24]

Paton argues that establishing each of these establishes that space is a form of sensibility (more properly, a form of outer sense), that thus space is unintelligible except with respect to a human observer.

To be sure, Kant was obviously convinced that the whole problem of the "applicability" of (especially) geometry in a very general way helped support this argument that space is a pure form of sensibility.[25] We could thereby account for the connection between the theorems of geometry and, say, rules of measurement in experience. But Paton's use of the "applicability" issue here seems to me quite premature. For one thing, the issue of applicability is not fully addressed by Kant until he attempts to prove the first "principle" of the understanding, the Axioms of Intuition. Prior to that proof, Kant even writes once that

> through the determination of pure intuition we can acquire a priori knowledge of objects, as in mathematics, but only in regard to their form, as appearances; whether there can be things which must be intuited in this form is still left undetermined. (B147)

He goes on in this passage from the second edition Deduction to argue that the "supposition" that there are empirical intuitions given in accordance with these pure determinations must be deductively established, finally through an argument defending the objective reality of the category Quantity (that "all intuitions are extensive magnitudes").

That is, while it is surely a part of Kant's *explanation* of the applicability of mathematics, especially geometry, to say that space is a form of sensibility, it cannot be said that such is an element of his *proof* that space is such a pure form. The issue of applicability — indeed, the whole

---

properties of space? I believe that this is a general problem in Kant's whole methodology, and shall address it directly in chap. 3, sections 4 and 5.

23. Cf. Paton, *Kant's Metaphysic,* pp. 34 and 135.

24. Ibid., p. 166.

25. See especially B206 = A166; B196 = A157. As I shall argue below, though, it is instructive that both these passages occur in discussions of the Principles and nothing like them appears in the Aesthetic.

issue of the "empirical reality" of space — develops as a *consequence* of Kant's proof that space is a form of sensibility and so cannot be invoked as an element of that proof without an obvious *petitio*.[26] Rather, the key to Kant's idealistic move lies wholly in (1) once we add that this space is an intuition. He will try to *show* that, once we have proved that space can be represented independent of experience, then we know that in dealing with space we must be dealing with our own "mode of knowledge" (or *form*), and once we know that space is an intuition, a singular representation, we know that we are dealing with a mode or form of *sensible* knowledge, a form of sensibility. I turn now to these two components of the idealistic argument.

3. Space as a Form

The importance of this feature of Kant's argument in any assessment of his formal idealism should be apparent at this point. With some ingenuity, after all, it would still be possible to accept a good deal of what Kant says and explain it by appeal to a transcendentally realist theory of space, or by defending the claim that knowledge of relations in pure space is indeed a priori but finally analytic, that such determination might serve as a conventionally projected structure, *applied* to our experience, and requires no form of sensibility to explain its possibility. To counter such alternatives, Kant relies heavily, in a characteristic way, on what must be the case if we are to *know* what we have established about the representation of space. The first characteristic, that it is a priori, prevents the realist option, and the second, its being an intuition, prohibits the second. He makes this argument in quite a compressed way, though. There are two *loci classici.* The first is in the *Critique,* in the Transcendental Expositions, although its force can be separated from any direct reliance on Kant's theory of geometry.

> How, then, can there exist in the mind an outer intuition which precedes the objects themselves, and in which the concept of these objects can be determined a priori? Manifestly, not otherwise than in so far as the intuition has its seat in the subject only, as the formal character of the subject, in virtue of which, in being affected by objects, it obtains immediate representation, that is *intuition* of them; and only in so far, therefore, as it is merely the form of outer *sense,* in general. (B41)

The second passage containing this argument occurs in the *Prolegomena,* and makes much the same point in a more detailed way. There he begins with the apparently perplexing problem, "How is it possible to

intuit something a priori?" If we consider intuitions as intuitions of
objects, they would obviously seem to require the presence of the object,
and since Kant only allows one way in which we can be presented with
objects, such intuitions just could not be a priori. (Hence transcendental
realism must ultimately deny the apriority of our representation of
space.) We thus have to ask, as he does, "But how can the intuition of
the object precede the object itself?" The answer must be that a pure
intuition cannot be an intuition of an object at all, even though the actual
grammatical form of Kant's solution to the problem makes it sound as if
it is the intuition of a form, a special kind of object.

> There is therefore only one way in which my intuition can precede the
> actuality of the object, and be a priori knowledge [*und als Erkenntnis a priori
> stattfinde*], if, namely, this intuition contains nothing other than the form of
> sensibility, which form precedes [*vorhergeht*] in my subjectivity [*in meinem
> Subjekt*] the actual impressions through which I am affected by objects.[27]

Clearly, the basic element of Kant's case is the claim that there is no
other alternative to his, that we cannot account for the a priori character
of our representation of space if such a representation depended in any
way on the prior presence of some object, or content. Our only alternative is to explain this formal characteristic of all material representations
(that common to all of them, that they are in one space) by claiming that
it is "brought to" experience by the subject of experience, it is a subjective form. As Kant's own emphasis in the quotation from the *Critique*
indicates, once we further realize that this formal characteristic is *immediately* involved, prior to any conceptualization, in our apprehension of
objects, we are also required to say that this form is a form of sensibility;
that it is immediately involved in that mode of representing by virtue of
which such apprehension is possible. This requirement thus precludes any
view that spatial determinations could be "conceptually" determined and
judgmentally "applied" to some manifold. Any manifold, as sensed in
outer sense, is always already spatial.

    Obviously, this line of argument, since it depends so heavily on a
disjunctive syllogism (Exclusively *p* v *q* v *r*; ~p and ~q; therefore *r*) is
open to an attack which shows that Kant has not at all exhausted the
possible alternative ways of accounting for what the Metaphysical Expositions had established. Indeed, historically, the major area of controversy
about Kant's ideality doctrine was concentrated on just such a "neglected
alternatives" approach. More specifically, the objection holds that there
is no reason why space should not be considered *both* contributed by the
subject *and* not only a form of sensibility, but *also* as valid for things in

27. Kant, *Gesammelte Schriften,* vol. 4, p. 282.

themselves. This kind of approach initially became well known in the Fischer-Trendelenburg controversy, and was reformulated more precisely by Vaihinger.[28] But there is no reason to limit the approach to this "third" alternative. I want here only to indicate that this whole tactic is one way to object to the strong "only if" at the heart of Kant's idealism argument.

While there is a good deal of literature about this kind of response, I believe other commentators have shown that Kant was not guilty of this neglect,[29] and, in any case, this kind of objection is not the one I want to consider here. More important for the overall purposes of this study is another, equally obvious response to the argument made above, one central to the whole issue of Kant's formalism. Namely, one can ask whether Kant's own alternative does account for what he thinks needs to be accounted for, and if so, how. Kant has argued, in other words, that space is a pure intuition, and can be such if and only if it is a form of sensibility. I want to ask, prior to the problem of various alternatives, whether that identification at all helps us to understand, in any determinate way, how a priori representations of space are possible, and do necessarily underlie our empirical apprehension of particular, sensible objects. Is our ability to determine the pure properties of space *explained* by calling space a form of sensibility?

Before raising such a question, two points about this kind of approach must be made. First, in making his case about the forms of sensibility, Kant appears to go considerably beyond just what the Metaphysical Expositions had established. Instead of its only being the case that all empirical apprehension presupposes the "background" of one infinite magnitude, Kant's argument now also mentions that we must be capable of determining, again a priori, the properties of this whole. He appears just to assume that once he has established the priority thesis of the Expositions, he is entitled to assume that we are able to determine without the aid of experience that, for example, *in this space* which underlies all apprehension, two straight lines cannot enclose a plane, that triangles have 180 degrees, that the square of the hypotenuse is equal to the sum of the squares of the other two sides, and so on into increasing complexity. He is not, at this point, appealing directly to any claim about the syntheticity of geometrical judgments to establish the ideality thesis, but he does assume that this one space which underlies empirical appre-

28. Cf. Hans Vaihinger, *Kommentar zu Kants Kritik der reinen Vernunft* (Stuttgart: W. Spandau, 1881–92), vol. 2, pp. 136–37.

29. Henry Allison, "The Non-Spatiality of Things in Themselves for Kant," *Journal of the History of Philosophy* 14 (1976): 313–21. I have also seen a draft of an improved version of Allison's defense of Kant (from a forthcoming book), and believe it establishes that the classic neglected-alternatives approach depends on an incorrect interpretation of Kant's idealism.

hension must include various possibilities and exclude others, that it has its mathematical properties, and that we can determine these properties a priori. There is no argument for the existence of this mathematics and Kant clearly believes he does not need to establish that this pure space *not only* underlies experience, but that specific mathematical properties of this space can be determined.[30]

This assumption is important to stress, given the nature of Kant's argument thus far. Kant's argument from the nature of spatial representation could obviously be compared with arguments about the requirements inherent in our representation of God, if God is to be God. However, if we then go on to ask about the *being* of God such that we could know those attributes to be true to him, we have assumed, if such an exercise is to have a point, that we do know those attributes to be true of God and want to explain that ontological and epistemological possibility. It is this kind of extension I have in mind here — Kant's assumption that we *are* able to determine the characteristics of the one, infinite space necessarily involved in all empirical apprehension. With this assumed, the question raised above becomes relevant: How does claiming that space *is* a form of sensibility account for such a possibility?

Second, we need to note that Kant uses the word "intuition" in a way that deliberately exploits an ambiguity inherent in the notion. When Kant says that space can only be a pure intuition if it is a form of sensibility, we have to note that intuition (*Anschauung*) there can mean either the act of intuiting (*Anschauen*), or that intuited (*das Angeschauete*).[31] (The same ambiguity is apparent in the term Kant uses to help define intuition — representation, *Vorstellung*). This ambiguity is helpful to keep in mind when we note that Kant, for the most part, does not claim that space is some object known *by* pure intuition, but that it *is* a pure intuition. As we saw in the Metaphysical Expositions, this *originally* meant that space

30. Obviously, such an assumption about the existence of mathematics is far weaker than, for example, Russell maintained. Russell contended that Kant believed that Euclidean theorems could not be deduced from the axioms without construction, and therefore "based" mathematics on sensible intuitions. When Hilbert, adding some axioms, found a way to deduce such theorems logically, Kant's position was, according to Russell, rendered out of date. Cf. *Introduction to Mathematical Philosophy* (London: Allen & Unwin, 1960) and *Mysticism and Logic and Other Essays* (London: Allen & Unwin, 1959), p. 74. A similar well-known claim about Kant's supposedly dated reliance on Euclidean geometry was made by Hans Reichenbach, *The Philosophy of Space and Time* (New York: Dover, 1957). These claims seem to me to overstate Kant's dependence (cf. note 4 this chapter) and, in any case, to be more than Kant needs to establish the ideality claim.

31. Cf. the first paragraph of R. Aquila's "The Relationship between Pure and Empirical Intuition in Kant," *Kant-Studien* 68 (1977): 275; or George Schrader's remarks in "The Transcendental Ideality and Empirical Reality of Kant's Space and Time," *The Review of Metaphysics* 4 (1951): 517.

could only be represented as a singular representation. However, exactly what the idealism argument establishes is that this representation is a represent*ing,* an intuit*ing* by virtue of which all spaces are immediately apprehended as part of one space. This is just what Kant means when he claims that "this pure form of sensibility may also itself be called a pure intuition" (B35–36 = A21). As isolated in the Expositions, the notion that space was a pure intuition left unresolved which of the two senses of intuition was intended. Space could have been a singular object repre-sent*ed* in any apprehension of empirical space. The ideality argument claims rather that space must be an "intuiting," a mode of representing objects, and is only thereby a form of that intuit*ed,* a "form of intuition." Clarifying this ambiguity thus returns us to the question asked above more precisely: How does this sense of space as a pure intuition, an intuiting or immediate mode of representing sensible objects, help account for our (assumed) ability to specify the determinate ways in which the manifold must be sensibly apprehended?[32] Kant clearly believes this is the *only* way to account for such an ability and that obviously involves the weaker claim that it is *a* way.

4. Mathematical Methodology and the Problem of Sensibility

To raise this question, though, we shall have to appeal to a later section of the *Critique* and to deal with a contemporary controversy surrounding this issue. Kant's attempt to explain how his position on space accounts for the "methodology" of mathematics occurs, appropriately enough, in his Transcendental Doctrine of Method (B735 = A707 ff.). It is in this section that Kant tries to show how his account of space as a form of sensibility functions in the determination of what the specific modes of representing ("rules of sensibility") are. In investigating this section, it should be stressed at the outset that we have already arrived at a general

---

32. The interpretation of *Anschauung* as *Anschauen* is advanced in helpful detail by Hans Graubner, *Form und Wesen* (Bonn: Bouvier, 1972), p. 93 ff. Cf. some helpful remarks about the same issue by Peter Krausser, "The Operational Conception of 'reine Anschau-ung' (Pure Intuition) in Kant's Theory of Experience and Science," *Studies in History and Philosophy of Science* (1972–73): 81–87. The most detailed commentary on the pure intuition/form of intuition issue known to me is Buchdahl's in *Metaphysics and the Philoso-phy of Science*, pp. 514–615. Buchdahl notes that Kant is interested *both* in the question of the possibility of anything being located in space at all (explained by space as a form of intuition) and in the possibility of various ways of locating objects *determinately* in space and knowing their spatial properties (explained by the doctrine of formal intuition, involving concepts somehow). He goes on to argue that Kant's answer to this latter question need not, and probably did not, involve a commitment to one geometry as the form of appearances. See especially pp. 606–15. I argue here that the gap between Kant's general argument that appearances must be spatial and his *theory* of the specification of *any* forms

sketch of how Kant conceived of the relation between pure intuition and sensibility, and that nothing in that sketch so far appeals to what is sometimes referred to as a psychologistic account of intuition.[33] That is, nothing Kant says in the Aesthetic trades off the potentially psychologistic connotations of intuition, as if space must be "looked at" (an-schauen) to be determined, and is *thereby* connected with sensibility. Thus far that connection is derived wholly from two basic points, one assumed, the other established. Kant assumes that sensibility is the only mode of direct contact we have with the external world. Moreover, he takes himself to have proved that all such contact immediately involves objects of perception which are in one space. This involvement is not a result of judgment, nor is it directly given by the sensory manifold. Thus far he has argued that there is only one way both of these points could be made together — if space is a form of that sensible apprehension. Our task now is to ask how Kant thinks this line of thinking can be extended into an explanation of this mode of representing, and obviously a critical issue in that extension will be whether he can do so while still avoiding the psychologistic elements with which his position is often associated.

First, it is clear that Kant realizes that an explanation of this extension is required. In the *Prolegomena,* he admits that the general notion of space as a pure intuition underlying all apprehension by itself tells us very little about this space. The passage introduces so many additional elements to the account given thus far that it needs to be quoted at length.

> Now I ask: do the laws of nature lie in space, and does the understanding learn them merely by seeking to investigate the complicated meaning which lies in space; or *do these laws lie in the understanding,* and the way in which it determines space according to the conditions of synthetic unity, from which all its concepts proceed? *Space is something so uniform,* and in respect to all particular properties *so indeterminate that one should certainly not seek a store of natural laws in it.* On the other hand, that which determines space to be in the form of a circle or a cone or a sphere, is the understanding, so far as *it* contains the ground of the unity of their constructions. The mere universal form of intuition, called space, is therefore the substratum of all intuitions determinable to particular objects and in it of course lie the conditions of the

---

of our spatial awareness cause problems in Kant's theory of formality, however strongly or weakly one takes his commitment to Euclidean geometry.

33. I should mention that by "psychologistic" here and throughout this discussion I intend no reference to any specific theory of psychologism, especially any psychologistic theory of truth. Obviously, with the Principles established, Kant believes that mathematics has "objective validity" as a condition for the possibility of experience. But a kind of epistemological psychologism is at work if one claims that we are only able to determine the truths of mathematics by reliance on what the mind is able to *do,* think, imagine, or construct. Said a simpler way, the "psychologistic problem" I deal with here is the one Hintikka, Russell, and others worried about in the discussions cited below.

possibility and manifoldness of these. But the unity of the objects is wholly determined by the understanding and according to conditions which lie in its own nature, and so the understanding is the origin of the universal law of nature, because it takes in all appearances under its own laws and thereby a priori produces [*zu Stande bringt*] experience (as to its form) by means of which everything which can only be known through experience is necessarily subjected to its laws.[34] [my emphasis]

Now this passage, with its stress on the understanding and concepts, clearly indicates that we cannot account for our determination of the characteristics of space solely by appeal to its intuitional status. But it is also initially apparent how such an intuition will in principle function in Kant's explanation of these determinations. The "universal form of intuition called space" somehow contains within it the "conditions of the possibility and manifoldness" of all determinable particular intuitions. When he finally gets around to explaining this notion, in the section of the *Methodenlehre* entitled, "The Discipline of Pure Reason in Its Dogmatic Use," one idea will emerge in particular as explanation for this role of intuitions in determining the mathematics of space — "constructability."[35]

First, Kant draws a general distinction between philosophic knowledge and mathematical knowledge.

Philosophical knowledge is the knowledge gained by reason from concepts; mathematical knowledge is knowledge gained by reason from the construction of concepts. (B741 = A713)

Then, more explicitly,

Thus philosophical knowledge considers the particular only in the universal, mathematical knowledge the universal in the particular [*Besonderen*], or even in the single instance [*Einzelnen*], though still always a priori and by means of reason. (B742 = A714)

Elsewhere, Kant makes this same point by distinguishing merely logical possibility from real possibility.[36] That is, a concept is possible as long as

34. Kant, *Gesammelte Schriften,* vol. 4, pp. 321–22.

35. Kant's first clear account of construction in mathematics occurs in the 1763 essay, "Untersuchung über die Deutlichkeit der Grundsätze der natürlichen Theologie und der Moral," *Gesammelte Schriften,* vol. 2, p. 276 ff. It becomes a dominant and quite firmly held principle of his theory thereafter. It is, for example, a prominent theme of the opening pages of the *Eberhardschrift,* and illustrates the connection discussed below between constructive possibilities and real possibility. Cf. Allison, *The Kant-Eberhard Controversy,* p. 107 ff.

36. B271 = A224 ff. An interpretation of the connection between our determination of real possibility and a theory of synthetic a priori judgments has recently been made by

its markers are not internally contradictory, but in making this determination, we do not thereby determine whether the object designated by that object is real and, more to the point for the comparison with mathematics, whether it *could* be real.[37] We can, apparently, make this determination if we try to construct that concept in pure intuition. And with this method, we do seem to have a connection with a "form of sensibility." This construction would seem to involve a pure determination of the *sensibly* represent*able*. Anything constructable, any concept whose rule for construction we can follow a priori, sets the limits for the empirically representable. Anything not so constructable would be outside those limits (even if logically possible), since we cannot encounter anything in the material of experience which is not, according to this procedure, really possible. This is apparently what Kant means when he writes:

> Mathematics can achieve nothing with a pure concept, but hastens at once to an intuition, in which it considers the concept *in concreto,* but certainly not empirically, but only in an intuition which it has presented a priori, that is, constructed, and in which everything which follows from the universal conditions of construction must hold in general for the object of such a constructed concept. (B743–44 = A715–16)

Of course, it is just this psychologistic way of construing constructability ("what mental pictures are possible") that has generated so much well-founded criticism of Kant, particularly since Frege. To be sure, there are indeed passages where Kant unmistakably gives the impression that this is exactly what he means in appealing, within the methodology of mathematics, to the form of sensibility. For example:

> That space is a formal, a priori condition of outer experience, that the constructing synthesis *through which we construct a triangle in imagination is precisely the same as that which we exercise in the apprehension* of an appearance . . . these are the considerations that alone enable us to connect the representation of the possibility of such a thing with the concept of it. (B271 = A224) [my emphasis]

However, before the famous objections to psychologism in mathematics are relevant, even such psychologistic passages as the above have not made clear the extent of Kant's reliance on the "sensibly picturable." It *is* clear that he is struggling to find some way to distinguish between a logically possible "mathematics" (although it might not deserve that name in Kant) and the mathematics of *the* space against which our empirical

---

Gordon G. Brittan, Jr., *Kant's Theory of Science* (Princeton: Princeton University Press, 1978), pp. 13–28.

37. Cf. Kant's "ship's clock" example at B757 = A729.

apprehension always occurs. He has already argued that there must be *one* space, and thus this space cannot have incompatible, even if equally logically possible, characteristics. It might be open to him to claim that we just do not directly know what these characteristics are, that we can determine a priori various possible mathematics of this space and then, say, choose an alternative as this "background" which seems to fit best all that we do know about, say, the dynamical relations of bodies in space.[38] But Kant has also argued that space could not be "immediately" involved in the apprehension of empirical regions and bodies unless it were a form of sensibility, and if it is a form of sensibility, it must be possible to say something about *it* independent of any knowledge of the material of experience. Thus, Kant cannot but try to explain the limitations actually inherent in various possibilities and impossibilities of *this* space. But, given all this, this need not mean that the key notion in determining these limits, constructability, need be a test of our psychological powers of imagination. For one thing, the triangle example cited above should not lead us to think that Kant believes that our ability to construct the "look" of a triangle in pure intuition is what is directly involved in the empirical apprehension of a triangle, as if this were how the form of sensibility requirement figures in mathematics and explains the limits of constructability. Quite obviously, we do not have to generate successively a three-sided figure in order to *perceive* any empirical triangle. Nothing Kant says in this passage implies this reliance on the construction of a sensible "look," and the earlier passage from the *Prolegomena* suggests rather that the determination of *rules* of construction "depends" on the understanding, not the (reproductive) imagination. This suggests that we can *begin* to answer our question — Just how does the claim that space is a form of sensibility figure in Kant's explanation of mathematical methodology? — in a way more indirect than is usually attempted. Briefly, that involvement need not mean that such a methodology directly involves trying to discover whether a spatial concept is purely "sensible" or not. Rather, we might first of all note that Kant's general interest is in explaining the status of the results of mathematical reasoning. Kant could argue that he has already demonstrated that these purely determinable characteristics of space just must *be* the forms of sensibility. This would mean that the notion of a form of sensibility would not function directly as the *source* of constructable intuitions (in the sense of psychological limits) but the mathematically defined constructables simply *are* the forms of sensibility in the loose sense just defined.

This interpretation suggests that Kant's reliance on the form of sensibility to explain what space is serves only to offer a *transcendental* account

38. Cf. H. Poincaré, *Science and Method* (New York: Dover, 1952), pp. 93–116.

of why some concepts turn out to be constructable and others not (i.e., because there must be one space underlying all empirical spaces, and as we have seen this means that it must be a subjective form of sensibility). Thus it would be quite possible for Kant to be wrong about the limits of constructability, *not* because he relied on a narrow psychologistic use of sensibility in mathematics, but because he did not realize the extent of possible constructability in mathematics, even though he could still be right that space is an ideal form of sensibility. Intuitionists generally must confront the (for Kant "transcendental") question of *why* certain concepts are constructable and others not, and Kant's answer about one space underlying all apprehension (a form of sensibility) is an answer to that kind of question.

There is an analogue here to Kant's transcendental procedure elsewhere. Briefly, construction in mathematics serves a function analogous to transcendental deduction in philosophy. It establishes the objective reality of a concept, and does so a priori. Now, when Kant thinks he is called on in the Metaphysical Deduction, to explain why there should be a certain number of such pure concepts, and why they are these concepts, he appeals to the finite *forms* of human understanding, and offers his "clue" that all thinking is judging. We do not, though, "deduce" a concept *by* trying to prove it is a form of judgment and, likewise, we do not try to construct a concept by showing it is a form of sensibility. But we do try to offer an explanation of the *status* of these concepts by showing they *are* subjective forms of the thought of an object. That is what the Metaphysical Deduction allows us to do. In like manner, I am suggesting, the Metaphysical Expositions allows us to *explain* the status of the results of mathematical construction, even while this account is not what we appeal to when we try to do mathematics.

Obviously, though, this can only be an initial comment and cannot end the discussion. We clearly still need to ask: If we do not appeal in any crudely psychologistic way to sensibility to determine what is "really possible," how *do* we determine the mathematics of the one space we already know must be (in the sense defined) the form of sensibility?

Unfortunately, a proper assessment of Kant's views on this issue would launch us into topics in the philosophy of mathematics which would require a book in itself to cover. However, it is important to note that recent scholarship on the issue, particularly by Beth, Hintikka, and Parsons, has done much to open up lines of interpretation which help correct some of the more simplistic interpretations of Kant, and which suggest ways in which his views might be considered as more in accord with post-Kantian developments in mathematics. Since the topic of these reconstructions bears directly on the issue at hand — how Kant's use of the form of sensibility in mathematics helps explain what he thinks such a form is — it will be helpful to conclude this section by considering these reconstructions. It is especially important for my purposes to consider Hintikka's interpretation since he is interested in interpreting the role of intuitions in Kant's theory of mathematics without *any* reliance on the forms of sensibility.

There are two main components to Hintikka's analysis.[39] First, he asks whether there is anything inherent in the very notion of intuition which would have led Kant always to connect intuitions necessarily with sensibility. He concludes that there is not. Second, he asks, if this connection is not essential to Kant's case, are there indications of a mathematical methodology which makes use of intuitions, but which would not depend on any connection with sensibility? Following some suggestions of Beth, Hintikka concludes that there are. I believe that these suggestions are valuable but that they go too far in abandoning the form of sensibility dimension.

In establishing the first point, Hintikka notes that Kant seems to give two criteria for intuitions, singularity and immediacy. The former tells us that intuitions do not represent by means of markers which several objects have in common, but rather pick out one and only one object. Hintikka suggests such representations are analogous to if not identical with what we would today call singular terms.[40] The latter criterion seems to imply that intuitions are possible by virtue of the direct presence of an object before the mind. At least, this appears to be what he means when describing empirical intuitions, and would certainly connect his doctrine of intuitions with sensibility (since sensibility is the only way objects can be directly present to human minds). Now Hintikka does not deny that Kant indeed believed there to be an important connection between sensibility and intuition, but he claims that Kant did not assume such a connection, and tried to argue for it. Such a claim is certainly in accord with much of what has been established in this chapter. Hintikka goes on, though, to point out that it is possible to consider Kant's theory of intuitions *prior* to, or independently from that connection, and that when we do, we can discern a theory of intuitions in mathematics which has no

39. Hintikka has written several articles on these topics, but for my purposes, I shall concentrate on two: "Kant on the Mathematical Method," in *Kant Studies Today,* ed. L. W. Beck (La Salle, Ill.: Open Court, 1969), pp. 117–40, and "On Kant's Notion of Intuition (*Anschauung*)" in *The First Critique,* ed. T. Penelhum and J. J. MacIntosh (Belmont, Calif.: Wadsworth, 1969), pp. 38–53. Further details of his interpretation can be found in the following articles: "Kant's 'New Method of Thought' and His Theory of Mathematics," *Ajatus* 27 (1965); and especially the four articles, "An Analysis of Analyticity," "Are Logical Truths Tautologies?" "Kant Vindicated," and "Kant and the Tradition of Analysis," published in *Deskription, Analytizität und Existenz,* ed. Paul Weingartner (Salzburg: Anton Pustet, 1966), pp. 182–272.
40. Hintikka, "On Kant's Notion," p. 43.

inherent connection with the notion of a form of sensibility. In such a theory, Hintikka argues, the immediacy criterion would just be a "corollary" of the singularity criterion and not independent of it.[41] Intuitions are singular representations and *thus* not mediately represented in the mind by common characteristics, but immediately present. This latter sense of the criterion suggests nothing particularly "intuitive" in the normal sense, that is, nothing "sensible" or picturable.

With this established, the second part of Hintikka's reconstruction is relevant. He argues that we can make a great deal of Kant's comments about methodology in the *Methodenlehre* (particularly his attempt to assimilate geometry, arithmetic, and algebra to the same method of proof); if we make use of this "austere" sense of intuition-as-singular-term.[42] For, when we examine how proofs are constructed in Euclid (clearly a paradigm case for what Kant was trying to explain), we do in fact find that a great deal depends, not on any direct appeal to "picturability" and thus no direct reliance on sensibility, but instead on a use of singular representations to establish a theorem. Roughly, that means that if we want to prove something about triangles, we represent an individual triangle, establish that claim about it (by the use of the axioms, postulates, other theorems, and the properties of this triangle), and then argue that, since the individual in question was selected arbitrarily, the same must hold for all such triangles. In Euclid, this procedure is especially relevant in the "setting-out" of this individual (the εκθεσίς) and in the "preparation" of the figure (κατασκευή).[43] And, more to the eventual point Beth and Hintikka want to make, this means that such arguments can be formulated in first-order predicate calculus, even while "making use of intuition" in the above sense. That is, if we want to prove $(x)(Px \supset Rx)$, we assume that some a such that Pa, establish $Pa \supset Ra$, and conclude $(x)(Px \supset Rx)$. The key notion in this reconstruction is the explanation of the εκθεσίς by means of existential instantiation, and the claim that this is what is (at best possibly) meant by Kant's appeal to intuition in his theory of mathematics. Further, this interpretation also depends on being able to show that

> if a proposition B of geometry is proved by a proof which appeals to axioms, A_1
> ... A_n ... then in general, the conditional $A_1 \& ... \& A_n \supset B$

41. Cf. Hintikka's reply to Parsons's objections in his "Kantian Intuitions," *Inquiry* 15 (1972): 342.

42. I should mention here a preliminary objection to Hintikka's whole approach: that Kant does not have a doctrine of "singular terms" in the contemporary sense. See Manley Thompson, "Singular Terms and Intuitions in Kant's Epistemology," *Review of Metaphysics* 26 (1972): 314–43. I believe Thompson is correct as far as he goes, but am interested in other aspects of Hintikka's analysis here. I return to some problems raised by Thompson in chapter 6.

43. Hintikka, "Kant on the Mathematical Method," p. 360 ff.

is synthetic; at any rate an appeal to intuition is made over and above any which is made in verifying the axioms.[44]

Now these interesting suggestions raise a number of problems. For one thing, it is undeniable that mathematical proof for Kant *must* make use of intuitions to establish theorems, and it is not clear whether an analogous argument can be made about this use of intuitions in such proofs. Also, Kant appears to have believed that the axioms and postulates of a geometry already limit the range over which individual variables may range. This limitation thus already makes use of the "constructable" possibilities determined by these axioms and postulates, and directs our attention back to where Kant seems to have thought the role of intuitions most significant — in limiting the axioms which could be posited. That is, as Parsons has pointed out, Kant's view seems to be (if the arguments of his mathematician-pupil Schultz can be trusted) that "mathematics fails to be analytic just because in its deductive development synthetic *premises* must be used."[45] That is, Schultz believed that *if* all the axioms were analytic, so would be all the theorems. But for our purposes, this reconstruction highlights some more general issues in Kant's use of the form of sensibility in his theory of mathematics.

First, the difference between the two criteria is stronger[46] and more directly relevant to the issue of sensibility than Hintikka appears to allow. We have already established that it is the "epistemological question" that Kant asks himself at B41 and in the *Prolegomena* that already establishes the idealism claim about space. That is important to keep in mind here since the immediacy criterion is an *epistemological* classification of intuitions. The singularity criterion tells us what kind of representation intuitions are, and the immediacy criterion tells us how such representations could be known, especially a priori. Now there is obviously a weak sense in which the immediacy criterion is epistemological for Hintikka too: all singular terms are represented without the mediation of common markers, but directly or immediately. In the case in question, they are individual free variables. But this is true of all individual representations, even those in logic (as Beth and Hintikka are also concerned to claim), and does not yet address the question most at issue in Kant's epistemo-

---

44. Charles Parsons, "Kant's Philosophy of Arithmetic," in *Philosophy, Science and Method,* eds. S. Morgenbesser, P. Suppes, M. White (New York: St. Martin's, 1969), p. 578. See Parsons's concise summary of the Beth-Hintikka position on pp. 578–80.

45. Ibid., p. 580.

46. Parsons points this out, but for a reason which seems to me mistaken (that there can be singular representations, such as definite descriptions, which are not "immediate"). I agree with Kirk Wilson that these latter would not be called singular representations by Kant, but concepts "used" in a singular way. Cf. his "Kant on Intuitions," *Philosophical Quarterly* 25 (1975): 247–65, esp. 252.

logical classification of intuitions. That question has always been: How could we represent an individual region of, relation in, or figure *in space* prior to or independent of the presence of an actual region or object(s)? When he then tells us that *these* representations must be immediate, he must mean that either they are possible only by virtue of the presence of an object before the mind, or that we can a priori determine the characteristics of the *one* space immediately underlying all empirical apprehension, and can do so independent of conceptual analysis, logical derivation, or empirical apprehension.[47] Such relations and characteristics are always immediately involved in any empirical apprehension, and not derived from them. Thus a pure or formal intuition is immediate by being a "partial" representation of the one whole space with which we are in immediate contact in pure intuition. All along Kant has insisted that this pure determination of the properties of this one space is possible, and that it is only possible if this space is a pure form of sensibility.

Thus, I am suggesting, the immediacy criterion already involves Kant in his claims about the forms of sensibility. A formal intuition is an intuition of *the* space underlying all apprehension, a representation of that whole with its "parts" — relations and figures within it. It is not a conceptual or empirical representation, in that sense immediate and pure, and thus makes possible what we are able to do in (at least) geometry. And, again, this would not be possible unless space were a pure form of sensibility.

Of course, this appeal to the immediacy of our representation of pure space does not mean that proofs are not needed in mathematics, just that such proofs must always ultimately be *grounded* in *the* pure intuition, space, which underlies any representation of a part of space. This appears to be what Kant meant when he said in the *Prolegomena* passage quoted earlier that "the mere universal form of intuition, called space, is therefore the *substratum* of all intuitions determinable to *particular* objects and in it of course lie the conditions of the possibility of the manifoldness of these." Or, in the second edition deduction, "But space and time are represented not merely as forms of sensible intuitions, but as themselves intuitions (which contain a manifold) and are therefore represented with the determinations of the unity of this manifold" (B160–61). Or, in the Aesthetic, "This form *as a pure intuition,* in which all objects must be determined, can contain principles of the relations of these objects before all experience" (B42 = A26) [my emphasis]. Finally, I think this view is

---

47. Not to mention that there is simply too much textual evidence linking intuition with sensibility in quite a strong way. Cf. B299 = A240: "The mathematician meets this demand by the construction of a figure, which, although produced a priori, is an appearance present to the senses." Hintikka wants to admit this connection, but I shall argue below that the issue cannot be discussed as separately as Hintikka would like.

directly confirmed by the way Kant actually makes use of the immediacy criterion in the key passage at B41, cited earlier.

In sum, if we keep in mind the original idealistic implications of Kant's epistemological question about pure intuitions, and the fact that he thinks he has established that there can only be one space, it can be concluded that the immediacy criterion cannot be fully understood apart from Kant's commitment to space as a form of sensibility. Admittedly, this whole situation is considerably murkier when we try to construct a corresponding interpretation for the role of a pure sensible intuition in arithmetic. Parsons has offered some interesting suggestions about that possibility,[48] but I am interested now in a more general problem still remaining in Kant's whole approach.

This will be apparent if we note that Hintikka freely admits that considerations like the above are indeed relevant to what we are now investigating — Kant's various reasons, including his reflections on mathematics, for concluding that space must be a form of sensibility. But Hintikka, in a way reminiscent of the argument suggested by Paton, claims that this issue arises only when the question of the "applicability" of mathematics to space is raised. Like Paton, he thus appears to argue that a chief *reason for* Kant's claim that space is a pure form of sensibility is just that fact, that the mathematics of space as determined a priori is the mathematics of "this world." Or

> The mutual relations of the individuals with which mathematical reasoning is concerned is due to the process by means of which we come to know the existence of individuals.[49]

This process is, of course, sensibility for Kant. However, it seems to me that if this is admitted, it renders problematic Hintikka's separation of the *procedure* of mathematics from reliance on "sensibility." The above claim, together with all else we have seen thus far, would seem to mean that the following Hintikkan picture of Kant's reasoning is not possible: we determine the mathematics of pure space a priori by virtue only of the reasoning about individuals peculiar to mathematical proof; admit that this mathematics does apply with certainty to any space we could experi-

---

48. Parsons is able to demonstrate a connection between mathematics and the senses by attention to Kant's remarks about symbolic operations, a connection evidenced very early in Kant's corpus (1764), even before the ideality thesis was developed. See especially, "Kant's Philosophy of Arithmetic," p. 589, and the remarks on time, pp. 550–91. Parsons admits though that his position appears to undermine Kant's distinction between logic and mathematics, p. 590.

49. Hintikka, "Kant on the Mathematical Method," p. 373. The claim is very similar, down to the use of the problematic locution "due to," to Paton's at p. 170 of *Kant's Metaphysics of Experience,* vol. 1.

ence; and then conclude that space must therefore be the form of
sensibility, and that this means that "the process by means of which we
come to know the existence" of *these introduced individuals* must have to
do with sensibility. What I have been arguing, and what the above
passage itself seems to support, is that Kant thinks he has established
prior to any transcendental exposition that space must be a form of
sensibility, that he appeals to that *result* to account for how we determine
the mathematics of this one space, and then uses these results to *explain*
(in a way which must involve the Principles) the applicability of mathematics. This difference in approach is quite important, I now want to
argue, because it reveals that Kant's case faces a difficult problem, one I
shall claim recurs again and again in his attempt to determine *what* the
forms of experience are.

5. Kant's Indeterminate Results

In order to state that problem, it might be best to begin with a summary
of the claims argued for thus far. I have attempted to present an
interpretation which locates Kant's argument that space is a form of
sensibility in his "exposition" of what is required if space is an a priori
intuitive representation. I then suggested that this argument is open, not
only to the objection that Kant has failed to consider all the alternatives,
but to the claim that his own alternative does not account for what he
thinks must be accounted for. More specifically, this objection raises the
demand that Kant explain how the claim that space is a form of sensible
intuition does account for our ability to determine a priori the characteristics of the one space in which everything must be apprehended. I then
admitted that the simplest way to answer this question was inadequate.
Kant does not appear to mean that the sensibly representable is how we
should understand the appeal to the use of the forms of sensibility in
order to explain what goes on in mathematical knowledge. His remarks
about arithmetic and algebra, as well as the lack of any direct textual
evidence for such a view of constructability, rule out such an alternative.[50]

---

50. I admit again that there are plenty of passages where Kant connects intuitability with
sensibility (e.g., B299 = A240), but he nowhere directly interprets that connection to mean
that the limits of intuitability are to be identified with the limits of imaginability. I also
assume that, should anything like the latter be his position, he would have to deal with
immediately obvious objections — such as: "what can be sensibly imagined" is contingent,
and depends on individual talent, etc. He never even begins to address the problem of
constructability in these terms. Finally, there is a very clear passage in Allison, *The
Kant-Eberhard Controversy* which decisively distinguishes intuitability from imaginability.
See the discussion of the difference between being able actually to construct, and having the
rule of construction, p. 127. See also the difference between "image" and "sensible" on
p. 134.

But, in discussing Hintikka, I also claimed that a reconstruction which eliminates all such appeals to sensibility eliminates too much. This is so not only because it eliminates a possible explanation of the applicability of mathematics, but because Kant's whole idealism argument depends on his being able to show that the only way space could be representable a priori is if it were a form of sensibility. This claim is supposed to account for what we are able to do in mathematics, and thus is involved in a strategy which must be accepted or rejected as a whole. And if we reject the idealism argument (which I believe must be done if we are to reconstruct the *Methodenlehre* in the way Hintikka suggests), much of Kant's case for his whole formal idealism collapses.

We are thus still faced with the problem of explaining the relevance of the forms of sensibility claim to our ability to provide a priori the mathematics of space. This question comes down to an explanation of how we are able to say anything determinate about such forms of experience. (As will be clearer in later chapters, we must be able to do this in a way consistent with the claim that these forms are the forms of all objects of experience and not simply "subjectively" imposed, be the real world as it may.) In sum, if the psychologistic way of explaining this determination is too crude, and Hintikka's reconstruction is too severe, what options are left?

To be sure, one reasonable way to respond to all this is to insist that this kind of question just asks for too much, that Kant simply believed that there was a certain "givenness" in the mathematically constructable, and there was no "explanation" for why certain things are constructable and others not. This is indeed a reasonable response, but I have tried to show throughout this chapter that we cannot accept it without rejecting an essential component of Kant's only argument for the formal ideality of space. That argument turns on an epistemological question which commits Kant to proving that no adequate representation of space and its parts is possible unless space were a form of sensibility. Moreover, in, for example, the Eberhard polemic, Kant clearly believes only he, and not the Leibnizians, can account for what happens in mathematics, and he at least believes he has done so by the use of the form of sensibility claim.[51]

However, if we consider in a general way Kant's transcendental strategy thus far, the problems encountered in this and the last chapter do not

---

51. Allison, *The Kant-Eberhard Controversy*, p. 110, and p. 120. This latter passage, incidentally, supports my interpretation above about when the issue of "applicability" enters Kant's argument, against Paton and Hintikka. Kant does not argue that *because* appearances are always given in accordance with the mathematically possible, the latter must be based on forms of sensibility. Rather, it is because mathematics can only be determined if space is a form of sensibility that appearances can then be said to be given in accordance with these forms.

seem very surprising. We might reasonably expect that there should be quite a large gap, difficult to traverse, between, on the one hand, the claim that experience would not be possible if based wholly on the given matter of experience, and on the other hand, what we appeal to in order to establish *what* these formal elements are. In this case, Kant's commitment to what can only be termed a radical formalism means that he has to try to explain the determinate character of these forms in strict isolation from any appeal to experience, and certainly without any appeal to, say, abstract entities, "existing" in some roughly Platonic sense. If he tries to account for the specific forms of experience by appeal to "what is established in mathematics," his argument is far too ad hoc, and begs the question he set himself in his idealism proof. If he tries to appeal to "what can be purely representable," he ends up with far too narrow a conception of mathematical methodology, and one which would encounter several other problems with respect to mathematical properties like infinity. If his procedure is reconstructed such that no direct connection with sensibility is assumed, it again becomes quite difficult (as in the first alternative above) to integrate that reconstructed methodology into his idealism argument.

It would be premature to conclude anything here from these problems. But we already can suggest that it might be possible to preserve Kant's critique of empiricism, and even accept the further claim that experience requires a subjective, formal component, and not then go Kant's further step and argue that these subjective conditions must be *formally specifiable,* without appeal to any "material" component whatsoever. Admittedly, it would take quite a lengthy discussion to understand what this loosening of Kant's strictly formal and strictly a priori methodology would be like. All I want to suggest at this point is that Kant's own initial account of the form and matter of experience leaves us with far too material or formless a notion of that matter, and far too formal or indeterminate a notion of that form. It doesn't seem possible to explain, except in an ad hoc and question-begging way, how we determine what these forms are, or what might be contributed to such an investigation by the matter of experience. To be fair, it should be admitted that Kant confronts these problems as a direct result of his attempt to specify a priori the necessary conditions of experience, and they are therefore not simply incidental, poor arguments. Once such a "turn" is taken, as admitted above, it is expectable that it will be quite difficult to know "what to appeal to" to establish what these conditions are. All I have tried to show thus far is that Kant's conception of form does not give him much room to maneuver in answering that question.

Further, I hope to be able to show that these problems reappear at other crucial points in Kant's enterprise, and that the balance of such evidence suggests that Kant's idealism, while generally defensible, en-counters more and more difficulties the more that idealism is construed as a formal idealism. Or, more broadly, the more Kant conceives of philoso-phy's task as an independent analysis of the "rules" for knowledge, prior to and divorced from experience of all kinds, the more such difficulties emerge. Again, though, I want to develop these difficulties internally, in terms of Kant's own concerns. To do so, it is necessary now to turn to his analysis of the other foundational source of human knowledge, concepts, the "form of the thought of an object."

4
Concepts

But a concept is always, as regards its form, something universal which serves as a rule. (A106)

PURE CONCEPTS

1. The Metaphysical Deduction

In the following two chapters, on Kant's theory of concepts and schemata, I divide up his discussion in a somewhat unusual way. Besides considering his theory of pure concepts and transcendental schemata, I discuss separately — and with more attention than either Kant or commentators devote to the issue — his theory of empirical concepts and empirical schemata. I do so mainly in order to understand what Kant thinks a concept or schema is. Of course, there are special and complicated issues involved in his theory of pure concepts and schemata, but I shall try to show that part of the most important and revolutionary aspect of the Transcendental Logic is the explanation that *all* concepts are "forms of the thought of an object," or *rules* for judgment about objects. If that is the case, I argue, then we should be able to explain all concepts in terms of this theory. After all, one continual problem of concepts has been the problem of concept generality, the one-over-many character of all concepts. This problem is not essentially different with concepts like "cause" or "substance" than it is with concepts like "man" or "body." And if Kant is right about what, in general, concepts (as "forms") are, he should be able to demonstrate the relevance of his analysis, and his solution to the problem of generality, to both cases. The problem of the schematism is even more complex. Besides showing in what sense a "schematization" for concepts can be said to be required, it also has to be shown, as a point of interpretation, that Kant did believe such a question relevant for empirical concepts. And that issue in itself will introduce interesting complications.

Further, there is another, more systematic reason for focusing so much attention on Kant's theory of "the empirical." It has become apparent thus far that one essential element in Kant's ability to maintain the theory of formality he does is his separation between "spontaneity" (in both the understanding and pure intuition) and receptivity, or sensation. But there would be quite a gap — indeed, an abyss — in his theory if he could not successfully bring these elements "back together again," and if he could not explain the relation between the formal, a priori requirements for "thinking anything at all" and "thinking this or that" in particular. No theory of the "possibility of experience" would be very interesting, or ultimately coherent, if we had no way of understanding in any detail the relation between that structure of possibility and "actual" experience. For example, we might then be left in the position of being able to demonstrate that our thinking of any objective event was intimately tied to our thinking of it as in some causal relation to some other, but unable to understand ever how some particular event could be an instance of that required causality. Explaining the *relation* between "form" and "matter" is, as it has always been when issues are raised in such terms, just as important as understanding each separately, and is a problem particularly well illuminated by Kant's theory of empirical concepts. Moreover, it simply *is* the problem of the schematism, in both its pure and empirical aspects. Said another way, it should be admitted at the outset here that it is indeed hard to isolate these questions from many of Kant's other concerns, as hard as it has proved to be with his theory of sensations and intuitions. However, consideration of these topics has, I hope, already indicated why the interrelation of many of these issues is itself important for the concerns of this study. That is, questions like: What are the forms of experience and why does Kant think they are specifically what he thinks they are? Why should they be construed as subjective, and so only the form of phenomena? and What is the relation between such forms and the matter of experience? are all different, separable issues. Accordingly, one might be inclined to admit that, for example, Kant indeed did not pay enough attention to the last question, even while one might claim either that he need not have, given his interests, or less strongly, that such neglect does not create problems for the better-known aspects of his idealism. However, we have already seen that an interrelation of these topics is, on the contrary, central to Kant's defense of such foundational principles as his theory of the understanding, or indeed, of his everywhere underlying characterization of form itself. If *that* notion cannot be defended, or if the implications to which such an account necessarily leads cannot be (implications which are reflected in all the questions posed above), then Kant's project as a whole is threatened.

What follows, then, is just a continuation of the problem of Kantian "formality," in all its dimensions, and that first of all means asking *why* Kant believed concepts should be understood as he does, a question separate from and prior to his more famous concern with the "objective validity" of concepts (an issue I shall take up in chapter 6).

His explanation of, especially, "categorial" formality occurs in his introductory discussion of the Transcendental Logic, and especially in a section he chose in the second edition (B159) to call the "Metaphysical Deduction." In the latter section especially, there are two elements in Kant's exposition which form the basis of a great deal of what he wants to claim in his famous Transcendental Deduction. First, he propounds a theory of categories, more precisely a theory of what categories are, which differs dramatically from that prominent in the tradition stretching from Aristotle to Leibniz. In that tradition, a search for a "table of categories" had been a search for a list of the primary predicates of all beings, that predicable of something just by virtue of it *being*. In keeping with his claim that the "proud name of Ontology" must yield to an "analytic of the understanding," Kant reinterprets the notion of category by closely associating it with that of the "forms" or "rules" of *judging*.[1] Categories are not primary predicates or kinds of being, but rules for judging about beings, not forms of objects but "forms of the *thought* of objects." However, even while Kant makes extensive use of the "logical" forms of judgments and syllogisms to explain his notion of intellectual formality, he also must distinguish categorial formality from what he calls mere "logical" formality. This means explaining the difference between forms of thought *simpliciter* and forms of the thought of objects, which latter forms can still be determined a priori, prior to experience of objects.

This analogy with logical forms of judgment and this differentiation from them make up the heart of the Metaphysical Deduction. For the central strategy in the section, aside from a good deal of important scene setting for the Transcendental Deduction, is the claim that a transition can be made, a derivation of sorts *from* the "Table of Judgments" *to* the "Table of Categories," all by virtue of what Kant calls — in what is for him an odd, almost Pickwickian use of a word — a "clue" (*Leitfaden*). It is this clue that supposedly will allow us to understand what the quantity or quality of a judgment has to do with judgments of quantity or quality, or what the logical notions of ground and consequent, or subject terms, have to do with the concepts of causality or substance. Throughout this section Kant makes clear that, in order to answer this last question, we must return to his theory of "materiality" and to the relation between the

1. Cf. "What all this amounts to is that to apply Ockham's strategy to the theory of categories is to construe categories as classifications of conceptual items. This becomes, in Kant's hands, the idea that categories are the most generic functional classifications of the elements of judgments." Wilfrid Sellars, "Towards a Theory of the Categories," in *Experience and Theory,* eds. Lawrence Foster and J. W. Swanson (Cambridge: University of Massachusetts Press, 1970), p. 45. On the further similarities between Kant and Sellars, see below, note 22.

forms and matter of experience, as stipulated by his formal idealism. As just noted, with pure concepts, this will mean understanding how "categories" differ from "logical rules" of judgment, or even how "Transcendental Logic" in general, while an a priori formal enterprise, can be said to differ from "General Logic." And Kant himself attempts to make this distinction by using just these familiar, if occasionally abstract, notions of form and matter. He tells us, for example, that categories differ from forms of judgment because into the former we have introduced a "transcendental content" (*einen transzendentalen Inhalt*) (B105 = A79). This mysterious notion appeared in another form earlier in the section when Kant claimed

> Transcendental Logic . . . has lying before it a manifold of *a priori* sensibility, presented by transcendental aesthetic, as *material* for the concepts of pure understanding. In the absence of this material those concepts would be without any content, therefore entirely empty. (B102 = A77) [my emphasis]

It obviously requires more explanation than Kant gives it.

More specifically, in the first half of this chapter, two issues are relevant to the issue of formality. The first is important because Kant has been so severely criticized for his attempted "derivation" of categories in the Metaphysical Deduction. This is so not only because of Kant's legerdemain in producing his various tables, but because of the central issue: Kant's questionable attempt to introduce, quite suddenly, a pure, yet material use of concepts. It has been claimed that the central strategy of this section is either a nonsequitur[2] or that it reveals the presence of two theories of judgment and concepts, one of which stems from a period when Kant had a more traditional, less functionalist view of concepts.[3] I believe that both of these criticisms miss the point here by exaggerating Kant's intentions, and by not considering the relation between this section and the rest of the Transcendental Analytic. Understanding this architectonic relation is the first problem I shall address.

The second is the substantive issue itself — what categories are, especially since they are explained by the obscure notion of a "transcendental content." I shall discuss that issue, which involves the larger question of "General" and "Transcendental Logic," in section 2.

2. P. F. Strawson, *The Bounds of Sense* (London: Methuen, 1966), pp. 74–82.

3. Thomas Swing, *Kant's Transcendental Logic* (New Haven: Yale University Press, 1969), tries to divide Kant's "critical period" into two phases in which he first still tried to salvage some material use of reason, then came to realize that the human intellect was exclusively formal (had itself no access to objects), and proceeded to attempt a detailed demonstration of its proper relation to objects. See, for example, p. 170 ff. I do not think there is sufficient evidence to support this claim as an interpretation of the historical Kant, and will present a different view of, especially, the schematism, but Swing's emphasis on this "formal-material" problem is, I believe, quite appropriate.

Now, if we put aside for the moment the problematic nature of some of Kant's terminology and try for an overview, we can at least see the general force of Kant's claim about the relation between categories and forms of judgment. It is at least reasonable to suggest that the form of judgment, what we would today call the form of our language, has something to do with the basic ways we apprehend and discriminate the world. The fact that we think or speak in subject-predicate categorical judgments is surely not unrelated to our conceiving of the world in terms of substances and attributes. If this is so, it would seem a useful strategy, in any attempt to uncover the basic features of any concept of an object which we *could* have to look to the logical relations necessarily involved in the structure of our statements and inferences. This idea — that the way we think or speak about the world, that the forms of our conceiv*ing,* set the limits within which anything can be conceiv*ed* — became in itself, apart from Kant's particular theory, an extremely important one after him, at times drifting into psychologism, at times powerfully reasserted in contemporary logical terms by the Wittgenstein of the *Tractatus.*[4]

However, such a general overview does not get us very far in trying to understand the nature of the relation between forms of judging and forms of objects judged. However, it is important not to ask more of this section than is appropriate, particularly prior to the Transcendental Deduction and Schematism (even though it should be freely admitted that Kant was more responsible than any commentator for such exaggerated expectations). To see why this is so, consider the argument as a whole.

What Kant wants to claim in the sections from B92 = A67 to B115

4. Admittedly, such a schema for a deduction of categories is very abstract, and as so stated does not need to rely heavily on obtaining categorical candidates from general logic. Strawson, *Bounds of Sense,* p. 82 ff., is probably right that *such* a program, if pared down austerely, can only properly begin with the logical notions of an individual name and a predicate expression, and when considered "in terms of" objects of experience, can only yield the broadly categorical notions of particular (spatio-temporal) objects and a universal character, or category itself. It would seem a more expedient strategy to consider directly whether the general notion of an object of experience itself can be made to yield categorical rules necessarily involved if particulars are to be describable in conceptual ways at all, and then consider whether the particular character of our objects of experience (their occurring in space and time) yield any further, specific categories. Thus, instead of considering the logical notion of, say, a subject term in a categorical judgment, with respect to any object of experience, and so arriving at the category of substance, and then considering such a category in terms of our objects of experience, and arriving at the notion of permanence, we should first establish that we can have a full "weighty" experience of objects and then see if the requirements for this established possibility yield specific categories. To do so would thus be to place the Transcendental Deduction in its proper, central place, and to postpone the question of specific categories until this notion of "object" has been thoroughly analyzed and defended.

seems clear enough from the respective titles of these sections. He wants somehow to go *from* "The Logical Employment of the Understanding," and his specification of the "Logical Functions of Judgment," *to* "The Pure Concepts of the Understanding, or the Categories," and to accomplish this by means of a "clue" that explains this "*discovery* of all pure concepts of the understanding." Simply summarized, Kant argues that, first of all, we can specify the pure forms of judgment, the rules which prescribe all possible relations between concepts of judgment; that, in fact, there is a table of all possible functions of the understanding in judgment. While Kant gives the impression that this basic table has been around for centuries and requires only a bit of tinkering by him to produce the third form out of the first two in each group, material from the "silent decade" between 1770 and 1781 indicates a good deal more labor and a good deal more uncertainty about the results than Kant lets on in the *Critique*.[5] Further, claims for the systematic completeness of the table, even with these long-thought-out revisions, have never been easy to defend, Klaus Reich's interesting attempt notwithstanding.[6] All that is important at this point with respect to these remarks on judgment, though, is how much they intensify Kant's general characterization of "thinking." Considered "formally" in the logical sense, thinking is only a kind of activity, a unifying of representations supplied from elsewhere; that, simply put, the human understanding is "not intuitive, but discursive" (B93 – A68). It is primarily *this* conception of thinking which forms the basis for Kant's whole account of concepts. Originally defined, all concepts of the understanding should only be considered as what are here called "functions," as "the unity of the *act* of bringing various representations under one common representation" (B93 = A68). As we shall see in the next section, this emphasis on "the unity of the *act*" as the mark of conceptual unity functions as the cornerstone in Kant's account of some traditional problems with a concept's one-over-many quality. For now we can just note that the first step in Kant's explanation of the categories is a general characterization of the understanding, or thinking in general, as spontaneity — more specifically, as unifying *activity* — rather than an insight into anything like the "intelligible" structure of the world. This is what provides the distinctively transcendental beginning for the rest of his explanation.[7]

5. Kemp Smith, *A Commentary to Kant's Critique of Pure Reason* (London: Macmillan, 1923), pp. 186–201. The best short summary of Kant's twists and turns during this important period can be found in Michael Washburn's "Dogmatism, Scepticism, Criticism: The Dialectic of Kant's 'Silent Decade,'" *Journal of the History of Philosophy* 13 (1975): 167–76.

6. Klaus Reich, *Die Vollständigkeit der kantischen Urteilstafeln* (Berlin: Diss. Rostock, 1932).

7. For the sake of contrast, compare the very different view defended in the *Dissertation*, paragraph 3.

(It should also be noted here how much Kant's initial remarks indicate that his whole view of logic is entirely intensional. For him, clearly, logic was a logic of judgments, not propositions, a logic of the relations between concepts or between judgments, not an extensional logic, capable for example of formally defining truth functional relations between propositions. His is the logic of assertion, and so of the forms of assertion.)

Next comes the famous clue itself. It occurs, stated briefly, at B93 = A68: "Now the only use which the understanding can make of concepts is to judge by means of them." For the sake of the clue, the "only" in this passage does much of the work. *All* thinking is judging, this activity of uniting elements into higher unities. Since all thinking of objects is thus as well a judging, Kant tries to reason that the logical forms of all judging can also be considered the general features of all thinking about objects, again *if some way for considering* a priori objects in general can be found. The actual use he makes of such a clue, suspect though it is, appears at B105 = A79.

> The same function which gives unity to the various representations in a judgment also gives unity to the mere synthesis of various representations in an intuition, and this unity, in its most general expression, we entitle the pure concept of the understanding.
>
> The same understanding, through the same operations by which in concepts, by means of analytic unity, it produced the logical form of a judgment, also introduces a transcendental content into its representations, by means of the synthetic unity of the manifold in intuition in general. On this account we are entitled to call these representations pure concepts of the understanding and to regard them as applying a priori to objects.

Kant obviously simply overstates here what the clue of the Metaphysical Deduction allows him to do, particularly with this last phrase about being entitled to regard pure concepts as applying a priori to objects. Stated so boldly, it almost seems as if we are here at the end of the task of the Analytic rather than at its beginning. Kant seems to argue: There are definable forms of judgment in general, formulable into a complete table. All thinking is judging. When we thus consider all forms of thinking in terms of any possible object of thought (anything we could intuit), we thereby introduce a "transcendental content" into these pure forms and arrive at the categories. We would thus have proven that there are pure categories which have an a priori relation to objects, QED, contra Hume.

Of course, this is not what Kant means to say here. For one thing, he must *prove* (1) that no object could be experienced unless subject to some form of judgmental activity, a claim that is simply assumed in the above section. He also must go on to prove (2) that certain aspects of our experience, for example that it is spatial and temporal, place further restrictions on the kind of general description rules without which an object could not be experienced; and then he must go on (3) to apply these standards for categorical status to various candidates and develop a detailed account of our categories, particular concepts which have an a priori relation to our experience in particular. Such may in fact be the relation between (1) Deduction, (2) Schematism, and (3) Analytic of Principles. (More precisely, working out these various steps above will enable us to understand the difference, for example, between "ground and consequence," "causality," and finally "necessary succession according to a rule.") The task of the Metaphysical Deduction seems everywhere more tentative than the above impression would indicate. Kant explicitly moves from the Table of Judgments to the Table of Categories by suggesting that we "introduce" a "transcendental content" into this reflection, and there is ample reason to believe he thinks this introduction requires a good deal more explanation. It is true that when we consider the forms of thinking in general in terms of a "synthetic unity of the manifold in intuition" that something like a *possible* categorical status for pure concepts can be achieved. And it is true that Kant sometimes gives the impression that this "introduction of a content" is what he has done in the Metaphysical Deduction, and so has simply arrived at the Table of Categories, pure concepts which can already be said to relate to objects, *tout court.* Clearly, though, as the very next section of the *Critique* ("The Principles of Any Transcendental Deduction") makes clear, it is just this transcendental content which needs so much explaining. He becomes more specific in this and the next section by claiming that it is the "possibility of experience" in general which *alone* will provide this "content" for such pure concepts, and that such a claim as the one made about the categories (that they are required for a synthetic unity of any manifold) is just what must be proved. At this point in the *Critique,* we do not know what it means to suggest that a consideration of the possible ways we can and must think together or unite anything *in our experience* explains the "materiality" of the categories. Kant has neither assumed that we simply possess categories which have such an a priori relation to objects in general, nor attempted a quick inference from pure rules of thought to rules for the thought of objects (appearances to the contrary). As the wealth of detail that follows makes clear, he has instead proposed a *way* in which we should proceed in order to establish this relation.

In other words, Bird is surely right here that the task of this section of the *Critique* should be considered considerably weaker than it often is, and even weaker than Kant sometimes seems to characterize it.[8] We

---

8. Cf. Graham Bird on the "noncommittal" nature of claims made in the Metaphysical Deduction in *Kant's Theory of Knowledge* (New York: Humanities Press, 1973), p. 82 ff.

should not here claim that we have established once and for all *the* list of pure concepts, have demonstrated in what sense these categories are a priori related to all possible objects of experience, and thus leave to the rest of the *Critique* a kind of explanatory and specifying task. Instead, Kant here offers some criteria for categorical status, specifies in more detail what it means to call such categories a priori, and provides a few candidates for such a priori status, leaving to the rest of the *Critique* the difficult task of proving what is suggested here.

There are certainly indications that Kant has such a tentative project here in mind. At B81 = A57, he writes:

> In the *expectation,* therefore, that there *may perhaps* be concepts which relate a priori to objects, not as pure or sensible intuitions, but solely as acts of pure thought . . . we form for ourselves *by anticipation* the idea of a science of the knowledge which belongs to pure understanding and reason, whereby we think objects entirely a priori. Such a science . . . *would* have to be called Transcendental Logic. [my emphasis]

It seems reasonable to read the remainder of this section, prior to the Deduction with its self-imposed task of proving objectivity, as more specifically *anticipating* such a science than taking any large step *in* it.

However, even so tentatively stated, some important problems still need clarification. Aside from the above-mentioned difficulty of explaining the relationship between the four main sections of the Analytic — the Metaphysical Deduction, the Transcendental Deduction, the Schematism, and the Analytic of Principles — the nature of the various suggestions offered here requires further comment. This is particularly true of what seems to me the most important philosophic issue introduced in this section, the nature of categories.

2. General and Transcendental Logic

Once these architectonic issues are clarified, and Kant's claims are presented as modestly as they should be, the central philosophic issue still remaining is the explanation of what a "pure" category is; more precisely, what such a concept would be if the Transcendental Deduction can establish that there must be such pure concepts. Obviously, even such a statement of the problem already indicates that no full answer to this question is possible until the full argument of the Deduction can be presented and assessed. However, Kant does introduce here some crucial notions which should be discussed separately; for example, the relation of concepts to judgments, the need for some pure rules of judgment *überhaupt,* and the a priori status of the categories.

There are two places in the Metaphysical Deduction where Kant sketches his theory of judgment and the role of concepts in that theory.

Both passages are important for understanding his answers to the questions posed above. The first discussion occurs at B93–94 = A68–69.

> Judgment is therefore the mediate knowledge of an object, that is, the representation of a representation of it. . . . Accordingly all judgments are functions of unity among our representations; instead of an immediate representation, *a higher* representation, which comprises the immediate representation and various others, is used in knowing the object, and thereby much possible knowledge is collected into one. Now we can reduce all acts of the understanding to judgment and the understanding may therefore be represented as a faculty for judging [*Vermögen zu urteilen*].

Since judgment is thus defined as the unification of representations into higher representations, concepts used in such judgments are defined accordingly. They are representations by virtue of which other representations can be determined *in* judgment. "Concepts, as predicates of possible judgments, relate to some representations of a not *yet* determined object" (B94 = A69).

The important aspect of this definition is, as has often been noted, the central role Kant gives the activity of judgment.[9] That is, judgment is not defined simply as the unification of concepts, as if concepts could be understood "separately," apart from their relation to judgment. What is so striking in Kant's account is, rather, that concepts should only be understood in terms of their role in judgment, as "functions of unity" in judgment. Thus, when we understand a concept like "body," we primarily understand what role it could play in judgments. That means that we understand of what lower representations it could be predicated, such as "metal." (To understand the concept is to know how to *use* it. It thus cannot be understood apart from its potential role in judgment; as if, for example, we could understand it by itself, by understanding "the property" to which it referred.) As we shall see in the next section, this general characterization of concepts is what Kant means when he claims that concepts should be construed as "rules" for judging, a notion at the heart of his explanation of the "generality" claims made possible by the possession of concepts.

These definitions are then stated in different terms at B102 = A77 ff. There, instead of talking about judgment as a "result," to be analyzed into its logical components, Kant discusses the issue epistemologically, focusing on what the subject does in order to arrive *at* the original unification of representations. That is, he introduces his notion of "synthesis." In doing so, he is implicitly distinguishing the purely logical

---

9. Cf. the helpful discussion of Roger Daval, *La metaphysique de Kant* (Paris: Presses Universitaires de France, 1951), p. 62 ff.

analysis of judgment, offered above, from what he elsewhere calls the "real" use of the understanding in judging about objects. That is, "General Logic" abstracts from the "origin" of representations and classifies the various formal ways in which these representations are predicable of each other. Or, as Kant says, "By means of analysis different representations are brought under one concept — a procedure treated of in general logic" (B104 = A78). Typically, such a bringing together of representations could occur in a syllogistic inference. If we claim that some representations belong under one concept, and that latter under another, then the first group, or concept, belongs under the third. Various rules for such grouping together of representations can be given, for kinds of judgment and kinds of syllogisms. However, Kant also wants to ask how representations are synthetically "brought together" in the first place; not by virtue, that is, of what we know analytically about other representations and their higher or lower relations to each other, but originally, as a claim about objective reality. He thereby finally gets around to explaining the "transcendental logic" he had introduced at B82 = A57.

"What transcendental logic, on the other hand, teaches is how we bring to concepts, not representations, but the *pure synthesis* of representations (B104 = A79). By this he means that we investigate, not already synthesized representations, but the syntheses which made possible the classifications of General Logic. General Logic had presuppposed the truth of the claims about the relation of representations with which it begins. Once that is assumed, we just deal with representations as they are provided from elsewhere, regardless of content. But, Kant now points out, judgment in its real use does not merely classify representations under other concepts, but brings the synthesis of representations to concepts. That is, we *form* or *constitute* thereby the concepts presupposed by General Logic.[10] We claim that these representations belong together objectively under another representation or concept.

Since this issue will emerge again in a different way in the next chapter, we should note here that Kant is considering judgment from two points of view; he is not advancing two different theories of judgment. In *any* judgment, one concept is predicated of another according to the rules of General Logic. But we can either attend to the form of that relation, in what way a concept is said to be related to another, or we can note the content of the judgment and ask epistemologically how we know what the judgment asserts. (It is, by the way, only with this latter question, with respect to the content of the judgment, that the distinction between

10. On this point, compare Henry Allison's discussion of the issue, as it relates to the Eberhard polemic. *The Kant-Eberhard Controversy* (Baltimore: The Johns Hopkins University Press, 1974), p. 64.

analytic and synthetic can be relevant. It is not a distinction explicable in terms of the form of the judgment alone.)[11] In the former case we are, speaking loosely, analyzing the judgment "after" it has been made, whereas in the latter we are asking what was presupposed *in order* to make the judgment. "What the judgment asserts" can thus be answered either by isolating its logical form (it asserts a predicate of a subject, or a consequent of a ground), or by isolating the actual claim advanced, particularly where the judgment is synthetic (it asserts that the predicate "heavy" is predicable of "body," or that causal connection is predicable of all objects of experience).

Of course, the special problem in the latter case concerns synthetic a priori judgments. In such a case, we are asking: In what ways must all representations be thought together? And, for our concerns, the interesting aspect of that question will be: What do we have to *know* in order to answer that question? But for now, we should note how the above analysis of judgment in its logical and real use helps clarify the relation between General and Transcendental Logic, and thereby between pure concepts as "logical functions" and as categories. In part his explanation of that relation depends on a claim he seems to think is implicit in his analysis of judgment itself. As we have seen, Kant does not think we can account, even logically, for our possession and use of concepts except by reference to their role in judgment. But it is equally true that judgment is possible only by means of concepts, rules for unification. Now Kant never explicitly tries to defend the claim that there must be some general "logical functions of unity in judgment," and his theory of logic is not sophisticated enough to support very much that would be metalogically interesting. But this kind of consideration of the relation between concepts and judgment is clearly part of his implicit justification for such an assumption. That is, concepts could not be used in judgment unless there were some concepts (rules) which define what judgment is.[12] And his consideration of the relation between General and Transcendental Logic seems based on the same kind of preliminary expectation about the real use of judgment — i.e., that there must be some concepts which define what "counts" as a judgment about objects.

That is, all Kant seems to mean by asserting that connection is the suggestion that, just as there must be "higher order" rules in logic which define the possible relations of representations, considered formally, so we might "expect" that there must be, a priori, rules for *any* synthesis of representations. This expectation arises because "the same function

11. Admittedly, this claim, to be fully defensible, requires more comment. Again, however, this interpretation is supported by remarks in *On a Discovery*. Cf. Allison's discussion, p. 56.
12. Ibid., pp. 64–65.

which gives unity to the various representations in a *judgment* also gives unity to the mere synthesis of various representations *in an intuition* (B104–5 = A79). The logical functions of unity in judgment specify formally how judgmental unifying may be attained. Since we can only know anything about objects (= anything intuitable) by making a judgment, these functions of *unity,* we might reasonably expect, *are* the ways in which objects come to be known, in which a synthesis of representations can be said to represent an object.[13]

Admittedly, this still gets us no farther than "candidates" for categorial states.[14] But Kant's explanation of this expectation or clue does establish what he thinks a category is, and specifies the problem to be addressed in my next two chapters: How is it possible to consider the functions of unity in thinking with respect to any intuitable object? How do we establish what this "transcendental content" is? His account also already tends to eliminate a possible answer to such a question, and points us in the appropriate direction. That is, it is already apparent that it is not possible to establish this content for pure concepts by reflection merely on the "*thought* of an object of experience." In the two passages quoted above which deal with the issue of "pure materiality," Kant has already indicated that the answer to this question depends on being able to assert something *about* anything which could be immediately given to human observers, the manifold considered (hypothetically) distinct from functions of thought. He has claimed that without the "manifold of a priori sensibility" concepts would be "empty" (B102 = A77). In other words,

13. One way to put this point about the categories is suggested by Arthur Melnick in *Kant's Analogies of Experience* (Chicago: University of Chicago Press, 1973), p. 40 ff., especially p. 45. He argues that the categories should be seen as "epistemic concepts," concepts which do not straightforwardly "apply" to objects, but apply to objects only insofar as these objects could be subject to our judgmental forms. The categories are the features objects must have if they are to be subject to our forms of thought. I agree that this is part of Kant's understanding of the relation between categories and judgment, but will suggest some problems with this strategy, especially in the next chapter, concerned with Kant's theory of judgment, and in chapter 6, on the Deduction.

14. In other words, while Kant cannot defend the transition from any table of judgments to a table of categories, he may be able to defend the relevance of *some* consideration of the forms of judgment to the search for categorical structure. We might then just suggest that the subject-predicate form of some judgments could serve as a "clue" in our attempt to determine the categories (and, after all, that is all Kant says it is). We would then, to continue the example, try to prove that all objects of experience must be subject to our forms of thought (the Deduction), and so be led by our clue to establish "substance" as a candidate for categorical status. We would go on to establish the limitations substance would have given the particular form of our experience (substance is schematized as "permanence"), and *then* try to show that such a notion of substance fulfills the requirements of categorical status established in the Deduction. Admittedly, the transition from subject-predicate to substance is weak, but "clues" are not the same as "evidence."

we must be able to establish a relation between *our* ways of thinking
together representations, and those representations as given. Or we must
be able to prove that objects do fall under these concepts, not just that
our functions of unity are involved in our *thinking* about objects. And
again, pure intuitions will be crucial in understanding this "pure content,"
as we shall see in the next chapter.

Thus far, then, the Metaphysical Deduction has established what Kant
thinks categories are, and has provided some initial explanation and
defense of that position. All concepts are "functions of unity" in judgment, and should only be understood in terms of this production of unity
in judgment. Concepts can be considered real or material concepts when
the unity produced is a unity of content, when a "synthesis" is "brought
to a concept," and categories when that content can somehow be considered a priori, when a pure synthesis is brought to a concept. Kant
believes this is the proper way to consider concepts and categories
because he believes that "the only use" we can make of concepts is "to
judge by means of them." Because this is so, categories *are* forms of
thought, rules for our unification of representations (or, later, "subjective
conditions"), but this unification must then be shown to be objective, not
merely to express the way we "think" about objects. We thus still need to
understand in more detail *how* this a priori relation between form and
content can be established if categories are so defined, and *whether* Kant
can, within these definitions, establish the objectivity of such connections.

However, there is one further, important element of the theory of
categories dealt with here; what it means to accord these concepts an "a
priori" status.

3. The Apriority of Categories

Occasionally, Kant defines the a priori status of the categories in "genetic" terms, implying that the origin of such concepts is what is decisive.
We would thus claim that some concepts are a priori because they have
never been *derived* from experience, but "lie ready in the mind." In the
initial passages of the Transcendental Logic section, he remarks that by
this "analytic of concepts," he means

> the hitherto rarely attempted dissection of the faculty of understanding itself,
> in order to investigate the possibility of concepts a priori by looking for them
> in the understanding alone, as their birthplace, and by analyzing the pure use
> of this faculty. (B90 = A65–66)

He goes on to speak of these pure concepts as "seeds" and "dispositions"
of the understanding "in which they lie prepared," and we seem to be
dealing with some form of an innate ideas thesis. Later on, however,
Kant is very clear that the question of derivation is not at all central to

the problem of the status of such concepts, that their "birthplace" is not, as this passage suggests, the mark of their a priori character, but that rather their "use" is all important.[15] That is, a claim that we possess concepts a priori is a transcendental claim; it is a claim about a kind of *knowledge*. In this case, when we claim to have a priori concepts we mean to assert that the concepts can be known to have a relation to objects in general without our having to appeal directly to experience of objects to establish that relation. A priori does not mean "not derived from experience" but "known without appeal to experience." The question the deduction will pose is thus not: Can we discover in the understanding (as birthplace) concepts which lie there (like seeds) prior to any actual experience? but: Can we identify and justify a *use* of concepts which establishes a relation to all possible objects of experience which does not justify that use by appeal to what we have experienced?

In order to understand fully this distinction between a priori and a posteriori, we need to return again to Kant's notion of synthesis, since he tends to try to explain the distinction as an epistemological one by using this notion. In section 10, Kant builds his case for the special status for these concepts in the following way. First:

> By synthesis, in its most general sense, I understand the act of putting different representations together and of grasping what is manifold in them in one act of knowledge [*in einer Erkenntnis*]. Such a synthesis is pure if the manifold is not empirical but given a priori, as is the manifold of space and time. (B103 = A77)

While such a description of this "pure synthesis" appears to commit Kant again to a view of the content of pure concepts which holds that we simply "possess" such a pure manifold and so also "possess" rules for the synthesis of this manifold, as well as to a strange separate synthesis which "occurs" prior to "the" empirical synthesis, later explanations do not bear out such an interpretation. Again what Kant means by a "synthesis a priori" is a connection of representations whose warrant is not derived from experience, not a synthesis which occurs before experience. While some recent commentators have attempted to interpret the "a priori synthesis" more literally,[16] as an activity which must "occur" prior to or

---

15. Kant is quite clear at B117 = A85 and B118 = A86 that the a priori nature of concepts is an issue relevant to their "a priori *employment*" (*Gebrauch*).

16. See the recent article by Paul Guyer, "Kant on Apperception and *A Priori* Synthesis," *American Philosophical Quarterly*, vol. 17, no. 3 (1980): 206–12. Guyer rightly sees that how one understands Kant's talk of an a priori synthesis depends finally on how one construes his notion of "mind-imposed unity." My own interpretation of that notion is considerably different from Guyer's, and accordingly my interpretation of the a priori synthesis is different as well. See chap. 8, section 1.

along with every instance of empirical knowing, Kant's own words make clear he is using "a priori" as an adverb, to explain the kind of justification involved, either directly in synthetic a priori judgment, or as a presupposition for empirical knowledge. Thus, "By this pure synthesis I understand that which rests upon a basis of a priori synthetic unity" (B104 = A78). I understand him to be saying here, by "rests upon a basis," that the category (that is the concept as applying to objects) is so *known* to apply a priori, without appeal to experience. His example bears out this interpretation. When we count, we presuppose a rule for counting, like the "decade," a claim which does not mean that we formulate the rule prior to or along with each instance of counting. (The situation here is similar to that of "pure intuitions" making possible empirical intuitions. Cf. the triangle example on p. 76 above.) If this general line of interpretation is correct, we should expect that an attempt to "transcend" the formality of rules of thought, and so arrive at rules for the thought of an object, should occur by considering the "unity" or connection which we can specify a priori necessary for any experience, and then showing that precisely this unity is what is supplied by the rules for all synthetic connection.

This is in fact suggested by the claim, "Pure synthesis, represented in its most general aspects, *gives* us the pure concept of the understanding" (B104 = A78). In other words, if we can establish a priori that a "synthetic unity" is necessary for any manifold of experience, and can prove that such a unity would not be possible without general rules for such unifying, we will have established the a priori status of pure concepts; we will have proved their relation to objects in general without a direct appeal to experience of objects. "Pure synthesis" will "give" us pure concepts by showing us the *way* to establish the objectivity of the unity prescribed by such rules, and how to do so a priori. In this sense, "pure synthesis, represented in its most general aspects" is just another way of expressing the principle of the Transcendental Deduction which Kant hopes will justify the objective status of the categories — the a priori notion of "the possibility of experience." To ask "whether there is a pure synthesis" is just to ask whether we can establish a priori the necessity for a synthetic connection in any manifold. If we can, the rules for such a connection will be "concepts a priori."

Obviously, at this point, a full assessment of all these claims about categories would have to involve much of the rest of the *Critique*. However, as suggested at the beginning of this section, we can begin to assess Kant's general theory of concepts apart from the details of the Schematism, Deduction, and Principles, if we see whether his account can deal with a variety of standard issues relevant to any account of concepts. That is, with respect to empirical concepts, the general problems of "form and matter" will be different from that for categories, but just as important in understanding Kant's overall theory of formality. In that context, we need to understand whether his account of the derivation, objectivity, and generality of such concepts can be justified within his theory of "rules" and discursivity, and if not, what that might say about his theory of concepts as a whole. Assessing the issue in that context is one way of assessing Kant's chief reason for interpreting categorical formality the way he does — his theory of an exclusively discursive understanding. More specifically, the precise "problem" of empirical concepts for Kant arises partly from his admission that there can be "usurpatory" concepts, which seem to be genuine empirical concepts, or actually derived from experience, but which can be shown to be pseudoconcepts (like "fate"). Such an admission raises directly the problem of correct and incorrect derivation, and so a "proper" relation to objects. Partly, as stated above, the problem concerns just what an empirical concept is. Such questions (what such a concept is and how it can be said to be correctly derived and so objective) are often treated by Kant as if they were unproblematic. However, as we shall see, he has a number of things to say about this issue, not always consistent. In the following, I'll deal in a more extended way with his attempt to explain the notion of concept by the notion of "rule" (4), his remarks in the *Logik* on concepts, "Merkmale," and concept formation (5), his scattered remarks on the acquisition and even "deduction" of empirical concepts (6), and some of the problems his account raises (7).

EMPIRICAL CONCEPTS

4. Concepts and Rules

What, then, are empirical concepts for Kant? When I say that I have or have acquired a concept of red, or of body, what is it, properly understood, that I *have*? We have already seen some indications of Kant's answer to this question. For example, he writes:

> Whereas all intuitions, as sensible, rest on affections; concepts rest on functions. By function I mean the unity of the act of ordering various representations under one common representation. (B93 = A68)

> But a concept is always, as regards its form, something universal which serves as a rule. (A106)

Ambiguities aside for the moment, Kant's twin claims here — that "having a concept" is like being able to *do* something, or like having a certain ability (n.b. "By function I mean the unity of the act"), and that the universality of a concept derives from its serving as a repeatedly applicable rule for discriminating appearances — have seemed to many a remarkable advance over the dogmatisms and empiricisms, "representation of 'the general'" and "faint copy" theories that had preceded him. Looking ahead at the implications of this view, Bennett, himself leaving aside some ambiguities and offering what appears to be high though historically inverted praise, writes:

> [Kant's] actual working use of "concept" is . . . rather thoroughly Wittgensteinean. For him as for Wittgenstein, the interest of concepts lies in the abilities with which they are somehow associated.[17]

And, looking back at the difficulties Kant has overcome, Wolff, summarizing a central aspect of his entire Kant interpretation, writes:

> The paradox of a multiplicity which has unity without losing its diversity — the problem which the ancients called the one and the many — is resolved by the notion of rule-directed activity.[18]

Such interpretations seem to have singled out, quite justifiably, a central, revolutionary aspect of Kant's "transcendental philosophy," and one especially prominent in contemporary theories. In passages like "The Logical Employment of the Understanding" (B93 = A68 ff.), "Transcendental Judgment in General" (B172 = A133 ff.), and "The Schematism of the Pure Concepts of the Understanding" (B170 = A137 ff.), Kant does claim that the "logic of concepts," or an explanation of what it means (1) to acquire (in the case of empirical concepts), (2) to have, and (3) to apply concepts, can be explained by looking at the logic of acquiring, having, and applying rules for certain activities.[19] With this definition, Kant departs from both the empiricist doctrine of concepts as "faint copies" of, or as "built up" out of, prior sense impressions, and the rationalist claim that concepts are somehow "more distinct" ideas, although on the same continuum as sense-ideas. What is decisive in this departure is not just that Kant realizes that concepts are different from certain kinds of mental contents, like sense-impressions; his apparent claim is that they are not, simply speaking, introspectable mental con-

17. Jonathan Bennett, *Kant's Analytic* (Cambridge: Cambridge University Press, 1966), p. 54.

18. R. P. Wolff, *Kant's Theory of Mental Activity* (Cambridge: Harvard University Press, 1963), p. 123.

19. Admittedly, after the "transcendental turn," it is difficult to separate these questions from one another. However, (1) and (2) do raise different, even though related, questions: (1) is especially involved in a comprehensive Kantian philosophy of science and (2) raises some traditional problems of ontological commitment. Both such issues will be treated below, as far as Kant's discussion of them allows. I discuss (3) separately in the following chapter.

tents or representations of objects in the strict sense. He does include concepts under the genus "repraesentatio" in his analysis at B377 = A320, and in the *Logik* he calls a concept a universal (*repraesentat. per notas communes*) or reflected (*repraesentat. discursiva*) representation.[20] But he also makes clear that this should not be taken to mean that concepts represent some special object; for example, abstract objects. In the *Critique,* concepts are said to represent only "mediately" (*mittelbar*) and "by means of a marker which several things have in common" (B337 = A320). In the *Logik,* they are said to represent "through common markers." The concept is thus a rule for thinking together a number of individuals each of which possesses a "marker" picked out conceptually (and so represented) as the principle of grouping. While on many post-Platonic accounts, the occurrence of concepts as predicates in judgments (particularly certain kinds of concepts, categories) had seemed to commit us to a special object denoted by that general term, an object exemplified in many particulars, Kant's account denies the necessity of that commitment, while also trying to explain what many nominalists could not — the *normative,* restricting role of concepts in our conceptual scheme. Hence the notion of "rule," and, as we shall see, the interpretation of rule as "condition."

The empirical concept of body, for example, is not some "fainter" mental content, derived from livelier sense-impressions of bodies. Neither is it a more distinct representation of what is confusedly perceived by the senses. And, although Kant never mentions any alternative other than the above Humean or Leibnizian ones, it is clear that he would also regard as untenable any claim that a concept actually represents some intelligible entity, some universal or Body-ness, whatever the ontological status of that entity. All such alternatives — empiricism, rationalism, classical or medieval concept realism — interpret the distinction between sensibility and the understanding mistakenly. Neither sensations nor concepts are representative in the traditional sense; sense-impressions, except as conceptualized or discriminated, are "blind" and so uninformative and hardly foundational in the empiricist sense. Concepts, on Kant's theory, express only the capacity of the understanding to unify and discriminate passively received sense-impressions and cannot be said to represent the "intelligible" structure of the world. The only alternative left for the concept of body is the one Kant gives us in the rest of that A106 passage:

> So the concept of body serves as a rule for our knowledge of outer appearances with respect to the unity of the manifold which is thought in it. It can be a rule for intuitions only insofar as it represents, in any given appearance, the

20. Kant, *Logik, Gesammelte Schriften,* vol. 9, p. 91.

necessary reproduction of the manifold, and therewith the synthetic unity in its consciousness [*die synthetische Einheit in ihrem Bewusstsein*].[21]

Admittedly, this passage is a tangle of seemingly confusing and even inconsistent claims. One can begin to understand it, though, by seeing that its central thrust is very much the one we have been insisting on. A concept is "something universal" (we shall have to say more about this *etwas*) which "serves as a rule" for the "synthetic unity" of any "one" consciousness. That unity is the unity "of the act" of thinking together various representations. Any intuited "this" can be a "this-such" or "of-a-kind," or, really *determinate,* only if a rule is applied connecting that intuition ("synthetically") with other intuitions (or remembered intuitions) "in one consciousness." Or, finally, to say that "one" concept includes or refers to "many" representations is not to assert a problematic relation between one abstract entity (like a universal) and many other entities. It is only to express that a rule can be *applied* in *many different instances of intuiting.* As indicated earlier, we can say that concepts thus do not *refer* to anything; they are *used* universally and do not name a universal.[22] While there were certainly philosophers before Kant who also denied that concepts could be explained by "universals," it is Kant's insistence on this notion of "rules" for "activities" (called in various places "synthesis" or "judgment"), and his attempt to see this activity as the central component in all consciousness, which make his position so distinctive.[23]

However, contrary tendencies are also obviously present. As noted, a concept is still "something universal," even though we might be tempted

21. There are obviously a number of ways that this analogy with rules could be expanded. For further elaboration, see L. J. Stern, "Empirical Concepts as Rules in the *Critique of Pure Reason*," *Akten des 4. Internationalen Kant-Kongresses, Teil II*, vol. 1 (Berlin: de Gruyter, 1974), pp. 158–65, especially p. 161, and John J. Economos, "Kant's Theory of Concepts," *Kant-Studien* 64 (1973): 63–70. Additional, relevant passages in the *Critique* which attempt to explain and defend concepts as rules include: A106; A108; A121–28; B174 = A135; B197–99 = A158–60; B238–56 = A193–211.

22. Sellars offers a useful explanation of the problems of a concept's "content." Cf. Wilfrid Sellars, "Towards a Theory of the Categories," p. 71. In fact, Kant's theory of concepts is in many ways the ancestor of Sellars's theory of *inter*linguistically definable concepts, his claim that the appearance of singular terms which refer to abstract entities can be explained as ways of talking about particular linguistic episodes. See *Science and Metaphysics* (New York: Humanities Press, 1968), chaps. 3 and 4.

23. This interdefining relationship between concepts and judgments is brought out in Kant's response to Eberhard. Cf. Allison, *The Kant-Eberhard Controversy*, pp. 139–56; and Allison's remarks on the problem of judgment and intuition, pp. 46–92. The properly logical role of spontaneity in concept formation is brought out well in Jürgen Mittelstrass's "Spontaneität. Ein Beitrag in Blick auf Kant," republished in *Kant: Zur Deutung seiner Theorie von Erkennen und Handeln*, ed. Gerold Prauss (Köln: Kiepenhauer und Witsch, 1973), pp. 62–72.

to see this "something" as fairly neutral. It could just mean that the notion of "concept as rule" will help explain the universality of concepts, and not that concepts refer to universal things. However, Kant also says not that a concept *is* a rule, but more cautiously, that it "serves" as a rule (*dient . . . zur Regel*). This prompts us to ask, What is it that serves as a rule? We might say that just about anything can serve as a rule, if we speak loosely enough, and the context in which it serves is clear. Some pictured universal, or introspectable particular can *serve* as a rule, at least in the obvious sense of: let anything which resembles this X be judged to be an X. Further, as noted, Kant is still fond of saying that a concept "represents." Now, although he properly and incisively, in rule language, says that it only represents the "reproduction" of some manifold (in the way a rule loosely "represents" a certain order of action: do this, then do that, then do this, etc.), he *also* says that it represents something called the *synthetic unity* of that manifold. If we emphasize the synthetic quality of this unity, we can say that such a phrase just repeats Kant's claim that a concept-rule tells us how to connect, or unify the manifold in successive ways. But this will not do; he also claims that it represents a unity of this reproduction, again raising questions about what this general unity looks like in any analysis of concepts. And in the earlier quoted passage (B93 = A68), Kant had spoken of the "one common representation" under which the rule directed activity of the understanding (often called judgment) brings various other representations.

In order to understand what kind of a synthetic unity "serves as a rule," we clearly need to add to the notion of rule what Kant says about concepts and their "components" elsewhere. We find that, while Kant does not return to any "representation of 'the general'" model, he does have a good deal to say about what *is* represented by concepts.

5. Concepts and Markers

In his discussion of concepts in the Jäsche edition of the *Logik* (1800), Kant explains that these rules consist of several *Merkmale,* semantic "markers" or "characteristics," which, as an aggregate, or list, function as an *Erkenntnisgrund* in the recognition of some other conception, or some intuition. His full claim is:

> A marker [*Merkmal*] is that in a thing which makes up part of the knowledge of it, or — which is the same — a partial representation insofar as it is considered as cognitive ground of the whole representation. All our concepts are therefore markers, and all thinking is nothing but a representing through markers.[24]

24. Kant, *Logik, Gesammelte Schriften,* vol. 9, p. 58. In making use of Jäsche *Logik*

Kant further asserts that in concepts of experience (an *Erfahrungsbegriff* or empirical concept), these characteristics are "synthetic," or subject to much possible "addition," and so, empirical concepts are "indefinite," and capable of no complete definition.[25] This also seems to imply that all such characteristics are acquired empirically, leaving the *sense* of the concepts dependent wholly on these contingently collected defining marks (or, the concept C is just this collection, $\{M_1, M_2, M_3, \ldots\}$).

Besides, then, the rule analogy, the *Logik* adds two more distinctive elements to Kant's theory of concepts: each concept is an indefinite collection of "markers," and each concept functions as an *Erkenntnisgrund*. Both elements, though, raise problems for other Kantian doctrines. Before dealing with how these "characteristics" are acquired, consider the results of the *Merkmale* claim for his analytic/synthetic distinction. For one of Kant's most familiar examples of an analytic judgment, "All bodies are extended," involves just such supposedly indefinite empirical concepts.

In such a judgment, there seem to be some markers of the concept which are not "added on" through experience, but are somehow "already thought" *in* one of the markers that *is* derived from experience. That is, each of the markers that make up the "indefinite" definition of some concept is itself a concept which can be expanded by analyzing those markers involved in the "very thought" of such concepts. Thus, even though all of a concept's markers are derived from experience, some internal characteristics of a concept's individual markers can be asserted to be analytically true of such markers.

Of course, it has always been difficult to say exactly how this distinction between analytically contained and synthetically added predicates is to be made, but the *Merkmale* theory, I think, makes it even more difficult. In the first place, with empirical concepts, it is clear that no "definition" of a concept's markers can be considered the proper way to understand these analytically (nonempirically derived) characteristics. Beck has already shown[26] that "true by definition" has a special meaning in Kant, and only confuses Kant's notion of analyticity when introduced into that context.

---

here, I am aware that, while the publication was in some sense supervised by Kant, questions can be raised about its relevance as a source of "critical" doctrines. See, for example, the remarks made by H. J. de Vleeschauwer, *La Deduction transcendentale dans l'oeuvre de Kant* (Paris: La Hage, 1934–37), vol. 1, p. 42, and Reich, *Die Vollständigkeit der kantischen Urteilstafeln,* pp. 22 and 25. I do not believe, though, that any use here made of the *Logik* is not in keeping with the caution such commentators advise. Cf. also James Collins, "Kant's Logic as a Critical Aid," *Review of Metaphysics* 30 (1977): 440–61.

25. Ibid., p. 59.

26. L. W. Beck, "Kant's Theory of Definition," reprinted in R. P. Wolff (ed.), *Kant: A Collection of Critical Essays* (New York: Doubleday Anchor, 1967), pp. 23–36.

As Kant puts it:

> Since one cannot become certain by any proof whether all markers of a given concept have been exhausted by complete analysis, all analytic definitions must be held to be uncertain [*unsicher*].[27]

When a series of markers is used to define a concept, we can never be sure that we have correctly picked out and associated markers which delimit this concept and no other, can never be certain that we have included a sufficient number of markers to distinguish it, and above all can never provide a *complete* definition of the concept. With empirical concepts, definitions are of no help in specifying the distinguishing markers already thought within a concept and those added by experience. Indeed, Kant seems to have little direct interest in such definitions. They provide a convenient way of organizing our knowledge, but only that.

> What purpose can be served by defining an empirical concept, such, for instance, as that of water? When we speak of water and its properties, we do not stop short at what is thought in the word "water" but proceed to experiments. (B756 = A728)

Only what he calls "synthetic real definitions," or constructed definitions in mathematics can be certain and complete a priori.

But again, if *all* an empirical concept's markers are derived from experience, any attempt to specify a marker as belonging to that concept will have to depend on experience. The *same* will hold for the amplification of any one of a concept's markers selected for analysis. That amplification would also seem to rest on the experience we've had. If it doesn't, if a marker can be included in the list of markers for a given concept independently of experience, then the concept itself, considered as the collection of *such* markers, would not seem to be empirical but pure. Such would be the case because the concept is not some definable, independent notion which *has* markers; it *is* some indefinite series of markers used to delimit and discriminate it from other concepts. It is thus hard to see how some markers could be ascribed to the concept without any appeal to our experience (unless, again, we want to say that the basic, delimiting markers of the concept are so knowable a priori because the concept *itself* is pure). It should be clear too that Kant does not want to solve this problem by claiming that there are some characteristics which we come to know empirically and, once we have them, then treat as analytic. The way in which we come to know these characteristics fundamentally determines how the predicate *is known* to be true of the subject term.[28]

27. Kant, *Logik,* p. 142.
28. The difficulty of reconciling Kant's theory of concepts with his theory of analysis and definition is pointed out by W. H. Walsh, *Kant's Critique of Metaphysics* (Edinburgh:

Of course, it is not difficult to imagine *some* markers of a concept which seem to be analytic markers but which do not thus require that the concept itself be pure. All empirical concepts could be said to possess the marker of self-identity and to be still clearly empirical. Aside from such a rather unilluminating example, however, it is hard to think of another where the *Merkmale* theory would not provide difficulties.

It is also clear that Kant never meant that *only* pure concepts could serve as subjects of analytic judgments. Thus, he must have in mind here the above-mentioned distinctions between those markers of a subject-concept without which that subject itself cannot be thought, and those added in experience, which can be listed in an "analytic definition" once, as logicians, we have a "given concept." Indeed, something of such a distinction is present in the distinction between "necessary" and "contingent" markers, and in the discussion of the "logical essence" of things. Kant thus distinguishes "primitive and constituting markers" and goes on in the passage to write: "The logical essence is indeed nothing other than the first ground-concept [*Grundbegriff*][29] of all necessary markers of a thing (*esse conceptus*)." Thus, all concepts must have such an *esse conceptus,* and some are given for further analysis with an empirical history and so can even allow an indefinite analysis.

But again this notion makes it hard to see how empirical concepts can be said *themselves* to be derived from experience. The above distinction allows us to say that many of a concept's markers are added on empirically and separable "later" by logical analysis. However, if there are some aspects of the concept, necessarily inherent in it independent of experience, on the *Merkmale* theory anyway, the concept itself would seem to be pure (or, at least, "mixed"). If, in other words, we want to claim that an empirical concept like dog is derived from experience, and we also want to say that, nevertheless, basic markers of the concept are accessible by analysis independently of experience, we can at least ask the familiar, How do we then draw the line between such essential markers and those helpful in its delineation but true of it only on the basis of experience (such as animal vs. maximal and minimal height)? Why not claim that all the concepts' markers are derived from experience? There could, of course, still be differences between more inclusive or more basic markers, but no marker in an empirical concept could be said to occupy the privileged position of "already being thought in the concept of the subject," simply because all of such a concept's markers are derived from experience.

Edinburgh University Press, 1975), p. 8. It emerges in the *Critique* quite explicitly at B755 = A727.

29. Kant, *Logik,* p. 61.

One other way to state this problem is to notice Kant's remark on how much is already presupposed by general logic, apparently either when it attempts some imprecise analytic definition of a concept or when a concept is analyzed into analytically "contained" and synthetically added predicates or markers. That is, it should not be surprising that the epistemological status of these markers (how they are known to be connected with other markers) is not illuminated much by the task of general logic. As he puts it:

> General logic . . . abstracts from all contents of knowledge, and looks to some other source, whatever that may be, for the representations which it is to transform into concepts by process of analysis. (B102 = A76)

And in the *Logik*:

> Universal logic, therefore, doesn't investigate the source of concepts; not how concepts, as representations, arise, but simply how given representations are conceptualized in thought [*zu Begriffe werden*].[30]

Given such restrictions on the task of logic, it would not be correct to expect an explanation from it about distinctions which it everywhere presupposes. However, it is still not clear how the basic distinction between analytically contained and synthetically added predicates can be made, given the claim that a concept *is* just some set of markers. There seems little reason not to consider all the predicates of an empirical concept, and all the subsequent markers involved in any one marker of that concept, to be based on experience. At the very least, the marker theory itself does not seem to clarify how such a distinction between markers is to be defined.

Perhaps this issue will seem less puzzling if we investigate just how Kant thinks empirical concepts *are* derived. If "no concepts can first arise by way of analysis" (A77 = B103), how do they "arise"?[31]

6. Derivation

Kant does claim in the fourth section of his *Logik* that "the form of a concept, as a discursive representation, is at every point produced," and in the sixth section he proceeds to tell us how they are produced. There

30. Ibid., p. 94.
31. By concept acquisition here, I mean concept *learning* and thus mean to avoid all Lockean-Leibnizian problems about innateness. Cf. Bennett's helpful discussion, *Kant's Analytic*, pp. 95–99. It should also be emphasized that "explaining" such acquisition is transcendental, and not psychological. Kant is interested in what is logically indispensable in such acquisition, and not in what happens in the mind when learning occurs. While this distinction is more problematic than it sometimes appears, it should at least be clear that Kant's interest in concept acquisition is not like Piaget's.

the *logical* act of concept formation is said to occur by means of "comparison" (*Komparation*), "reflection" (*Reflexion*), and "abstraction" (*Abstraktion*). He gives an apparently straightforward example.

> I see, for example, a fir tree, a willow tree, and a linden tree. In first of all comparing these objects with one another, I notice that they are different from one another with respect to their stems, branches, leaves, and so forth; but subsequently I now reflect [*reflektiere*] only on that which they have in common, the stem itself, the branch itself, and the leaves themselves, and I abstract from the magnitude, figure, etc. So I arrive at [*bekomme*] a concept of tree.[32]

A central activity in such an analysis is "reflection," earlier defined as "how different representations can be conceived in one consciousness [*in Einem Bewusstsein*]." Now, although some features of this account appear more "psychological" than "logical," Kant is generally clear in this section that this abstraction is meant to be the result of the work of "pure reason" in fixing the markers that will count as those covered by the concept, and is not a mere "association" of empirical representations. However, just because of this legislating role of reason it is hard again to understand how this account explains the *derivation* of the concept.[33]

In the first place, as is often the case with descriptions of such derivations, a good deal of conceptual "work" seems to have already gone on here. For one thing, the sensory manifold seems already to have been experienced in some determinate way prior to this analysis; I am able already to recognize three associable objects, and to have sufficient conceptual clarity to recognize branches, stems, and leaves as such. Indeed, the process described here seems more like our making much clearer to ourselves a concept we already have than to be a genuine derivation. As such, this reflective procedure would be helpful in "arriving at" as general a concept of tree as we can isolate, but would not account for the origin of the concept itself.

Further, such a description, appearing as it does to resemble a simple abstractionist account, must be read together with other claims about the

---

32. Kant, *Logik*, p. 95.

33. Mittelstrass is again helpful here: "Denn auf die hier gestellte systematische Frage, was wir eigentlich tun, wenn wir von Begriffen sprechen, gibt es nur die Antwort: Wir stellen uns nicht vor, sondern wir führen logische Handlungen aus, indem wir mit Hilfe von Prädikatoren und Regeln, ohne auf etwas Aussersprachliches wie eben Vorstellungen angewiesen zu sein, unsere Begriffe konstruieren" ("Spontaneität," p. 69). This formulation itself makes necessary the qualification which we are treating here as problematic. "Die Logik, in disem Fall, eine Begriffstheorie, nicht dafür verantwortlich ist, welche Unterscheidungen 'in der Wirklichkeit' getroffen werden sollen, sondern nur dafür, wie unter Voraussetzung dieser schon getroffenen Unterscheidungen, und d.h. der exemplarischen Bestimmungen, Begriffe abstrahiert werden können" (ibid.).

power and limits of this kind of analysis. Kant has already insisted that
"no concept can arise by way of analysis," and, in spite of the way such
comparison, reflection, and abstraction help in organizing and ordering
the knowledge we *already have,* it remains true that "every analysis
presupposes a synthesis." Or, he puts it in the *Critique*:

> Synthesis of a manifold (be it given empirically or a priori) is what first gives
> rise to knowledge. This knowledge may, indeed, at first be crude and confused
> [*roh und verworren*], and therefore in need of analysis. (B103 = A77)

Thus, we still need to ask how we acquire the empirical rules for that
empirical synthesis, and how concepts function in that knowledge. Kant
does have some things to say about this acquisition, but his remarks are
not without ambiguity.

In the first place, he is clear that such a derivation cannot be a
straightforward "abstraction." He claims that it is always incorrect to
speak of "abstracting something" from the manifold of appearances.
Instead, one always *abstracts from* such a manifold, or *constructs* a
concept out of it. When this claim is coupled with Kant's constant
insistence that there is no intellectual receptivity, no Aristotelian *nous
pathetikos,* any abstractionist theory of concept formation seems excluded. However, by excluding such abstractionism, Kant does not also
mean to deny that it still makes sense to claim that empirical concepts are
derived from experience. It is true that he means to deny that universals
are "read off" from an intuited manifold by an abstracting intelligence.
Cognizing is always something we *do* in Kant (*Spontaneität* is one of his
defining marks for *Verstand*), and so we *construct* or make empirical
concepts in an imprecise, never completable response to experience. As
he puts it,

> All empirical concepts must be seen therefore as constructed [*gemachte*]
> concepts, whose synthesis is not arbitrary ["willkürlich," a term of art in Kant
> for mathematical concept construction] but empirical.[34]

However, this account raises a problem similar to the one encountered
before. There, we found it hard to say how a group of such characteristics
could be thought together as *one* concept unless there were defining
marks of the concept not empirically acquired, but essential to the sense
of the rule. Since this would seem to require some nonempirical ground
of *knowledge* for those predicates, we found Kant opting for a theory of
indefinite concepts and a loose notion of the analytic definition of a
concept. Now a similar problem emerges.

A rule, as we have seen, is supposed to function as a *ground of*

---

34. Kant, *Logik,* p. 141.

cognition (*Erkenntnisgrund*) for the "unity" of some empirical manifold. This means first of all that some concepts "contain" others. For example, the concept of metal is an *Erkenntnisgrund* for the concepts of gold, silver, and copper. Metal includes more than any one of these concepts, and so each of these individual concepts can only be represented "through it." By being a more general representation, such a concept provides the *Grund* within which individual concepts can be differentiated.[35] At the level of empirical apprehension, the same relation would apply. Having some empirical concept means that, given the empirical apprehension of a sufficient list of *Merkmale,* we can judge some "this" to be a "this such," a dog, a horse, or quark. To call a concept such a *Grund* is, then, just to point out that more specific representations can be thought "through it." ("So können alle diese Dinge, die in so fern unter ihm enthalten sind, durch ihn vorgestellt werden.")[36] The difficulty here, though, is whether Kant can describe the *concept* as the "ground" of cognition (which he does) or whether, focusing our attention now on how the concept is acquired, he also has to say something (which he does not) about those features *in* the manifold, or due to some conceptual activity, which warrant the collection of markers together as *this* rule. This is especially difficult since those features are themselves concepts or properties, requiring again an analysis of that by virtue of which such primary apprehension is warranted as well.

We could say that the collection of "markers" that defines some such rule is "warranted empirically," but the rule is supposed to be only an *Erkenntnisgrund,* or that by virtue of which the empirical manifold can be determinately apprehended as such *in the first place.* It does not seem at all useful to claim that the source of some rule is "experience," unless we are again willing to ask what it is *in* experience which warrants the rule's objectifying function.

Clearly the problem that is emerging here is that of what, precisely, we need to explain in trying to account, transcendentally, for our acquisition of concepts. And it is just at such a point that the apparently helpful analogy with rules seems to break down. Our first difficulty was accounting for the ground or source appealed to in thinking all these characteristics together as associable. As we saw, if we try just to appeal to "what has so far been associated in experience" as this ground, then not only do a number of problems arise for Kant's analytic/synthetic distinction, but the whole question is begged, since we originally wanted to know what there is in experience which does warrant this association.

We could end up giving Kant Hume's solution here and appeal to

35. Ibid., p. 96.
36. Ibid.

constant conjunction of properties. We could, that is, except for the second problem discussed above about derivation. We have found that it is only because of the possession of such a rule in the first place that any manifold is determinately associable. *Contrary* to Hume, it is not the case that impressions just by their occurrence generate a feeling of associability. Perhaps Kant's most decisive objection to Hume is his claim that it is the *mind* which must actively order and associate them, and this according to acquired rules. All of this makes understanding this acquisition even more difficult since, apparently, having the rule is a condition for the correct synthesis, and so, apprehension of the manifold.

Further, all such difficulties should make clear why we cannot simply associate acquiring a concept with learning a rule. Something of that analogy may apply, but if having "learned the rule" means more than just having learned to respond to sensory stimuli — that is, if it does mean having learned to make cognitive, and possibly wrong, *judgments* about the world (as it surely does in Kant, however the notion is interpreted elsewhere) — then acquiring the rule must entail some apprehension of the rule's foundation or ground.[37] And this last requirement has proved extremely puzzling, since possession of the rule seems required just for the apprehension of these associated characteristics. Put quite simply, Kant's well-known criticisms of empiricism (his insistence on the constituting role of concepts in the apprehension of any manifold) can be seen here in his account of empirical knowledge, and when it is seen, it becomes difficult to understand how any such *Erkenntnisgrund* could be acquired *from* the manifold.

Kant himself is more than a little ambiguous in his own explanations of what we have to explain or justify with respect to empirical concepts. He begins by noting:

> Many empirical concepts are employed without dispute from anyone. Since experience is always at hand for the proof of their objective reality, we believe ourselves, even without a deduction, to be justified in appropriating to them a meaning, an ascribed significance. (B116–17 = A84)

---

37. As is so often the case, Wittgenstein, for whom the notion of concept as rule is so central, poses this problem well, even if enigmatically. In the *Philosophical Investigations* (New York: Macmillan, 1965), he writes: "A rule stands there like a signpost — does the signpost leave no doubt open about the way I have to go?" (vol. 1, pp. 39–40). Of course, there is such a doubt ("sometimes") but Wittgenstein then claims this makes such a question "empirical," not "philosophical." As is well known, however, he does indicate *how* such empirical questions should be resolved: "I have further indicated that a person goes by a signpost only in so far as there exists a regular use of signposts, a custom" (p. 80). We cannot pursue his solution here, except to indicate that the question we are asking Kant here would reemerge about the origin of such customs, and especially about how we *interpret* and come to *trust* such customs.

However, Kant quickly realizes that this general statement won't do. There must be some limitation on what can *count* as an appeal to experience. Believers in witches, the ether, and the like all consider themselves to have "empirical" evidence for their claim. What allows us to say that such concepts are usurpatory?

Kant moves to correct this too hasty formulation by explaining more cautiously:

> And from it [the transcendental deduction] I distinguish empirical deduction, which shows the manner in which the concept is acquired through experience and through reflection upon experience, and which therefore concerns, not its legitimacy, but only the facts relevant to its possession [*Sondern das Faktum betrifft, wodurch der Besitz entsprungen*]. (B117 = A85)

We thus only "believe ourselves" (*halten uns*, A84) to use concepts without a justification and that illusion needs correcting by some kind of account. The "sense" of empirical concepts does need to be explained, and, as we have just seen, is so by an account of their "origins." But this leaves us in a strange bind. On the one hand, Kant seems to admit that a demand for a *quid iuris* for empirical concepts *does* arise, if for no other reason than to distinguish them from "usurpatory concepts." But, on the other hand, what is officially defined as that empirical deduction is explicitly said to concern *not* the concept's legitimacy (*Rechtmässigkeit*), but just the "manner in which a concept is acquired." In other words, their origin is explained, but their use is not justified.

To add even more to the confusion, Kant himself seems to point out this problem. In a passage just following the one we have been considering, he thanks "the illustrious Locke" for his "physiological derivation," but expressly criticizes this derivation sense of justification, and insists that such an account is *wrongly* called a "deduction" (and, apparently, was wrongly so called by Kant himself at B117 = A85). The context of this criticism of Locke is meant to show the need for a justification of pure concepts, but the limitations it rightly imposes on what a deduction, or *quid iuris* defense, is make it hard to see how empirical concepts could be justified, or distinguished from usurpatory concepts.

Now these empirical standards for entry into the conceptual order could, of course, include a number of candidates. The "ground" or warrant for empirical concept formation could be an appeal to "our pragmatic intentions," or even to abstract entities, "universals." Our only point thus far is that it is very hard to see how Kant does deal with this issue, and, what's more, the more he describes "empirical realism," the less it is clear how he *could* deal with it.[38] Consider, for example, how he

---

38. This issue is discussed in an intriguing way by Richard E. Aquila in "Kant's Theory of

attempts to make use of his own version of "practical" standards for such concept formation, in the *Critique of Judgment*. First, he restates some elements of his theory of empirical concepts.

> Empirical concepts have, therefore, their territory [*Boden* or *territorium*] in nature . . . but no realm [*Gebiet,* or *ditio*], only a dwelling place [*Aufenthalt,* or *domicilium*]; for though they are produced in conformity to law [*gesetzlich*], they are not legislative [*gesetzgebend*], but the rules based on them are empirical and consequently contingent.[39]

We have already seen how hard it is to define exactly how these concepts come to have their "territory" at all, and how difficult it is to carry through the suggestion that they are in *no* sense "legislative." Here, Kant considers another source or ground for the "unity of our empirical cognitions." That source is "reflective judgment," governed by a "principle of purposiveness," and is called a "subjective" source for our ability to associate "markers" together, not only in individual concepts, but in species, genera, and "systems" of science. As he puts it:

> This transcendental concept of a purposiveness of nature is neither a natural concept nor a concept of freedom, because it ascribes nothing to the object (to nature), but only represents the peculiar way in which we must proceed in reflection upon the objects of nature in reference to a thoroughly connected experience, and is therefore a subjective principle (maxim) of the judgment.[40]

It is the subjective nature of this demand or "need" for unity which, while it reveals how deeply connected Kant's version of empirical knowledge is with his theory of reflective judgment,[41] is of little help with our problem here. While the most general explanation for our association of

---

Concepts," *Kant-Studien* 65 (1974): 1–19. Denying the prevalent interpretation of concepts as exclusively rules or functions, Aquila argues that Kant *can* speak of concepts representing "contents"; indeed, they are "representatives of the general" (p. 4); and that he can do so without claiming they represent a universal. Thus: "A concept, on Kant's theory, is that element in a representation whose presence in an intuition would constitute that intuition as an awareness of something under one general description rather than another." But Aquila's "that by virtue of which" an intuition is recognized as falling under this and not that description *as* the concept's content (1) leaves out precisely Kant's interest; how such a general "feature" *could be known*, apart from some "recognition" or intellectual intuition which Kant explicitly excludes; and (2) does not address the further, completely nontranscendental, but required question of "*that* by virtue of which" intuitions *come to have* those "features" Aquila wants the concept to represent. In short, I think Kant should have a theory of concepts at least something like Aquila's, but if he did, he would cease to be "Kant," cease to be "transcendental."

39. Kant, *Kritik der Urteilskraft, Gesammelte Schriften,* vol. 5, p. 174.
40. Ibid., p. 184.
41. Cf. Gerd Buchdahl, *Metaphysics and the Philosophy of Science* (Cambridge: M.I.T. Press, 1969), pp. 504–6.

markers into concepts, species, and so forth, it is also the furthest removed from any connection with any "objective" or empirically based origin. It is still, I think, hard to see the range and limits of such "reflection," and hard to understand how the demand for order we impose on nature is at all guided by what we learn from nature. Finally, many of the issues discussed here about empirical concepts would need to be settled first, before this kind of an explanation of systematic unity would be relevant.

7. Kantian Responses

To anyone familiar with Kant's overall strategy, a number of possible responses suggest themselves at this point. One is certainly a stronger emphasis on the role of the categories in empirical concept formation. As it is often put, the categories are the basic rules (or "laws") *for* such concept formation. Schematized categories, in fact, tell us how to form empirical concepts.[42] On this view, if carried to extremes, we could say that the "origin" of empirical concepts *is* simply the understanding itself. The order it demands from experience is the basic ground for the kinds of empirical concepts we have and the specific ones we use just represent various, always contingent attempts by reason to satisfy these restrictions. As we have seen, empirical concepts are "made," not "abstracted," and rather than looking for something "in the manifold" to explain their derived status, we should realize that, as regards their form, empirical concepts might just as well be called a priori, originating wholly in the understanding's attempt to *prescribe* an order to nature. Once we assert, "To regard any principle or rule as a priori is to assert that their primary function is to serve the understanding," there seems no reason not to call such concepts a priori, even if contingent. And Schrader,[43] who advances

42. This is the interpretation proposed and defended in great detail by Wolff in *Kant's Theory of Mental Activity,* p. 130. Since Wolff makes more use of the notion of rule in advancing his interpretation than any other commentator, it is worth noting how the problem here developed is relevant to his case. In explaining conceptual as rule-governed unity, Wolff notes that such unity "is the apprehension in one consciousness of a variety of representations which were originally disjoint. By carrying them forward, the mind has made it possible to think them as a unity" (p. 129). The point made in this section could then be put: it seems that it rather has to be the case that some prior apprehension of such unity is required for the directedness and coherence of the mind's activity. Or, when he claims, "To say that mental content R represents object O is to say that R is one of a variety (= manifold) of mental contents which has been, or can be reproduced in the imagination according to the rule which is the concept of O" (pp. 133–34), our problem has been the status of "O" and the place such an ("abstract"?) object must have in accounting for the markers that make up the rule for the apprehension of O.

43. George Schrader, "Kant's Theory of Concepts," in *Kant: A Collection of Critical Essays,* ed. R. P. Wolff. The quotation is on p. 151.

this view, along with the above interpretation of the a priori, has some good evidence for this claim.

As we have seen, however, such an interpretation must reckon with what, if anything, is left intact of the idea of an empirical origin of concepts. It is possible on this view to claim that the "content" of empirical concepts still turns out to be supplied from experience, and so in that sense, empirical concepts are still empirical. But it is now difficult to understand how the prescription effected by these concepts can ever be corrected by experience. On Schrader's view, the basic difference between pure and empirical concepts has to do with respective "levels" of generality and not their "origin." But then, the system of empirical concepts, since restricted only by very general rules for their formation (categories), seems capable of ordering our experience in any number of ways. So long as "events" are still connected in the formally correct way with "causes," which events are associated with which causes in empirical laws seems on an interpretation like Schrader's to be a function of a wholly "internal" procedure of reason (more specifically, contra Schrader's discussion, of reflective judgment). Apparently any adjustment of this system of concepts comes not directly "from experience," but, one would imagine, from inconsistencies with other concepts and laws fashioned by reason "elsewhere" in the system of science.[44]

It may be that Kant's theory of concepts needs to be interpreted in this way to avoid some of the problems discussed here. But we should be clear how much of Kant's own claims are thereby given up. We have already seen that his own concept of an empirical deduction of concepts has very much to do with grounding the legitimacy of that concept directly *in* experience, and that when he comes to a point where he wants to interpret some further question as "empirical" he hardly seems willing to interpret that to mean the construction of another concept with which to interpret the manifold. In sum, while Schrader's interesting interpretation might be a helpful way of explaining the links between Kant and Hegel, it leaves the notion of "empirical" in Kant very dark.

Another response, related to the above problem of explaining both the

44. Much of this difficulty is brought out well in Buchdahl's claim for a "looseness of fit" between the conditions "imposed" on nature by the understanding and the "order" of nature regulatively determined by reason. Cf. *Metaphysics and the Philosophy of Science,* p. 470 ff. Buchdahl shows that empirical law-likeness is a task of reason in Kant (p. 501) but notes as well that the claim for an advance beyond the observation of contingent particulars to a more systematically ordered experience "is supported only by a number of heuristic and informal arguments" (p. 503). Many of Buchdahl's observations would make difficult an explanation of empirical concept formation which relied exclusively on the doctrine of the categories. See his discussion of the relation between the Second Analogy and empirical causal laws, pp. 641–72, especially section 3, "The 'looseness of fit' between transcendental and empirical levels."

constitutive *and* the derivative role of empirical concepts, is to appeal to
the general task of transcendental philosophy itself. One could argue that
Kant's lack of much attention to the problem of empirical concepts is no
oversight on his part, or certainly not an important one. Transcendental
philosophy has as its task only an analysis of those conditions of experience which are a priori accessible. If anything is clear from his brief
discussions of empirical concepts it is that they can barely be described
"formally" at all, their "boundaries" are always in a state of flux, never
fully definable, subject to alteration or even abandonment through experience; and that thus, aside from the kind of rules for their formation
given by the categories, nothing further can be said transcendentally
about them. Any question about whether such concepts correctly discriminate items in our experience can only be answered *in concreto,* in
connection with the rest of our empirical knowledge, and it certainly
cannot be answered formally or a priori according to a principle of
correct derivation.

Such a defense of Kant is more complex than it might initially seem; in
fact it goes to the heart of the formal nature of the transcendental
enterprise. The only way to respond to it briefly is to note that Kant has
not himself excluded these kinds of questions and many of their ramifications. He does seem to think that some general account of the "guidedness" of empirical knowledge is called for if his version of empirical
knowledge is to have any force. Many of his central arguments depend
directly on certain characteristics of the role of sensibility in empirical
knowledge, and even more important are his arguments about what such
a manifold *cannot* be said to do. (Cf. again his denial of representative
models of intuition, above, pp. 30–46.) Now, it may be that such
representative models do lead to unacceptable results and need to be
abandoned. But if such representative models are abandoned, then, as
has been made clear throughout this discussion, *some* alternative, "transcendental" account of empirical receptivity (and particularly of sensible
affection) is certainly called for. Such an account is hardly peripheral to
Kant's transcendental concerns. It is as important in an explanation of the
"empirical" elements in his complete epistemology as it is only dimly
present in scattered passages in his *corpus.*

Of course, to introduce the general problem of Kant's theory of
sensibility at this point is to reintroduce all the problems discussed in
chapter 2. Nevertheless, it seems to me fair to note, at this point, the
central importance of such an interpretation or rational reconstruction,
and to note again the basic problem such an interpretation would *continually* face. The difficulty involves just those elements of Kant's epistemology which mark his break from prior traditions, and which generate
so many valuable insights in the *Critique* — his theory that the under-

standing is wholly active, in no way passive, that it is exclusively spontaneity, and his account of the "material" or formless content of knowledge, sensations.[45] The familiar, by now classic difficulty of understanding
how both such aspects of our knowledge combine in any actual piece of
empirical knowledge is, I think, particularly well illuminated in the
foregoing problems with empirical concepts, an issue which forces Kant
to attempt some explanation of the derived, *yet* "formal" rules which
function in the understanding's organization of experience.[46]

Such an ambitiously general remark prompts another, final one. As
indicated, in his account of both pure and empirical concepts, a basic
element in Kant's theory is that they are, in his understanding of the
term, "formal" — concepts are rules for the thought of objects; they
classify *our* ways of knowing objects and not directly what objects are,
and so do not represent characteristics of objects, or special, abstract
objects. But we seem to continue to have difficulty understanding the
transcendental role "materiality" is supposed to play in human knowledge: in the account of sensations, the relation between empirical intuitions and pure intuitions, and now in the origin of empirical concepts. As
we have seen, Kant seems to see only one way to "save" philosophy's a
priori task, an account of the formal structure of any possible human
experience. But the often indirect, incomplete, half-hidden, and occasionally inconsistent arguments he advances in defense of "what we
appeal to" to discover that structure (now, we can say, in either its pure
or derived aspects), have so far fallen short and have, it might pre-
maturely be added, raised some doubts about the nature of an exclusively
formal analysis in philosophy. I think that such difficulties become even
clearer when one looks at the completion of the theory of concepts in the

45. I am suggesting here, first, that Kant *did* indeed attempt to break quite radically from
the Cartesian picture of knowledge as a kind of clarity or "glow" of representations, or as an
immediate grasp of some content, in favor of a thoroughly discursive picture of conceptual
activity. I think the evidence for this break is much greater than, for example, Rorty admits
in his "Strawson's Objectivity Argument," *Review of Metaphysics* 24 (1970): 207–44. However, I am also arguing that, just to the extent that Kant was successful in moving in this
"Philosophical Investigations" direction, he raises what will become *the* problem for such an
account, the "ground" for this activity, a problem which he does not seem to be able to
solve within the limits of his methodology.

46. There are, of course, other passages in Kant's *corpus* where this problem is dealt
with. It arises in an especially interesting way in the *Metaphysische Anfangsgründe der
Naturwissenschaft, Gesammelte Schriften*, vol. 4 (cf. especially p. 468 and pp. 476–77).
However, discussion of such passages would have to involve a detailed look at Kant's theory
of concept "construction" in science, too detailed for the scope of this work. I can only
assert that I think many of the difficulties discussed here would arise in that context with
respect to the precise empirical nature of concepts like matter, force, velocity, and motion.

Schematism chapter. The problem there — "applying" concepts to a manifold — will again raise some difficult problems with Kant's account of both pure and empirical concepts, and those difficulties continue to reveal the limitations in Kant's foundational notion of formality.

5
Schemata

This schematism of our understanding, in respect to appearances and their mere form, is an art concealed in the depths of the human soul, whose true activities we surmise from Nature and lay unconcealed before our eyes only with difficulty. (B181 = A141)

1. The Place of the Schematism Chapter

Throughout attempts by various commentators to come to terms with the *Schematismuskapitel,* probably the most obscure chapter in the *Critique,* there seems to have been as little agreement about Kant's intentions in this short section as there has been in assessing the general success of his attempt. The chapter has been called superfluous, unintelligible, an architectonic anachronism, as well as the most important in the *Critique,* the key to the central argument of the Analytic. In the following I shall not be directly concerned with defending an interpretation of Kant's intentions, and shall only briefly present what I take to be the most reasonable reconstruction of what Kant thought he was doing in the chapter. My main interest will be to continue the discussion of concepts begun above. That is, having examined the problems of the origin and status of concepts, both pure and empirical, within Kant's theory of their formality, the next question that will arise, at least for Kant, is the problem of their *application (Anwendung).* Again, my interest will be assessing how the notion of a concept as a rule could include a successful, "transcendental" account of the application of such a rule in "judgment." And, again, that will require both a discussion of pure concepts and their "transcendental schemata," and a separate discussion of a most obscure and rarely discussed topic — empirical concepts and their schemata.

From Kant's perspective, the Schematism chapter appears to be more an explanatory pause in the course of his argument than any decisive new step in it. Of course, he also leaves no doubt as to his view of the importance of such an explanation, and seems to regard it as fundamental in understanding the shift from a transcendental discussion of concepts to synthetic a priori judgments.[1] But it is also true that much of this section

1. Although he leaves out discussion of many problems the chapter raises, H. J. Paton's

mostly provides additional crucial details of Kant's theory, a further explanation of just what the Transcendental Deduction *had* done in restricting the use of pure concepts. For example, for all its expressed importance, Kant refers back to the Schematism chapter infrequently, and often only in a summary manner, using the notion of a schematism just to repeat the general claim that categories can only have a sensible use. He does not seem to appeal to any "results" specifically arrived at there in order to advance his case elsewhere. Indeed, many of the basic doctrines of the Schematism are so much supplemented by revisions in the second edition (particularly with additional remarks on the "schematic" importance of space, as in the *General Note to the System of Principles*),[2] that it becomes understandable why so many commentators have been troubled about its exact "place" in Kant's whole argument. The Schematism never assumes the status or relative clarity and distinctness of his doctrines of intuition, concept, judgment, and idea, and, in terms of our question, seems a quite unusual appendage to the theory of the forms of experience.

I think, though, that one can understand its position in the development of Kant's argument just by beginning with this realization of its deliberately expository, or backward-glancing, character, and by considering it in terms of the problems of formality thus far developed. With that in mind — and also keeping in mind that, in order to present a continuous discussion of Kant's theory of concepts, we have not yet examined the details of Kant's argument in the Deduction — Kant's overall strategy could be summarized as follows.[3]

Kant intends, by virtue of his clue, to derive from the forms of judgment "categories," forms of the thought of any object. We noted that it was probably best just to regard these derived categories as "likely" candidates for such pure concepts, that their specific derivation would have to occur later, and that the most important result of the Metaphysical Deduction lay in revealing what Kant thought concepts *are* — rules

---

commentary on the Schematism is still one of the clearest available. See *Kant's Metaphysic of Experience* (New York: Macmillan, 1936), vol. 2, pp. 17–24.

2. B288 ff. In this section, in speaking of a demonstration of the possibility of things in conformity with the categories (supposedly the task of the Schematism), Kant claims we need "outer intuitions." This appears to mean there that in order to understand the "sensible" use of any category, we must understand each in terms of human, spatial awareness: not just as modes of time consciousness. But no specific such schematism is provided; although one could argue that such is what occurs in the construction of concepts in pure science, as explained partly in *Metaphysische Anfangsgründe der Naturwissenschaft*.

3. In some details, the following parallels the accounts given by Paton and Bird. Norman Kemp Smith notices a number of tensions relevant to such an account, but again writes them off as evidence of Kant's "conflicting" views of concepts. *A Commentary to Kant's Critique of Pure Reason* (London: Macmillan, 1923), p. 334 ff.

for synthesis or, as expressed later, judgment. He then takes himself to
have shown, in an argument we shall look at in detail in the next chapter,
that synthesis is necessary for any experience, and that pure concepts,
nonderived rules, are necessary for any synthesis. He then extends his
argument, partly in the Deduction and partly in the Schematism, to prove
that, in particular, no possible content of *human* experience could be
experienced except in terms of pure rules for unity.[4] That is, he specifically "applies" his general argument to possible contents of a spatio-
temporal or intuitively enformed manifold. Then, having defended his
proof for the necessity of pure concepts in experience — a proof based
on the "possibility of experience" — *and* having explained the relevance
of that principle to the form of our experience (especially, but not wholly,
in the Schematism) he will go on in the Analytic of Principles to show
how the notion of a conceptual rule for synthesis, when considered in
terms of the particular form of our experience, yields synthetic a priori
judgments. In other words, once we know *how* to prove the objective
validity of pure concepts (by means of an appeal to the possibility of
experience), know that such a proof shows the necessity for some pure
concepts, and then *introduce* the specific characteristics of *our* experience
(that is, its spatio-temporal character), we can proceed to use that proof,
in terms of that (human) experience, and attempt a proof for a specific
judgment about all objects of experience. Without the "introduction" of
these characteristics into the argument, concepts could not be "applied,"
could not yield judgments.[5] Rules for the synthesis of any manifold would
have no specific relevance to the human sensible manifold. As it is, the
Principles are the *result* of the application of pure concepts to the form of
our experience, and the justification for a claim of a priori application is
thus made in terms of the argument of the Deduction, applied to any
specific features of those forms of experience which we can discern a
priori.

4. This latter element of Kant's proof introduces a complicated difficulty which will be
central in the following chapter's discussion of the Deduction. Kant's statements of his own
formalism often make it sound as if the forms of experience were simply "imposed" a priori
on the material of sense. As will become apparent in more and more detail, though, he is
also deeply concerned to show that this imposition is not "blindly" applied, that all objects
of sense can be shown to be subject to the subject's forms. Since he attempts to attain this
"perspective" on all possible objects of sense *formally* (that is, universally, nonempirically),
the attempt will be a crucial test of the syntheticity of his enterprise. In this context, this
problem of an application that is not simply an imposition is the problem of "judgment,"
and, as we shall see, the problem arises in empirical contexts as well.

5. Also, without this introduction, Kant's single strongest claim against all prior metaphysical traditions would lose its force — his claim that such metaphysics "amphibolously"
confused conditions for the thought of objects with conditions for objects themselves, and
that he alone had given pure concepts "content."

It is with respect to this latter aspect — discerning the specific features of our form of experience — that the problem of the Schematism enters. If we know that some pure concepts are required for experience to be possible, and want to know further in what specific terms a pure concept could be individually defended as a necessary condition for human experience, then, as Kant seems to think, we need to know *how* ("in what terms")[6] a pure concept could condition the possibility of and so a priori determine a specific kind of manifold — a human, sensibly apprehended manifold. We need to provide a schematization in general for any possible concept, and then show how specific schemata could be used for candidate categories in a full proof that they are specifically conditions for the possibility of our experience.

Such at any rate appears to me the best general statement of what Kant thought he was doing. The important features of his strategy are first, that the Schematism is an attempt to explain *how* the understanding accomplishes what the Deduction proved that it must, and second, in doing so makes clear that for Kant the central problem of the Schematism should be considered a problem of *judgment,* specifically the problem of judgmental application.

Admittedly a very great deal remains obscure. Some of that obscurity, though, diminishes in the actual details of this enterprise (though certainly not all, or perhaps a good deal of it), and some can be eliminated by a larger view of Kant's theory of concepts.

For example, the Schematism can be said to expand Kant's understanding of the formality of such concepts. The schema of a concept is just that aspect which renders a "schematized concept" more than a "form of thought." In those terms, Kant understands a pure concept not just as a formal law of thought, more too than the form of the thought of any

6. This transcendental "how" question must, though, first be carefully distinguished from what we can call a "psychological" how question, a question explicitly excluded from the first *Critique* by Kant himself in his response to Ulrich in the *Metaphysische Anfangsgründe der Naturwissenschaft, Gesammelte Schriften,* vol. 4, p. 574 ff. That question only asks "what happens" in the mind when application does occur; the transcendental how question explains the conditions for application, or what *must* be the case for application rules to be meaningful. Further, this how question must be distinguished from what we can call a "teleological" how question, one which asks "how" we can assume that appearances, as given, do regularly conform to the a priori restrictions of the knowing subject; that is, how we could assume application in order to explain it. Thus that teleological question does not ask, By virtue of what homogeneity can a rule be applied? but, By virtue of what can we assume that there will be a homogeneity? And such a question is answered in detail only in the *Critique of Judgment.* Moltke Gram has some helpful things to say about this "how" question in *Kant, Ontology and the A Priori* (Evanston: Northwestern University Press, 1968), p. 88, and Eva Schaper discusses, in a general way, the relevance of the Schematism to the third *Critique* in "Kant's Schematism Reconsidered," *Review of Metaphysics* 18 (1964): 267–92.

object, but as the specific form of the thought of any object of *our* experience.[7] Thus concepts are not just rules for combination, and are also more than rules for the synthesis of elements in any manifold, but are rules for the synthesis of elements in a human, spatio-temporal manifold. In effect, then, the schema will provide what was earlier mysteriously called the "transcendental content" for categories, will specify the "material" reference to objects that makes categories more than subjective rules for our thought, but a priori determinations for all objects of thought.

Also, apart from their role in this explanation of a Kantian category, the Schematism also throws some light on details resulting from the Deduction, and thus also has a role to play in the proof structure of Kant's Analytic. We now, supposedly, know that categories determine any manifold of sense, and that they specifically determine the unity of a spatio-temporal manifold. Once we understand *how* that comes about, how a manifold could be said to be "a priori determined," we can go on to (1) develop the specific "mode of determination" for each candidate category, and (2) using the proof strategy defended in the Deduction, examine in detail whether any individual category — defined in those terms, terms specific to our forms of experience, in short whether any schematized category — can fulfill the requirements of a necessary condition for the possibility of experience, as they have come to be defined.

This all sets for the Schematism an unusual and difficult task. Kant has set himself the goal of preserving the purity and formality of categories (he wants to continue to claim that categories do not represent universal properties of objects in general), while establishing, still a priori, a connection between such categories and all possible objects of sensible experience. Of course, the ultimate goal still remains to prove that objects do fall under the categories, in clearer language that the categories are universally and necessarily applicable to all objects of any human sensible manifold. Clearly, though, along the way to that goal, Kant has to explain how, in what terms, such pure rules could determine the material of a human sensible manifold. But that kind of understanding seems to presuppose access *to* all possible objects of experience, a way of

7. Thomas Swing has claimed that there are really two theories of concepts at work, often in conflict, in the Transcendental Analytic, one which retained a somewhat precritical view of the relation between pure concepts and the intelligible world (a view which would make the Schematism otiose), and a properly critical theory which demands an explanation for concept materiality. See *Kant's Transcendental Logic* (New Haven: Yale University Press, 1969), pp. 54–78. As I am presenting it, the conflict at issue is not a result of traces of pre-Critical theory, but, again, a result of Kant's decision that his methodology must be formal, and his hesitancy to explain his claims for synthetic results by asserting simply that such forms are subjectively "imposed" in the "construction" of experience. The Schematism is such a confusing chapter just because *that* conflict is most of all in the foreground.

saying something about all *objects* of experience, and not just more about the "form of the thought" of all objects.[8] As one might expect by now, to do so Kant appeals to his notion of the *form* of our immediate experience of all such objects, specifically to the form of inner sense, time.

2. Transcendental Schemata

Even such a brief restatement of Kant's probable intentions reveals at once how much is at stake in the Schematism chapter. Although mostly explanatory, what Kant seeks to explain here is something which has come to be quite important for the theory of forms of experience. It has become clear that Kant does not regard pure concepts as logical conditions for the intelligibility or meaning of the concept of human experience, nor does he regard them as psychological dispositions of the human mind. They are to be understood as "conditions for the possibility of experience," a position that commits him to proving both that human knowledge would not be possible except if organized and discriminated in general ways (in "modes" of knowledge) not derived from experience, and *how,* in terms of what features of experience itself, such an unusual "a priori determination" is to occur.[9] His own preliminary remarks on the issue spell out what he regards as this "peculiarity" (*Eigentümliche*) of transcendental philosophy.

> But transcendental philosophy has the peculiarity that, besides the rule (or rather the universal condition of rules) which is given in the pure concepts of the understanding, it can at the same time specify the instance [*den Fall*] to which the rule is to be applied. . . . It must formulate by means of universal but yet sufficient characteristics the conditions under which objects can be given in agreement with these concepts. (B174–75 = A135–36)

Later, the Schematism is said to "deal with the sensible conditions under which alone pure concepts of the understanding can be employed" (B175 – A136), and to be the first part of the whole "Doctrine of Judgment."

How, then, can such sensible conditions be specified? What do we appeal to in defining them? In what sense, especially what a priori sense, do these schemata specify the instances to which pure concepts can be applied? Kant's answer to this question is couched in some of the most mysterious technical terminology yet employed. Simply summarized, all

8. This all anticipates again much of the next chapter's discussion of the second-edition Deduction.

9. The situation here is similar to, say, a Leibnizian who claims that ultimately substance is monadic, and who is then called on to "save the phenomena," to explain *how* phenomenal unity could look as it does, if reality is so described.

the above occurs by means of a schematism of the understanding; these schemata are called "products of the transcendental imagination"; they are to be both "pure" and in "immediate relation" to all possible objects of experience; and in general, such a schematism is said to be "temporality." In slightly less technical language, the Schematism specifies that categories are to be considered conditions of human experience *by* being considered modes of our time consciousness.

Each of the various components involved in this answer requires special comment. However, it would also be fair here to charge that the question itself of a transcendental schematism has not yet been clearly presented. To do so, one first needs to return to the whole context of a schematism as it is presented by Kant — the context of "subsumption" and "judgment."

We know already, from the preceding chapter's discussion, that Kant's interpretation of concepts and their universality will require a corresponding interpretation of what it means to apply a concept, or to subsume instances "under" a concept. In fact, "recognition in a concept," as he will come to call such subsumption, occurs only in terms of what will be called the synthesis of apprehension and reproduction. As his general theory of concepts demands, recognition in a concept is thus not to be interpreted as the "reflection" of an "original" in an image, nor in terms of class inclusion judgments. Rather, recognition is the consciousness of the unity effected by the application of the rule. Kant's replacement of a "Concept-Instance" model by one which calls for a concept, as a rule, determining the synthetic unity of any individual, can be seen especially well in the statement of the famous *Restrikstionslehre* that the categories have only a sensible use (B165 ff.). Although he seems there to describe concepts having instances corresponding to them, he quickly demonstrates that he means by this that concepts are involved in judgments only insofar "as they can be *applied* [*angewandt*] to empirical intuitions."[10] Knowledge, by means of judgments, occurs when a universal rule is applied to the material of intuition, and determines the unity of these intuitions in this or that way, not when individuals are recognized as instances of a general type.

The same kind of ambiguity about what Kant means by subsumption under a concept in judgment occurs in the first paragraph of the Schema-

10. This unique Kantian theory of "subsumption" is one of my disagreements with L. Chipman's explanation of the schematism in "Kant's Categories and Their Schematism," *Kant-Studien* 63 (1972): 36–50, especially 45. I want to investigate in more detail than what he, one-sidedly I think, calls Kant's "constructivist" and "subjective" interpretation of subsumption. It should also be noted that what Kant means by "determining judgment" is not what he means by predication, which always does involve the subsumption of one concept under another. In fact, the former is a presupposition of the latter.

tism chapter. The first sentence of that paragraph speaks quite traditionally of the "subsumption" of an object under a concept, even of an object
being "contained" under a concept, and of thus the necessity for a
homogeneity (*Gleichartigkeit*) between concept and object. The description here almost sounds as if concepts should be considered representative
of παραδείγματα, or εἴδη, for which there are sensible εἰκόνα; all of
which would seem to raise for Kant, in his own expression, the problem
of *das Dritte* between such, as surely as the τρίτος ἄνθρωπος is raised for
Plato.[11] According to everything said so far about the nature of concepts,
Kant should be concerned, not with how an object is subsumed under a
concept, but how, and in what cases, a rule for synthesis is applied in
determining any *Erkenntnismaterie*. We are supposed to have already
realized that there can be identifiable instances of a concept only as the
result of applying a rule, that there can be further logical analysis of these
results only as the result of synthesis. Kant himself indicates quickly that
he means subsumption just in this admittedly unusual and very idealistic-
sounding "determining" sense. (He had already stressed the problem as
one of applying pure concepts to appearances, at B171 = A132.) In his
subsequent discussion it becomes ever clearer that the familiar "One-
Many" problem for him is not "by virtue of what are many subsumed
under one," but that it is: by virtue of what can a rule determine a
manifold a priori to produce the unity that makes speaking ("later") of
many under one possible (recalling again his insistence that the analytic
unity of any concept presupposes a synthetic unity).[12] Throughout, a
concept remains universal as a universally applicable rule for synthesis,
not as a genus or universal type. Thus the question of the Schematism
chapter, with respect to subsumption, must be how a *sensible* manifold
can be *conceptually* determined, not how instances are recognized as
having some common predicate. Indeed, it is always Kant's view that the
latter kind of analysis presupposes the former.

What, though, could it mean to apply a rule and "determine" a
manifold a priori? Much of what it means comes down again to how Kant
interprets the results of the Deduction. It is Kant's position that no
amount of reflection on the data of sensible intuitions can yield evidence

11. Although I do not think Kant is guilty of the particular confusion he charges him
with, H. W. B. Joseph points out well the Platonic affinities with Kant's doctrines of
concept and schema. See "The Schematism of the Categories in Kant's *Critique of Pure
Reason*," in *Essays in Ancient and Modern Philosophy* (Oxford: The Clarendon Press:
1935), pp. 266–302.
12. Admittedly, this talk of determining (*Bestimmen*) sounds like a totally "constructivist" interpretation of Kant's formality. It will, though, be precisely the task of the
Schematism to show *how* this determining is not wholly "subjective." Admittedly, this
schema will be provided for transcendental judgment by the "imagination," but an imagination guided by the characteristics of all objects of sense.

of, say, causal connection between events. It is also his position that experience would not be possible unless such data could be organized and thought together in terms of some causal rule. He concludes from this, after an extended analysis of the "unity of experience" as a whole, that causality is a necessary, subjective rule for all experience. However, in interpreting what this result amounts to, Kant also holds that such a subjective, a priori stipulation of what could be experienced cannot be said to occur wholly from "the side of thought," if you will. Although he is maddeningly ambiguous at times, he is often crystal clear in wanting to avoid the view that we *simply* have to "think" of the world as causally ordered — however it may be in itself. He often quite clearly and somewhat proudly states that he is not trying to prove that any thought we could form of objects is subject to categorical rules, but rather that all *objects* are so subject.[13] To do this, he introduces this section on *judgment* to explain how these categorical rules determine a manifold (i.e., specify what kinds of unity could be experienced) in terms of *its* (the manifold's) immediate properties, in terms of those properties all objects of experience immediately share just by being intuited. Understanding how the categories determine the manifold a priori, once we realize that this is what Kant means by "subsumption," means understanding them in terms of our conditions for receptivity, and that is undertaken to demonstrate that the understanding does not wholly "spontaneously" determine what could count as an experience of an object.

Some of this could be put, as it often is, by saying that the schematism explains the "sensible" meaning of the categories.[14] Although Kant does not really have what a post-Fregean community would recognize as a coherent theory of meaning, there is something to this characterization.[15] Kant agreed with Hume that the categories were not derived from experience, and yet that they could have only a sensible meaning, that

---

13. For evidence of Kant's ambiguity on this point, compare what he says at B289: "We can never get further than proving that without this relation [causality] we are unable to *comprehend* the existence of the contingent, that is, unable a priori through the understanding to know the existence of such a thing — from which it does not, however, follow, that this is also a condition of the possibility of things themselves [my emphasis]," with what he says at B138: "It [the synthetic unity of consciousness] is not merely a condition *I myself require* in knowing an object, but is a condition under which every intuition must stand in order *to become an object for me*" [my emphasis].

14. The notion is Walsh's. See his "Schematism" in *Kant: A Collection of Critical Essays,* ed. R. P. Wolff (New York: Doubleday Anchor, 1967), p. 74 ff.

15. That is, Kant seems to be thinking of the following kind of consideration: however generically similar, "causality" could mean something quite different in the context of God's creative power than in the context of the powers of intuition and conceptualization possessed by humans. How to specify that context and the restrictions on "meaning" it demands, without doing so a posteriori, is the task of the Schematism.

they should be understood only in terms of some possible object of experience, and not in terms of some mysterious, metaphysical property of any object. And the Schematism just represents his attempt to explain how this could be, how the categories could only have a sensible meaning, even if they are not derived from experience. He does this by explaining how each of the categories has only a sensible *use*. The concept is explained, is shown to have a meaning that is relevant to our experience, not by pointing to a variety of instances, or hunting for foundational impressions, nor by stipulating that the "rules of the thought of an object" simply constitute the form of any sensible object, but by understanding the use of the rule in terms of some universal, a priori, and above all formal characteristic of any received manifold. And again, that use must be specified formally. We have to be able to understand causality not just as a rule connecting ground and consequent, but must understand what such a rule would mean in its sensible use. We must be able to specify the kinds of instances in which such a rule could be applied to in our experience. And to do *that*, Kant now claims, we need the strange ability of "transcendental judgment."[16]

Kant begins to explain what is involved in this transcendental judgment in the introductory section for both the Schematism and the Analytic of Principles, "On Transcendental Judgment in General" (B171 = A132). This passage also indicates that the problem of a transcendental schematism might be called that of the "conditions for the possibility of judgment," and that by the possibility of judgmental subsumption under a concept Kant means understanding how a rule is applied. But at this point, Kant himself goes on to stress how unusual such a discussion is. If the issue is, "under what general sensible conditions" (where, as will be clearer later, "under what conditions" = schemata) rules are applicable — i.e., if we attempt to specify these conditions — our only possible answer seems to be further rules, which would again need judgment's "guidance" to be employed. If we are in the position of understanding

---

16. This is a good place to point out that such an attempt by Kant does not fall victim to G. J. Warnock's famous criticism that it is senseless to stipulate that someone has a concept and then wonder if he can use it. See his "Concepts and Schematism," in *Analysis* (1948–49): 77–82. What else could understanding the concept mean than understanding how it is used? This problem has, I believe, been effectively and variously answered elsewhere. See Moltke Gram, *Kant, Ontology, and the A Priori* (Evanston, Ill.: Northwestern University Press, 1968), p. 87 ff., and Schaper, "Kant's Schematism Reconsidered," p. 271 ff. It should only be pointed out here that there is some sense indeed to the notion of a scientist, for example, having a well-formed, perhaps hypothetical concept, understanding it, and being unsure to what set of facts the concept could be applied. There is no more mystery in that than there is in a judge wondering if this is a case of second- or first-degree murder, or in anyone understanding the notion of ground and consequent and wondering how that notion should be applied in our particular experience.

what a causal connection, or substance as a rule for synthetic unity, means, and want to know how we would apply that rule within the peculiarities of human experience, the only answer seems to be a further rule for synthesis (necessary succession or permanence), which would raise the supposed problem of judgment all over again. Such a problem would be analogous to a logic teacher confronted by a student who claimed to understand some set of rules for correct inference, and could follow what went on in an example of their application, but who could not himself apply the rules correctly. The teacher might provide further application rules ("in such a situation, it is often expedient to apply this rule before that one, or always simplify these kinds of expressions first"), but the student still might have trouble recognizing *when* he is supposed to follow *these* rules. As Kant himself insists, it is in the nature of rules always to require guidance from judgment, and not to be able to give guidance to judgment. However, schemata, which turn out to be limiting rules for the application of the categories, appear to do just that, all adding even more to the complexities of this section.

At this point, two things need to be said about Kant's attempt. One concerns the general problem of judgment, the other the peculiarities of transcendental judgment and transcendental schemata. The former is particularly important in the light of various problems discussed in earlier chapters. As has been continually obvious, an enormous amount of Kant's case rests on how he interprets the respective roles played in experience by sensible intuitions and by concepts. The former he characterizes in terms of passivity and materiality, the latter in terms of spontaneity and formality, rules for that spontaneity. Now he introduces a third, mediating element — judgment.[17] In general, this sudden introduction alters somewhat the overall picture of experience so far sketched. We are now to understand as involved in experience not just the active discriminating, classifying, ordering, and uniting of the understanding, directed on a passively received, "material" content, but also a kind of "insight" into which rules for discriminating, ordering, and so forth are to apply to specific manifolds. Once we face *that* problem ("application") we might be tempted to do a number of things in responding to it — formulate further rules, claim that one either sees when the rule is applied or doesn't, or that no further problem needs to be addressed once we have the rule, that the rule itself specifies under what conditions it is to be applied. Many of the difficulties of the Schematism chapter stem from the fact that Kant appears to say all three at various points, and a number of

17. *Urteil* and *Urteilskraft* are both regularly translated, as judgment, creating some ambiguity. It is the latter, literally "the power of judging," that is at issue here, not the former, which, if considered in the context of an extensional logic, we would consider a "proposition."

different issues need to be disentangled before any coherence can arise from his position. But the first thing to notice is just the unusual properties of this faculty of judgment. His account of what is later called "determining judgment" (one has the universal and seeks to apply it, as opposed to "reflective judgment," where one seeks to formulate a universal) often sounds like the kind of "intellectual" or at least vaguely nonsensible intuition he is everywhere at pains to deny. It sounds like an apprehension of a manifold that is neither a passive reception of material nor a spontaneous synthesizing. (In fact it almost sounds like the Platonic *noesis*.)[18]

But before broaching the general problem of judgment, and in particular its relevance to empirical investigation, one should note the special problems of transcendental judgment and the transcendental schematism. For here, Kant does appear to think that transcendental judgment is guided by something other than the meaning of the concept itself in its application to all objects of experience, that, at least in this case, specifying conditions for applications are possible and necessary. For pure concepts of the understanding, the Schematism could just be said to specify further the meaning of the concept itself ("for us"), and in that sense to help explain the conditions of its application. That is, the question of a schematism for pure concepts only asks about "the possibility of application," not for rules specifying actual application. We don't now want rules that will specify whether this or that series of events *is* causally connected (a decision that always requires judgment in its still ambiguous empirical use), but for the rules that specify the conditions under which this could ever be a question (or how, the terms in which, this is a legitimate question to pose empirically). We will come to know in a general way, from the Deduction, that this broad schematism for understanding pure concepts is the "possibility of experience." This chapter, looking toward transcendental judgments about all possible objects of experience, makes clearer how that principle works. As indicated, judgment is still always required in empirical investigation, but we must now explain how that judgment could be possible, in what way the categories set the limits within which an empirical judgment can be made. And specifying the categories in that way is transcendental judgment.

Since the task of a transcendental schematism is to explain how there can be a universal determination of objects in general,[19] such a schema must be a universal feature of all appearances, and must be formally

18. Again, though, as will be discussed in more detail, it is *Einbildungskraft* which does the work of Platonic and Aristotelian *Nous*. This is more grist for Heidegger's mill, as is effectively demonstrated by Hermann Mörchen, *Die Einbildungskraft bei Kant* (Tübingen: Max Niemeyer, 1970), pp. 110–22.

19. And not simply an imposition of order on a manifold.

universal, not some mere empirical predicate. Since all objects of experience, inner or outer, are subject to the form of inner sense, time, such
becomes Kant's general solution to the problem of a transcendental
schematism. This schema will help explain the terms in which the categories apply to appearances because it is both a necessary feature of all
sensible appearances, and yet is a purely formal feature of those appearances, thus formally specifiable as the a priori mode of categorical
determination. The categories are thus said to determine appearances by
virtue of the understanding's "affecting" inner sense, and since the form
of inner sense is time, the categories are to be understood as modes of
time consciousness. It is in these terms that the schema does not help us
in, say, making individual causal judgments, but provides the method, a
specification of the rule of causality in terms of the form of our experience, by which these empirical judgments can be made. In short, the
transcendental schema does not provide a rule for discovering the content
of such judgments, but further specifies their form.

Kant goes on to explain this "schematic" explanation of a concept's
applicability by contrasting a schema with an "image" (*Bild*) as a candidate for such an explanation. Although a transcendental schema is said to
be a "product of the imagination [Ein*bild*ungskraft]," it is not for that
reason to be considered an image, a *Bild*. The most important reason for
not considering a schema an image is that a schema has no "particular
intuition" as its "goal," but instead is said to aim at the "unity in the
determination of sensibility." A schema is thus said to be a *Methode,* not,
as any image must be, a particular representation. So far, such a claim is
straightforward enough. As Walsh points out,[20] part of understanding the
meaning of a concept must involve more than understanding the strict
semantical significance of its definition, more than being able to shuffle
around synonyms in that definition. And it must involve more than being
able to produce one or two examples of the concept. To be sure, if one
could do all that, one would have thereby some understanding of the
meaning of the concept. But to understand the full, say experiential
meaning of the concept, one would have to be able to produce a whole
series of various examples, and it is this added ability which Kant seems
to be trying to get at with the notion of a schema as a "method." Of
course, it remains unclear how a schema is really supposed to differ from
the concept, a problem that will become especially troublesome with
empirical concepts, but I think the general explanation Kant is trying to
present is not all that mysterious. And this denial that a schema for a
concept is a particular representation is also consistent with all our earlier
emphasis here on just what Kant thinks a concept is.

20. Walsh, "Schematism," p. 76.

That is, if concepts are rules, or functions, then any discussion of their sense or meaning can only occur in terms of the method of using them. Thus, to say that the categories have only a sensible meaning is not to say that categories only represent sensible instances. Again, in that sense, there are no sensible instances of categories. Categories are applied to a manifold and function as rules determining how that manifold is to be understood. It makes no sense to speak of some empirical causal connection as an instance of a causal rule. In the first place, "causality" is a pure concept. It has no direct sensible counterpart at all. There are no "substance" or "causality" instances, always only this or that substance or causal connection. Moreover, there are no "instances" of *rules*. Sensible *Materie is* an individual object or event only because such pure rules determine it to be so construed. And in Kant's terminology, all of this is formulated by saying that for pure concepts, the imagination specifies schemata, not images to explain the objectivity, or the experiential, more than merely logical, meaning of such concepts. In sum, we now have three terms related to one another: (1) concept — a rule for synthetic unity; (2) schema — a method projected by the transcendental imagination specifying the conditions under which it can be used; and (3) image — some individual example of a concept, resulting from the use of the rule, as specified by the schema.

Granted, the terminology at this point begins to overload already strained circuits, but the point Kant wants to make with the claim that pure concepts have no images, but have transcendental schemata, is again not all that impenetrable. To understand the concept of "substance" synthetically, that is, in terms of the objects of experience and not just as the concept of that which is always subject and never predicate, we cannot search around for "images" or instances of substance. (Indeed, as we shall see, that is a deceptive way of proceeding even for empirical concepts.) We cannot because there are no such images. There are no substances as such in experience; there are just houses, mountains, dogs, and so forth. Thus the experiential meaning of substance, the sense in which the concept is a rule for the unity of our experience, must be discovered in "transcendental judgment" by specifying the general conditions for the concept's application, by determining the method of application.

Thus, for transcendental schemata, one problem among many others that could be raised against this doctrine is *how* such could be done. What exactly happens in such a transcendental judgment to allow us to "connect" a pure concept with all objects of sensibility?

Thus far, the situation Kant has arrived at is supposed to look like this: through the Transcendental Deduction, we know that all experience must involve synthesis, and that pure concepts are indispensable in synthesis.

We have a list of potential categories as such concepts, taken from the forms of judgment (a derivation considered reasonable since all thinking is judging). We now have provided schemata for these categories that explain what each could mean in terms of our experience. And we can then, in the Analytic of Principles, go on to prove that these schematized categories are necessary conditions for our experience.

So, we understand the quantity of judgments categorically by construing that concept as a rule for the synthesis of the homogeneous in experience. By "schematizing" that category, we restrict its meaning to the synthesis of a manifold of our experience, that is, as a synthesis of an always temporal manifold. This specifies the meaning of the category of quantity as, in our experience, *number,* and our next step would be to prove that denumerability in particular is a necessary condition for our experience. And so on with other categories. The category of substance is schematized as permanence through time, the only meaning it could have for our experience; causality is understood as necessary succession. To be sure, much could be said against the particular arguments used by Kant to support each of these schematizations. It is also not clear whether the schematized category is different from, or more restricted in meaning than, the pure concept. Are we, for example, to understand that the notion of ground and consequent could only mean "for us" necessary succession, or that the schematized category in this case includes both that notion and the idea of some event having its ground "internally" in another event?[21] But the major problem relevant here is the general one — how the use of the pure intuition, time, directs or restricts our attempt to formulate transcendental judgments applying the categories to all objects of sense. As we have seen, Kant does not consider it a happy accident that our a priori conditions for experience are indeed applicable to objects of intuition as they appear to us. As given independently of our cognitive activity, such objects are one and all a priori subject to the categories, and that is a fact which requires explanation. Further, aside from some unfortunate slips into straightforwardly idealistic language (the "we get out of experience what we put there" locutions), Kant is also clear that this fact cannot be explained by asserting that the categories wholly determine what an object of sense is. In that case there would be no role for "givenness" in the final determination of experience at all. So some way must be found for thinking of all objects of intuition "at once," as it were, and a priori. As just seen, his solution is to appeal to the form of all intuition, inner or outer, time. He does not mean that the schema is itself simply a pure intuition, but that schematization involves a judgment about those characteristics objects of intuition must have if they are to be combinable into a unified, conceptually determined time-consciousness.

21. Cf. Paton, *Kant's Metaphysic of Experience,* vol. 2, p. 70.

So, finally, we have a specific question: What is it to form such a judgment, and especially to do so formally and a priori? In the first place, although often suggested by some interpreters, we cannot thereby just be forming a further rule. We don't now want, as Wolff suggests, rules which will specify how to use the categories in forming empirical concepts. Something like such a function may be part of what schematized categories do, but the problem with schemata is one step earlier. It involves what we appeal to to formulate a schematized category. Further, Kant's own comments cited earlier on the proper relation between rules and judgment seem to preclude interpreting a schema as itself a rule. And finally, such an interpretation does not help in explaining the central problem of the Schematism — how a formal rule for judgment can be extended to include an a priori relation to all objects of experience. As Gram concisely points out:

> A rule cannot give us the full story about a Kantian schema because Kant must show what in experience corresponds to a category; and no amount of discourse about the structure of other parts of our discourse will suffice to show what kinds of objects fall under the categories that Kant lists.[22]

Gram goes on from such remarks to offer his own interpretation of schemata in terms of "pure intuitions," instead of rules. Much of his interpretation involves a complicated, radical, often innovative reinterpretation of Kant's whole theory of judgment, and this is not the place to discuss it. But his overall attempt is quite relevant to the problem just posed and should be touched on here, however sketchily.

In essence, Gram argues that there is a noticeable difference between what Kant says he is doing in his theory of judgments and what he actually does. He has a "hidden theory" of judgment. Thus, explicitly, Kant says that in synthetic judgment, a concept not contained in the thought of another is connected to it on the basis of some "third thing," some actual experience or some reflection on the possibility of experience. Arguing that this definition will not finally distinguish analytic from synthetic judgments, and will not reveal the nature of Kant's break with Leibniz, Gram argues that Kant's use of the doctrine of synthetic judgments involves him in a different theory, one where a synthetic judgment does not involve two concepts at all, but "an expression for individuals," that is, intuitions, and a concept. Thus, a synthetic judgment does not connect two concepts on the basis of intuitions; it asserts *that* intuitions fall under concepts. He argues that concepts and intuitions are both considered representations by Kant (that intuitions, in short, *can* function as semantic entities in Kant's theory); that we cannot represent intuitions

22. Gram, *Kant, Ontology and the A Priori*, p. 100.

by means of concepts, that all judgments of experience are judgments based on empirical intuitions, and therefore that any judgment of experience must contain an element which does not stand for a concept.[23] So the problem of genuinely synthetic judgments a priori is not, Can we combine two concepts independent of experience? but, Can we discover independent of experience, and assert (in the judgment), that objects fall under concepts?[24] Now this theory leads to the consequence that in a priori judgments, we are directly making a claim that all intuitions (functioning as the subject term in such judgments) fall under a concept. We thus need a pure intuition to do that, and providing that pure intuition is what we *do* in schematizing concepts.

Independent of the specific interpretation of schemata, it seems to me that this interpretation not only wanders far from Kant's own explicit or implicit views, but poses a number of difficulties which Gram doesn't answer. He leaves very dark how he wants one to take the notion of an intuition functioning as a semantic entity in judgments. There are so many passages in Kant's theory of experience, aside from the details of his theory of judgment, where he quite clearly refuses to admit the possibility either of a direct experience of individuals, or their place in

23. There is one passage in particular in Kant which seems to support the view that intuitions can be considered unique, nonconceptual representations *in* a judgment; B376–77 = A320. Manley Thompson has suggested an interesting interpretation of the passage in his "Singular Terms and the Intuitions in Kant's Epistemology," *Review of Metaphysics* 26 (1972): 314–24, which does not involve, and indeed opposes, the major elements of Gram's interpretation. Cf. note 24 below.

24. It certainly seems as if Kant's epistemology, with its emphasis on the distinction between sensibility and understanding, and its claim that "determinative judgment" is the "application" of a rule to an individual, would be much more adequately expressed in a logic which took as the basic form of assertion F(a), not S is P. (Cf. chap. 4, note 4.) Thompson, who attempts a reconstruction of Kant's theory with the help of first-order predicate calculus, admits immediately, though (p. 325), that Kant himself "speaks repeatedly of predication as a relation between two concepts rather than between a concept and an object subsumed under it," and he then tries to resolve the problems this creates for his overall interpretation. But for our purposes, the value of his interpretation lies in the arguments he advances to show that "intuitions" could not be considered the subject term of judgments in Kant, "Singular Terms," p. 326 ff. It thus would remain true that, while all knowledge (pure or empirical) requires intuitions (a sensible or pure immediate contact with individuals, or the individual forms of outer and inner sense), *such* individuality is never conceptually expressible. Kant himself claims that there can be no *infima species* (*Logik*, paragraph 11), and that we specify the singularity of our use of concepts by convention. Said one final way, following Thompson, even if what Gram calls Kant's "hidden theory of judgment" approximates the assumptions of an extensional logic (objects falling under concepts), that general logic would still only be "first order quantificational logic plus identity but minus proper names or other singular terms that are in principle eliminable" (p. 334); or more straightforwardly, "If we ask what does constitute a linguistic representation of an intuition for Kant, the answer, I think, is simply that for Kant an intuitive representation has no place in language, where all representation is discursive" (p. 333).

judgment, and the issue has so many other ramifications in other areas of the critical philosophy, that much more would have to be said than Gram does before such an idea could be clear. Moreover, as far as I can see, there is still a difference in Kant between *what* a judgment asserts and the *ground* for asserting it. When I assert "All bodies are heavy," I am not asserting anything *about* my intuitions. I am asserting a connection by means of empirical concepts — a connection which I know to be true by virtue of my intuitions. Likewise, in synthetic a priori judgments, while it is necessary for me to know something about all objects of experience to make the claim (and it is the great virtue of Gram's book to point that out clearly), *that* is not what I asert *in* such a judgment. I assert by means of concepts *that* all events succeed one another according to a rule; I do not see why that is an assertion about how I know that to be true.[25]

But aside from such problems, one is left, I think, still very unclear in

25. Gram, on the other hand, argues in the following way: It cannot be the case that concepts are the sole constituents of judgments about experience. If that were so, then (1) "This sugar is white," where "this sugar" is taken to be a conceptual item, would not be distinguishable from (2) "Sugar is white," and they must be distinguishable since the truth of (2) is compatible with the falsity of (1) (p. 37). However, while it is true that "this sugar" does not pick out by its form alone, or "denote," the particular entity judged about, Kant is everywhere insistent that *no* semantic entity can do *that*. Just calling "this sugar" an intuitive rather than conceptual representation certainly solves no problems. In other words, when Kant says that no concept can represent *in concreto,* I do not take him to mean that, therefore, something else must represent *in concreto.* Rather, as always in this theory, representative or even extensional analyses of concepts miss the point; concepts denote only by their *use.*

Finally, I should add here that Gram has recently published a much more detailed defense of his interpretation of Kant's theory of judgment, "The Crisis of Syntheticity: The Kant-Eberhard Controversy," *Kant-Studien* 71 (1980): 155–80. In this article, he directly responds to the objection I have raised here. In sum, I have claimed that Kant does not have two theories of judgment, but is simply interested in different issues when discussing General Logic, concerned as it is solely with the form of judgments, and Transcendental Logic, concerned as it is with the epistemological ground of such assertions. The core of Gram's response to this charge is, "The assertion that something does fall under a concept demands a different kind of judgment from the assert (*sic*) that one concept is contained in another. The former is about the relation between our judgment and things; the latter, about the relation between two components of the judgment." To this I would reply (1) that nothing in Kant commits him to the view that, in the judgment "All men are mortal," if we regard the subject term as a concept, and not some Grammean "expression for intuitions," we are thereby committed to interpreting that judgment as *about* the relations between *concepts*; and (2) in responding to the objection, Gram admits that his theory does not require that "intuitions are *literally* parts of Kant's synthetic judgments [my emphasis]," and that "intuitions are still extrajudgmental parts of the world even though the way we talk about them is not" (p. 180). I would add that this same differentiation is relevant to Kant's understanding of the "real" as opposed to the merely "logical" use of *concepts,* and equally well explains how concepts can be subject terms of synthetic judgments without that fact committing Kant to the view that such judgments are *about* such concepts.

this interpretation about what exactly a pure intuition, functioning now so importantly, actually is. Gram never gives us much of a straightforward account of pure intuitions, independent of how they function in his reconstruction of Kant. It sometimes sounds like the account of mathematical concept formation we have already seen. We have pure concepts, and try to schematize them intuitively. The "pure objects" (Gram's phrase) which we come up with count as the meaning of the concept for us. But this, besides directly violating many of the things Kant says about the differences between proofs in mathematics and philosophy,[26] would return us to all the problems found earlier with the notion of pure intuitions. In short, if there ever was a case *obscurus per obscurius,* the attempt to explain schemata by means of pure intuitions would be it.

But Gram does point to a genuine problem. As he insists, the notion of proving a connection between concepts on the basis of a reflection on the possibility of experience is hardly much more satisfactory than his own attempt to invoke the use of pure intuitions. On the traditional view, we always end up describing only what is essential for or what makes possible the *thought* of an object, and would not then advance a genuinely synthetic claim. And he is also right that it is in the Schematism where Kant tries to show how this is not what he is doing; where he tries to break out of the strictly formal realm, even while still doing so a priori. But without knowing more about how pure intuitions can function in providing this link with all objects, we are still left wondering how such access to all objects is to be transcendentally obtained.

In fact, we seem left with the position that, for example, the homogeneity of the manifold is just *due* somehow to the demand of thought, specified in more detail, but still formally, as the thought of the successively denumerable.[27] And, if transcendental philosophy is to remain formal and a priori, it is hard to see how the situation could be otherwise. When that notion of formality must be confronted with the cherished goal of preserving the synthetic results of transcendental philosophy, Kant's position threatens to turn into a totally "constituting" version of idealism, or to echo with the claims of traditional metaphysics about an ability to "intuit" intellectually. However, when the issue is pure concepts, it would be unfair to press Kant's case much farther here, unfair because he had a great deal to say about this issue in the Transcendental Deduction (particularly in the closing stages of the second-edition Deduction). The

26. For Gram's account of the relation between his theory and Kant's account of mathematics, see *Kant, Ontology, and the A Priori,* pp. 45–47 and 74–76.

27. On this "constructivist" account of idealism, such conditions are "objectively valid" even though only conditions for our thought of objects just because we only know our own thoughts (= appearances). I have already indicated in chapter 2 why this seems to me far from Kant's view of his idealism, and will have more to say in chapter 7.

most the Schematism can do, at least in the terms used here, is to point to and illuminate the issue there, especially this latter problem of how Kant's position as a whole is to remain both formal and synthetic. Besides the above reflection on how that could be the case, the logical possibility of such an enterprise needs to be defended in detail, and so this discussion of pure concepts should be suspended until then. At this point, the Schematism can serve mostly to highlight how much and for what reasons this kind of issue in particular, indeed the issue stressed throughout the last few chapters, became *the* issue most problematic for the philosophers greatly influenced by Kant. The problem of how to schematize pure concepts, and Kant's lack of success in defending it clearly, is just what Fichte, for all his obscurity, saw clearly in raising the problem of the "deduction" of the "*nicht-Ich*" from the "*Ich*," and in his substitution of a kind of "*Streben*" for such a unity in place of a full theoretical account. Indeed, I would venture to say that this issue above all — the kind of transcendental judgment clearly required in this chapter — is one of the best ways to view the entire complex of problems in the philosophic movement known as German Idealism.[28]

But beyond such issues, there is still left an important, general problem within Kant's account. If the problem for pure concepts is how they could specify conditions of our sensibility and still be pure and formal, there is still the problem of the application of empirical concepts to a manifold. The problem there is still *how* we should understand the application of a formal, even if derived, rule to a sensible, "material" manifold. Such a problem will reveal a continuation of the difficulties found earlier with the relation between a priori conditions and empirical knowledge, a problem that is especially intriguing here because, again, of the many odd things Kant says about this faculty of judgment. In sum, the problem now becomes, If it has been proved that there must be categories (say, substance), and I know the terms of the connections demanded by that rule, permanence in time, *how* do I determine when an empirical rule for some substance does apply? What, in short, is the relation (if any) between an empirical concept and its schema?

3. Empirical Concepts and Empirical Schemata

Kant is not very helpful in answering this question, as the various, conflicting interpretations in much of the literature indicate. In the first place, he seems to vacillate between contradictory extremes, from claiming that concept and object in the empirical sciences are so "homoge-

---

28. Some aspects of this connection between Kant and German Idealism, particularly Hegel, are outlined in my "Hegel's Phenomenological Criticism," *Man and World* 8 (1975): 296–314.

neous" as to require no special discussion of "applicability" (B177 = A138) to claiming that concrete empirical instances are so heterogeneous from concepts as to require always the production of schemata in order for there to be correct application (B180 = A141). His first statement on the whole problem already involves him in some of these ambiguities.

> In all other sciences where concepts, through which objects are thought universally, are not so different and heterogeneous from those [*von denen*] which represent the object *in concreto,* it is unnecessary to offer an explanation about the application of the former to the latter. (B177 = A138)

This passage is meant to contrast the empirical case with that of pure concepts, and obviously intends to claim that the application of concepts to that from which they arose is not a problem there, as such application was for such pure concepts. There simply doesn't seem to be any problem with regard to what empirical concepts apply to; any answer other than the empirical manifold just wouldn't make sense. But it is hard to see how Kant's account can end there, and even harder to understand just what this exclusion of the question of a schematism is supposed to mean.

Consider the "from those" above. It is difficult to understand just what Kant might be referring to by the pronoun *denen.* He seems to mean *concepts* which represent the individual object, *in concreto.* If so, then of course, there is no serious problem of heterogeneity between concept and instance, since they are both concepts, but it is extremely difficult to imagine what one of these "individual concepts" might look like. It seems a contradiction in terms to say that a concept can *represent in concreto,* although a concept can certainly be *used in concreto* in the recognition of some individual content.[29]

Further however, the *Gleichartigkeit* here asserted is itself not as obvious as Kant seems to think it is. It does not seem that knowing the general markers of some empirical concept is at all the same thing as being able to use some collection of markers concretely, a fact which, as noted, Kant himself had pointed out in the introduction to this section. From the mere fact that empirical concepts have their origin in experience (a fact hard enough to explain), it does not immediately follow that they, as *universal,* have an unproblematic application to the manifold. For that to be strictly true, empirical concepts would have to be nothing but strung-along memories of numerous similar individuals and individual properties. That position, of course, is not only not Kant's (empirical concepts as rules are conditions for the apprehension of individuals, they are *Erkenntnisgründe*), but it would not make sense unless we can

---

29. Kant, *Logik,* paragraph 1, note 2.

describe *that similar* in many instances, a similarity by virtue of which we associate the individuals and properties into one whole. In short, while the origin of these concepts may be empirical, their status as *universal* rules, and thus the question of their application to particulars, is still as problematic as the old Aristotelian question of the relation between a καθόλου and the τόδε τι.

These difficulties begin to clear up as Kant moves radically in the other direction, in the seventh paragraph of the chapter. There he claims, "Actually, images of objects do not underlie our pure sensible concepts, but schemata" (B180 = A140). He then goes on immediately to extend this claim to empirical concepts as well (B180 = A141), claiming now that there is even less reason in this latter case for understanding any concept by means of an image (*Bild*) of it, by which he seems to mean the individual content (the *denen*) alluded to above. Images are always individuals; they are in fact the *result* of the concepts used *in concreto,* and they thus presuppose some method of application, some way of understanding how a universal rule, a collection of general markers sufficient to distinguish that rule from others, is applied in the face of sensible *Materie.* That is, he clearly insists we do need a schematism for empirical concepts. As we shall see, such an issue is different from that relevant to transcendental schemata, but important nonetheless.

Unfortunately, he does not provide many examples of what this schematization of empirical concepts should look like. There is only one famous example.

> The concept of dog means a rule according to which my imagination can delineate [*verzeichnen*] universally [*allgemein*] the figure of a four-footed animal without being limited to any particular figure, such as experience or any possible image which I can represent *in concreto,* actually presents. (B180 = A141)[30]

He goes on in the next sentence to call this procedure of delineating the schematism of these concepts. Thus, this *Gestalt* would be the schema. Such an opaque claim suggests two immediate problems — how Kant thinks he has adequately distinguished a concept from its schema, and what is the status of this empirical schema, this *Gestalt.*

Apparently, we have a concept, "dog," and then, as a result of the work of the imagination, some delineation "*allgemein*" of the figure of a four-footed animal; and, finally, an image of an individual dog. But it

---

30. Kant's use of "*allgemein*" here is difficult to translate. Kemp Smith's rendering "in a general manner" is confusing since the concept should *already* specify the manner of delineation; rather Kant seems to mean "the delineation in general" of a four-footed animal, etc. What seems to be "universally delineated" is the "*Gestalt.*"

seems straightaway that the rule which specifies the synthesis, being a four-footed animal, having certain other properties, and so forth, just *is* the concept dog. The imagination cannot provide a *Gestalt* for these qualities unless it simply follows the rule specifying those properties as "dog." Indeed, it is even hard to see what the significance is in struggling to make this distinction.

However difficult to make, though, and whatever point there may be in trying to make it, Kant himself is fairly straightforward about the importance of the distinction.

> The schema of sensible concepts . . . is a product, and, as it were, a monogram of pure a priori imagination, *through which and in accordance with which,* images themselves first become possible. These images can be connected [*verknüpft*] with the concept only by means of the schema to which they belong. (B181 = A142) [my emphasis]

Images, or any awareness of a particular instance of a concept, only are possible if a concept can be schematized; only through that schematization can these images be "connected" with the concept.

Kant goes on in the next sentence to indicate that even though all concepts require a schematism, the tasks of a schematism are different for pure concepts. They have no images at all, and so in their case we are not trying to understand the relation between a pure rule for synthesis and an individual content, a qualification on transcendental schematism we have already discussed. We want to understand the relation between these rules and all possible objects of experience. Apparently, on the other hand, the schematism for empirical and pure sensible concepts must come up with a way for thinking of a rule, a collection of *Merkmale,* in a way consistent with their use in judgmental application to particulars. One must add "apparently," since at the point where one would expect Kant to go on with the above contrast between types of schematism, he seems to lose interest in the problem, and dashes off with

> That we may not be further delayed by a dry and tedious analysis of the conditions demanded by transcendental schemata of the pure concepts of the understanding in general, we shall now expound them. (B181 = A142)

What he seems to have in mind here for empirical concepts, though, is not that different from the overall task of a schematism. Some way (usually attributed mysteriously to the imagination) must be found for thinking of a rule in terms of the content of experience. We don't, that is, simply encounter lists of *Merkmale* in experience, calling for or warranting the application of this rule and not that. Neither do we, especially in such empirical cases, merely impose a conceptual unity on a manifold. We have to understand the use of a rule in terms of the content of empirical judgment, and this poses a problem, since the rule is not a representative entity. It merely stipulates universal conditions for the recognition and connection of sensible intuitions. But — and now the problem — in *applying* such a rule, we must formulate a "schematic" representation of all these markers as a whole in order to use the rule to distinguish sensible contents. The *Merkmale* of the concept dog are "imagined" together "universallly" (*allgemein*) in order to use the concept, or to "connect" it with sensible particulars, "images." And finally, all of this seems to be another way of saying that conceptual *Merkmale*, as a rule for recognition, must be thought together as a representation of a universal object, even perhaps an abstract object, *a* "universal," for the concept to be applied.[31]

But this requirement introduces a number of problems into Kant's general theory of concepts. We already know that the list of *Merkmale* that define an empirical concept is indefinite, never completable. If that is so, then what does the "imagination" look *to* in thinking some set of markers together as a "universal" whole, a schematic totality? If Chipman, for example, is right that

> Kant's view seems to be that it is possible to apply empirical concepts to their instances because such concepts possess elementary sensible components which correspond to sensible features of the data which fall under the concepts[32]

then what is Kant's explanation of the ground for the *totality* of these "sensory components," the whole which makes possible the application of the concept in judging this to be a particular *kind* of thing? As we've seen, Kant imposes this required explanation on himself, with his own insistence on the necessity of judgment, and we seem here to have the closest thing to an answer in his account of the work of the imagination in providing a "*Gestalt*" for a rule, by means of which images can be connected with a concept.

In fact, this *Gestalt,* clearly itself not a rule, seems to approach the original meaning of σχῆμα. For an image to be thought under a concept, Kant now argues, the concept itself must be thought or represented *as a unity,* a totality of components. I must be able to imagine "dog-in-general" for the rule that is the concept dog to determine all possible dog images. We should note too that this *Gestalt* does not seem to be what Bennett has called a "private mental image."[33] It is a *universal Gestalt,* the

31. There is a highly metaphorical and occasionally helpful discussion of this problem by Friederich Kaulbach, "Schema, Bild, und Modell nach den Vorassetzungen des Kantischen Denkens," in *Kant,* ed. G. Prauss (Köln: Kiepenhauer und Witsch, 1973), p. 105 ff.

32. Chipman, p. 39.

33. J. Bennett, *Kant's Analytic* (Cambridge: Cambridge University Press, 1966), pp.

ground for the production of any *particular* image, whether privately conceived or empirically apprehended, and again seems more and more like an abstract object.

As indicated, however, it is still unclear how the imagination does this, and Kant's account is of little, no, or contradictory help in understanding how. Consider, for example, his remarks on the schematization of a mathematical concept, like "triangle."

> The schema of triangle can exist nowhere other than in thought, and signifies a *rule* of the synthesis of the imagination, *with respect* to pure figures in space. (B180 = A141) [my emphasis]

In this example Kant is unfortunately unambiguous in violating some of his own restrictions by claiming that the schema for a concept is itself a rule. But if this is so, then we are left wondering (1) how that rule is different from the concept itself, and thus how it could in any way help to solve the problem of application, and (2) how it can, as a different rule, in any other way do what we have suggested empirical schemata must do. According to the above, what an empirical schemata should do is provide a way of thinking of the unity of a concepts marker as a whole, and as *thus* applicable to instances. But if schemata are only rules, then not only do we have all the problems involved in (1), but now additional difficulties. In this case, if the schema for the concept triangle is itself a rule, then it is impossible for the triangle-rule to be *used* in the apprehension of images. Suppose we have a triangle rule. It is a triangle-rule and not, say, a square-rule because of what a triangle is (as determined in pure intuition), let us say because of its "form." Now, as already indicated, that form can be supplied neither by the intuition (which proceeds in accordance with the rule), nor by the *rule,* which itself must be formulated in terms of that whole. There must be some nonsynthetic "measure," which cannot itself be triangular, since it is that by virtue of which anything is, or is apprehended as, triangular. For a while now, we have been flirting with the suggestion that the imagination can supply this

---

141–52. That is, our problem does not directly involve the psychological issue of imagining a dog *indeterminate* enough to range over all breeds of dogs (but yet which would exclude foxes). The problem is rather how the rule, as a rule, is itself *determinate* enough to apply in "just these" instances. Thus, the issue is what we must presuppose in order to explain what the rule does, not what we in fact psychologically imagine. Bennett confuses this issue from the start by immediately collapsing concept and schema (p. 141). The difficulty Kant faces is simply the classic difficulty of a "whole" and its "parts." If the whole concept cannot be explained as just a collection of its parts, or markers (but must be an ordered collection of just these markers), then the whole must in some sense be prior to its parts, and thus make possible the determinacy of "this-such" a rule. Cf. also the *Critique of Judgment,* paragraph 77.

Platonic-sounding *Gestalt*. In this example, though, Kant claims that even the schema for a concept is simply a rule, leaving us in the dark about the source of that rule.

As noted, Kant's "dog" example is a bit more ambiguous about the *Gestalt* which functions as schema. We are, though, only told that this "figure" is produced according to the concept-rule. But what Kant does not say is how a "*Gestalt eines vierfüssigen Tieres*" can be produced just in accordance with a *rule,* since the rule itself does not specify a certain *Gestalt,* only a certain *Handlung.* Often Kant himself seems to face this lacuna squarely, as in the quotation which began this chapter.

> The schematism of our understanding, in respect of our appearances and their mere form, is an art concealed in the depths of the human soul, whose true activities we surmise from nature, and lay unconcealed before our eyes only with difficulty. (B181 = A141)

However much speculative freedom such open-ended remarks leave us, however, it is still not possible, within Kant's theory, to construe this work of the imagination as, speaking Platonically, "eikastic," as a dimly sensible grasp of an abstract object. If there is one unambiguous characterization of the imagination, in its transcendental aspects, it is that it is productive, it *makes.* Here especially, it makes schemata, "guided" not by an in-itself, but only by the concept as a rule. A schema, even an empirical schema is clearly said to be a "*Produkt*" of the pure imagination.

But such a characterization simply adds to the problem, leaving us again unclear what the imagination looks to, or is guided by, in forming this schema. And, finally, such a limitation places us in the same position as with the earlier account of the origin and status of empirical concepts. Formulated in terms of the strict separation between intuition and understanding, Kant's whole doctrine of concepts again seems to make the determination of the unity of experience either thoroughly ideal, or only explicable "nontranscendentally," in terms of a material content for concepts which he will not accept epistemologically. Now it has been clear throughout that it is just this separation between the roles of spontaneity and receptivity that provides Kant with his unique transcendental way around traditional rationalist and empiricist alternatives, and which allows him to formulate a theory of concepts that is free, supposedly, both from empiricist explanations of a merely psychological basis for the universality of knowledge, and from metaphysical commitments to either abstract or wholly mental objects. And here we simply find a large rift in the hegemony of his account, an occasional admission that the problem of "judgment" demands more from his theoretical enterprise than he can afford to admit, without sacrificing too much.

To be sure, the most important test for this whole theory of transcendental formality is yet to appear. And it is time now to consider whether many of the problems so far found in his account will also reappear in his most comprehensive case for the possibility of a priori knowledge in philosophy, his "Transcendental Deduction."

6

The Transcendental Deduction

But it is clear that, because we deal only with the manifold of our representations, and because any X which corresponds to these representations (the object), since it is supposed to be something different from all our representations, is nothing to us, the unity which the object makes necessary can be nothing other than the *formal* unity of consciousness in the synthesis of the manifold of representations. (A105) [my emphasis]

THE FIRST EDITION DEDUCTION

It is well known that the transcendental deduction of the pure concepts of the understanding is a labyrinth, full of false starts, abrupt stops, new beginnings, parallel paths, meandering side trips, and an end point so dimly recognizable that Kant himself seemed to have trouble finding it. Commentators, searching for a single, continuous argument, have been forced to jump continually from one section of the text to another, or to abandon all pretense of a textual analysis and offer an independent reconstruction of what Kant might have meant, must have intended, or should have said.[1]

Faced with such difficulties, it can sometimes be helpful to approach the text with a determinate, even if general, problem, and pick one's way through the details with a few fixed reference points always in view. Such points of view of course require numerous descents into the tangle of the argument itself, but they also allow an occasional glance above, points of orientation which, if they simplify somewhat the point of the argument, at least allow one to find a direction through the text, and may contribute to an understanding of at least some aspects of it. Such, in any case, is the

1. Two of the more extensive reorganizations of Kant's argument occur in Norman Kemp Smith's *A Commentary to Kant's Critique of Pure Reason* (London: Macmillan, 1923), with his division into "four stages," p. 203 ff., and R. P. Wolff, *Kant's Theory of Mental Activity* (Cambridge: Harvard University Press, 1963), p. 78 ff. The source for much of the reconstruction is Vaihinger's interpretation, based on the "patchwork theory" of the composition of the text. I will not be entering here into the historical or philosophic issues involved in the details of this problem, but will instead present the core of Kant's argument just as it develops in his own presentation.

intention of this chapter. It is not a commentary on the entire argument
of the Deduction, but rather an extension of the kind of analysis offered
thus far, a further and in many respects broader view of the Kantian
problem of form and formality.

The specific relevance of that issue to the Deduction is already prominent in the above quotation. Simply put: it appears that Kant believes an
analysis of what he calls the "formal" unity of consciousness can be made
to yield "the unity which the object makes necessary." Stated even more
directly at A109, "This relation [the general relation of a concept to an
object] is nothing other than the necessary unity of consciousness." Such,
in a nutshell, appears to be the solution to the problem of the objectivity
of formal conditions, as we have thus far developed it. In his language,
the rules for the subject's mental activity can be shown to be more than
merely formal, but to have a "material" reference, if it can be shown that
these rules are the "conditions for the possibility of experience." The
central tactic in that strategy will involve an analysis of the "unity of
apperception." And, with such an unusual solution to the problem of the
"relation to objects," we are clearly at the heart of Kant's transcendental
enterprise itself. Everything we have been examining thus far has been
pointing to and preparing for this section. Once Kant argued for the
"spontaneous" nature of the understanding, and the indeterminate nature
of the material of sensibility, we naturally wanted to know "by what
right" the understanding can so spontaneously, a priori, and with the
certainty and authority of necessity, legislate, and we are here to receive
Kant's unique answer: that the "ground" or basis for this legislation rests
in the requirements for a unified, self-identical subject.

Naturally enough, even with such a cursory statement as this of Kant's
strategy, the next question one wants to ask is simply what the "transcendental unity of apperception" *is,* especially if such a "formal" condition
for experience is to be made to yield an account of all possible objects of
experience. And, as just indicated, one of the most important aspects of
this claim about a unity of apperception is Kant's repeated insistence that
such a unity should only be understood formally, even though reflection
on the formal requirements for such a unity will finally allow us to
understand the relation between "subjective conditions of thought" and
"objects in general."

Initially, this claim to be operating at the formal level is not hard to
understand nor, given Kant's goals, to sympathize with. He wants to
discover some formal aspect of any possible description of the general
structure of human experience; that is, some aspect undeniable by
skeptical empiricists, rational dogmatists, or any other epistemological
claimant. As will be evident below, he thinks he has done just that by
arguing that no such candidate description could be successful without an

account of the simple fact that all my experience must be ascribable to one self, that diverse elements in one experience all belong to a single experiencer.[2] Having done so, he goes on to argue that only his account of *pure* concepts, which define a priori what can count for us as an object of experience, could do this job and thereby account for this required possibility, for the "transcendental unity of apperception."

Now, it is this strategy which makes it crucial to understand the *status* of the claim that "all my representations must be bound up in a unity," or that "the 'I think' must be able to accompany all my representations." Such a claim cannot be a contingent, psychological characterization of human minds, or else Kant's disputes with his opponents would simply be a debate about what the empirical evidence shows human beings actually do in organizing their experience.[3] When Kant, on the other hand, claims to be offering a formal analysis of the conditions for awareness, he must mean that he can offer an argument that will not be tied to any contingent description of human beings, but can show that any possible conception of experience is unavoidably tied to an assertion about a unity of apperception. Having done so, he must go on to show that only universally applicable, a priori, necessary objectivity rules can account for this unity. Clearly, then, it would be damaging to Kant's case either if a plausible account could be given of an experience in which there were no unity at all among representations, or in which that unity could be completely explained on the basis of rules acquired wholly from experience. And such are the alternatives he directly tries to exclude in the course of both versions of the Deduction.

2. It will, of course, cost Kant a great deal of labor to explain what it means to assert something about the subject's possible awareness of its own identity throughout diverse experiences, without thereby making a claim about the empirical (individual) subject of experience, or about any noumenal self. Sometimes he says that the assertion of the proposition "I think" *is* empirical, sometimes that it is a mere representation of myself as "intelligence," sometimes that it involves an ascription of "reality" to the self which is *not* an ascription of existence, a "reality" neither in the phenomenal nor noumenal world. See B422n for a discussion of all these claims. *Most* of the time, he asserts that this claim is only a "logical condition," and my intention here is to try to understand this characterization by contrast with an actual empirical awareness of self. That will take us eventually to an explicit contrast between apperception and inner sense.

3. The contrast between "logical" and "psychological" is tricky here, and was hardly as clear-cut for Kant as it supposedly is for us, after the nineteenth-century debates on psychologism. See G. Bird, "Logik und Psychologie in der Transzendentalen Deduktion," *Kant-Studien,* 56 (1965–66): 313 ff. It is also true that some sort of factual claim is necessarily involved. At the very least, Kant is assuming here that human beings, in distinction from animals, are, or can be, self-conscious. It is some "fact" about us that we can not only have, but *judge about,* contents of consciousness. This can then be called a formal condition of experience when we admit, as Kant insists we must, that no matter the details of any explanation of experience, this "fact" must be accounted for. Cf. the discussion by W. H. Walsh, *Kant's Criticism of Metaphysics* (Edinburgh: Edinburgh University Press, 1975), pp. 249–59.

In general, then, the focus for the following, the point of reference mentioned earlier, will be just this claim about the formal comprehensiveness of the argument. By formal comprehensiveness, I mean simply that Kant must show in a nonempirical way that there could be no coherent description of human experience which failed to explain the unity of apperception, and that no explanation of that unity could be possible except by means of pure concepts, categories which specify the general range of possible objects of human awareness.

Now, this way of stating the issue might seem to differ from Kant's own intentions, as formulated in his own terminology, but the issues sketched above, particularly as they will be developed into separate problems in sections 2 and 3 below, closely approximate Kant's own statements about the goals of the Deduction. That is, particularly in the first edition Deduction, he first claims that he wants to demonstrate "objective validity" (*objektive Gültigkeit*) of the categories. I take him here to be asserting, by contrast, that the categories can be shown to have more than "subjective validity." By the latter, Kant often means a merely "empirical" warrant for the synthetic claims we make in judgment. To prove objective validity is, thus, to prove that the synthetic connections universally asserted by means of the categories *are* justified a priori, and necessarily, ultimately by appeal to the formal requirements for a unity of apperception. It also seems, though, that Kant realizes it is something stronger to argue for the "objective reality" of concepts (*objektive Wirklichkeit*). (Although sometimes he clearly uses these expressions synonymously, as at B195 = A156.)[4] The latter demonstration would show that the unity prescribed by the categories is not only the nonsubjectively warranted (or "valid") unity of thought, but *is* all that an "object" could *be* for us (the categories *define* for us phenomenal "reality"). The clearest passage where Kant seems to have something like this in mind is at B150, and he appears there to mean just the above extension of the Deduction — i.e., a proof that nothing could be *given* which wasn't subject to the categories, an extension beyond the proof that the categories are "valid" for objects of intuition. Admittedly, it is hard to establish such distinctions in these precise terms,[5] but as the argument unfolds, I believe such a two-stage process is roughly what Kant has in mind.

To anticipate one final time, in keeping with the kinds of problems I

4. The use of "objectivity reality" is more frequent and prominent in the second edition, and will thus allow a more detailed investigation in sections 2 and 3 of this chapter. However, Kant does use the term in the first edition, as at A109–10.

5. The closest Kant comes is with his distinction between the intellectual and the figurative syntheses at B150 ff. Although I develop the distinction in different terms, I owe my own sense of the importance of the distinction, especially in the second edition, to Henry Allison.

have suggested emerge elsewhere in Kant's methodology, I shall suggest that Kant's attempt fails in a way which again raises some general issues about the nature of his "formal idealism." More specifically, I shall argue that his attempt at this kind of a comprehensive account, an account of the necessary conditions for any possible experience, founders on two important problems. One is his attempt to exclude formally, as "impossible," a purely "subjective" unity of apperception, a unification of the contents of consciousness based wholly on the empirical order of appearance, without appeal to any pure concepts. The second is his attempt to show, as was stressed in the last chapter, that his results do not, despite some of his formulations, establish only what is required for us to think or believe about the world. What I have called the comprehensiveness of his argument involves a claim not just that we must think together the contents of an intuited manifold in specifiable ways, but that it can be shown that no manifold could be intuited which was not subject to the categories.[6]

Both of these issues are central to the differences in the two versions of the Deduction. Accordingly, I shall first present a general summary of Kant's strategy in the first edition version, and then try to show how the second edition version, with its more direct account of the objective and subjective unity of apperception and its two-part structure, tries to deal with the issues raised above.

Kant first wants to claim "objective validity" for certain rules which prescribe a priori a variety of kinds of unity among representations. He will attempt this by showing that without such prescribed unity, experience would be impossible. The connecting link between these claims rests on his analysis of the supreme condition for all experience, the "transcendental unity of apperception," and his claim that such a necessary unity would be impossible without categorically prescribed unity. In that sense, the categories are necessary conditions for the possibility of experience, and so objectively valid.

The general structure of the proof immediately involves one in a variety of terminological problems. Two of the most prominent concern what Kant means by "necessary" conditions, and what he means by "experience."

As regards the first, although he offers little in the way of an independent account of this kind of a claim for necessity, the term itself suggests a number of different interpretations, interpretations which reflect well

6. These two problems are related directly to two recent controversies surrounding Kant's transcendental deduction. The former is relevant to the charge that no "transcendental argument" for a priori conditions is possible, that such an argument must be "spurious." The latter is relevant to the alleged dependence of transcendental arguments on some version of verificationism, at least in order to refute skepticism effectively.

some of the continuing difficulties we have been encountering with Kant's "formal" account. For example, a *strictly* formal view of this proof would construe the argument as essentially analytic and the talk of necessity and conditions as explicable in wholly logical terms.

Thus, to say that the categories are the necessary conditions for the possibility of experience (or for the unity of apperception indispensably involved in all experience) is *not* to say that the assumption of certain "objectivity rules" or categories will account for such a unity, that we can explain such a unity by appeal to such rules, but that *only* such rules will account for such a unity, and in that sense they are necessary conditions. We don't want to point to the requirement for self-consciousness as something that just needs to be explained, and then offer the categories as candidates for such an explanation. What we must show is something much stronger; that if there is experience at all, then experience is a priori subject to certain rules which prescribe connections which it must be possible for experience to exhibit. Said propositionally, if p is the fact of "the unity of apperception" (whatever that turns out to be) and q is "the objective validity of the categories," then we do not want to prove p, if q; but, p, *only if q,* or $p \rightarrow q$, where q is clearly a necessary condition of p.[7] While it is this strong requirement which causes Kant the most labor and gives rise to most of the well-known difficulties with the Deduction, it is also what distinguishes his version of a transcendental analysis from simply a regressive analysis of certain conditions which would explain certain undeniable facts about experience. If his enterprise is to be as radically formal as we have encountered so far, then his so-called "progressive" or synthetic methodology[8] must assume a very strong role, proving not that some assumed (sufficient) conditions will account for some initial postulate (be it the fact of Newtonian science, *or* the minimal conditions for experience itself), but that *only* certain conditions will account for what itself cannot be denied as a universal feature of experience.

However, while this interpretation of the relation between Kant's premises and his conclusion is quite appropriate, it cannot be the whole story of his strategy, a limitation which introduces the second problem mentioned above. For, just to the extent that this "connection" between premise and conclusion can be so strictly and formally established, the proof itself ceases to be interesting. On the above view of "necessary condition," we shall have proved that experience itself requires some a priori connection among representations only by beginning with a "con-

7. Cf. Wolff's discussion in *Kant's Theory of Mental Activity,* pp. 49–54.
8. The distinction between a regressive or analytic, and progressive or synthetic, methodology is explained in the *Prolegomena, Gesammelte Schriften,* vol. 4, p. 276.

cept" of experience which could yield such a conclusion. Hence arise many of the oft-discussed problems with the proof structure of the deduction — the "thick" and "thin" ambiguity popularized by Lewis (the claim, that is, that the deduction is based on an ambiguity in the meaning of experience),[9] and recently the "weighty" versus "weak" sense of an object of experience, used by Strawson.[10]

Indeed, Kant himself, in his discussion of transcendental proofs in the Discipline of Pure Reason, insists:

> Accordingly, the proof must also at the same time show the possibility of arriving synthetically and a priori at some knowledge of things which was *not* contained in the concept of them. (B811 = A783)

He explains that what establishes this synthetic advance beyond the mere concept of objects is "the possibility of experience," but that just leaves us back where we started, wondering how we could make any use of such a notion *without* simply analyzing what "was contained in the concept."[11]

9. C. I. Lewis, *An Analysis of Knowledge and Valuation* (LaSalle, Ill: Open Court, 1946), pp. 161–62.

10. P. F. Strawson, *The Bounds of Sense* (London: Methuen, 1966), p. 72 ff.

11. This problem has recently been the subject of dispute between Moltke Gram and Jaakko Hintikka. In "Transcendental Arguments," *Nous* 5 (1971): 15–26, Gram takes as Kant's criterion for a transcendental principle that it "makes possible the very experience which is its own ground of proof" (B765 = A737). According to Gram, this means that the conclusion of a transcendental argument must follow from a premise like "S knows (perceives) p," rather than from p alone. The *experience* (knowledge, perception) would not be possible unless the conclusion were true. But this inference could not be derived from a description of the object perceived. In that case, the conclusion would be implied directly from the concepts used to describe what we perceive. But the conclusion cannot be derived from the main or "epistemic" clause ("s perceives . . ."), since we would *already* have to know what it is for s to perceive or know something. Hintikka, in "Transcendental Arguments: Genuine and Spurious," *Nous* 6 (1972): 278–81, argues that Gram has paid too little attention to the transcendental quality of these proofs, that a transcendental argument for Kant is one which "shows the possibility of a certain type of synthetic *a priori* by showing how it is due to those activities of ours by means of which the knowledge in question is obtained" (p. 275). In that case, there is something quite distinctive in showing how what we do know presupposes certain universal features of *our coming to know*. But Hintikka provides no detailed account of how this connection is to be established, leaving Gram ample room for reply in his "Must Transcendental Arguments Be Spurious?" *Kant-Studien* 65 (1975): 304–17. For my purposes, two things need to be said about this controversy. One is that the notion of "establishing a presupposition" for experience can be made much more precise than Gram allows. Hintikka already points out the fallacious rejection of that possibility Gram offers (pp. 279–80), and, recently, Gordon G. Brittan, Jr., in *Kant's Theory of Science* (Princeton: Princeton University Press, 1978), relying on a paper of van Fraassen's, shows even more clearly how the relation can be defined (pp. 28–42). I shall not here enter into any discussion of the possibility of transcendental arguments in general, but shall suggest that while Kant does attempt a unique argument to establish the presuppositions for all experience (in a way that can be distinguished from implication), it fails just because of Kant's insistence that the proof be "formal," even if transcendentally not merely

And so the familiar problem — we need something more than an analytic connection between concepts (a procedure which would place far too much weight on the beginining assumption of such a proof) and something less than some claim which would assert something materially necessary about human experience, and something other than an empirical analysis of consciousness.

This strategy of Kant's, his attempt to prove something about necessary conditions for the possibility of experience in a way broader than that based on material implication or logical deducibility, is worth stressing here. For example, it would be initially correct to describe what Kant is doing by saying that he is proving that certain principles are required if we are to have experience of a spatio-temporal world of public objects. The categories are thus the conditions for the possibility of empirical *knowledge*; we could not explain the possibility of empirical knowledge unless the categories possessed objective validity. (Here the "possibility" of empirical knowledge does not mean that the categories are established by appeal to some set of true empirical propositions, but by reflection on the possible truth or falsity of any set of propositions about an objective, public world.) But that is only initially true, particularly since such an account would look very weak when considered as a response to skepticism about such categories. However the connection between such categories and such objective empirical knowledge is established, it would provide only a very limited defense of the categories, since the skeptic intends to deny that such public, objective experience *is* itself independently defensible. As we shall see in what follows, it must also be a part of Kant's proof to prove that experience in the broadest sense (considered as simply experience of objects of consciousness) *must* include a distinction between private and public, subjective and objective experience, *and* that this distinction cannot be made except by appeal to the categories. It is true, in other words, that Kant wants to establish the objectivity of the categories (or their objective validity) by proving that we could not make certain distinctions in experience without them; but he also wants to prove that we *must make* such distinctions (or that they have objective reality). It is the presence of both these steps in the Deduction which involves Kant in some of his most difficult problems, involving as it does a comprehensive rejection of the skeptic's candidate for experience. We need to know *both* in what sense we could not comprehend an experience without a distinction between objective and subjective succession, and in what sense only the assumption of the categories will account for such a distinction.[12] To see

---

logically formal. For more on the "presupposition" problem, see Patricia A. Crawford, "Kant's Theory of Philosophical Proof," *Kant-Studien* 53 (1961–62): 257–68.

12. Richard E. Aquila, in "Two Kinds of Transcendental Arguments in Kant," *Kant-Studien* 67 (1976): 1–19, has argued that the distinction drawn here between conditions for

how Kant attempt such a proof, we need to turn to the details of the first edition Deduction.

After a brief, four-paragraph restatement of some of these "principles" of the Deduction, Kant begins in earnest at A97. Many of the assumptions worked out thus far come immediately and forcefully into play, particularly his claim that the "unity" of any experience must be *effected* and is not directly experienced. "Knowledge," he claims, "is a whole [*Ganze*] in which representations stand compared and connected" (A97). As throughout, this unity of representations is promptly ascribed to "spontaneity," and Kant launches into a discussion of the various aspects of any synthetic connecting which could effect such a unity. As he himself points out in the Preface, his analysis here, belonging as it does to the strange discipline of "transcendental psychology," is still an analysis of the "subjective" side of this activity.[13] Simply put, that means that he has as yet asked no question about the "ground" appealed to by the subject in uniting some set of representations. He is only describing *how* such connection is possible, not yet proving, in some specific way, *that* it is. Instead of asking straightaway a question "of such extreme difficulty" Kant chooses to "prepare" the reader by, in effect, approaching that question indirectly, showing how the problem of connection, raised from the side of "subjective activity," *leads* directly to the problem of objectivity, and then what happens once that question is raised without a possible transcendent appeal to things in themselves.

Thus the course of the initial stages of the Deduction. Any connection

empirical knowledge, and the further claim that empirical knowledge could only be described as Kant does, should be seen as evidence of two different types of transcendental arguments in Kant, one transcendental with respect to conditions for an object being known, the other transcendental with respect to empirical existence. He shows that one sort of claim need not entail the other, and that Strawson's strategy for doing so, arguing that the existence of empirical objects is necessary for the existence of an empirical self, will not work (p. 7). Kant is guilty of many of the confusions between these procedures Aquila charge him with and convincingly documents. But Kant is also, at least, aware of the distinction (see B138), aware that an analytic condition for our knowledge of objects is not the same as a synthetic claim about empirical objects. In fact, I shall argue, that is exactly why the second edition version of the Deduction has two parts, as Kant moves from a claim about how we must unite our intuitions in order for there to be a possibly unified self-consciousness *to* a claim about the only kinds of intuitions of sensible objects we *could* have. One of the clearest statements of and defenses of the more limited interpretation of the Deduction (that Kant is only attempting to provide a "regressive" analysis of the conditions for empirical knowledge) is offered by Karl Ameriks in his "Kant's Transcendental Deduction as a Regressive Argument," *Kant-Studien* 69 (1978): 273–87. I shall argue, to the contrary, that there is ample evidence that Kant believed he could establish that no experience whatsoever could occur unless the categories possessed objective validity, and thus unless there were objective experience. That is why, I shall argue, he is so concerned to prove that knowledge of my own self is phenomenal, requires the categories.

13. A xvi–A xvii.

of elements in consciousness must, minimally, involve an "apprehension" of the elements to be unified, an ability to retain a memory of various such elements in uniting some together, and a rule that will prescribe which are to be retained, remembered, and thought together. It is with this last requirement that the "objectivity" question clearly becomes prominent, just as it actually does in the Deduction at A104 (within the section on the "Synthesis of Recognition in a Concept"). One function such a rule of connection is supposed to fulfill is to produce some claim about an "object" of representations, and Kant shifts his discussion at this point to an explicit discussion of that topic.

In doing so, he moves very quickly. Denying that we can provide some ground for this unity by direct appeal to an object considered independently of all representations (a concept of an object as only $= X$), he then states directly the claim that the rest of the Deduction must, in a variety of ways, support.

> The unity which the object makes necessary can be nothing else than the formal unity of consciousness in the synthesis of the manifold of representations. (A105)

In expanding his account of this "formal" condition, Kant gives it a variety of names, most often referring to it as "the transcendental unity of apperception," simply "transcendental apperception," but also, in describing this "transcendental ground of unity," associating it with "the understanding" or faculty of rules simply. As in:

> This thoroughgoing synthetic unity of perceptions is indeed the form of experience; it is nothing else than the synthetic unity of appearances in accordance with concepts. (A110)

The introduction of this condition means that, although no ground for the unity of representations can be found through some unmediated appeal to "objects" in themselves, we could not experience such representations at all without at least uniting them together in one consciousness. While this doesn't mean that I must think of these elements *as* parts of my consciousness, it must be possible for me to think such elements as one and all objects of *one* consciousness, just to be able to say that *I* experience them all. Of course, now the situation gets even murkier (around A108, and especially A111),[14] when Kant tries to specify just

14. At A108, Kant says that "this unity of consciousness would be impossible if the mind in knowledge of the manifold *could not become conscious* [my emphasis] of the identity of function whereby it synthetically combines it in one knowledge [. . . *wenn es nicht die Identität seiner Handlung vor Augen hätte*]." This requirement that the mind be able to be conscious of the identity of function is the basis of an important new interpretation of the Deduction, Dieter Henrich's in *Identität und Objektivität* (Heidelberg: Carl Winter, 1976). I am in agreement with much of what Henrich says, particularly his attempt to show that

what conditions are necessary in order to do that, and, rather vaguely, introduces the categories as the only possible explanation for such a unity.

> The objective reality of our empirical knowledge rests on the transcendental law, that all appearances, insofar as through them objects are to be given to us, must stand under those a priori rules of synthetic unity whereby the interrelating of these appearances in empirical intuition is *alone possible*. (A110) [my emphasis]

Of course, a very great deal more needs to be said before it can be claimed that *only* such a priori rules for synthetic unity (rules responsible for objective connection) can account for this unity of consciousness, and indeed in just what sense their doing *that is* what counts as having established objective connection.[15] It is clear enough that Kant's strategy is to prove that certain pure concepts are objective by proving that the synthetic connection they prescribe is necessary and universal, and to do so by proving that without these rules for distinguishing between objective and subjective connection, and for establishing the former, experience itself would not be possible. Again, since he wants to claim that *only* under this assumption could experience be possible, his attack is most vulnerable to a plausible account that showed a unified experience of an identical subject could be explained without such a priori, necessary rules. But before venturing into possible objections, one can fairly admit, as with Kant's classically transcendental account in the Aesthetic, a general plausibility to this argument. If there were *no* unity among representations, it would be very hard to make out what experience should be like. If cinnabar were sometimes red, sometimes white, sometimes heavy, sometimes floated in the air, if the pencils on my desk would

---

Kant intended to prove *all* our representations were subject to synthesis and categorical conditions, and his attempt to do so by taking the claim above as central. That claim is interpreted by Henrich to refer not to the simplicity of the self (pp. 48–71), nor to strict or Leibnizian identity (pp. 71–84), but to a requirement for a "moderate identity" (*gemässigte Identität*) of the self throughout all experience. Since the identity of the subject requires a sequence of states of that subject, and a transition between them, the subject, it is argued, must know a priori what it means to make a transition from state to state (pp. 83–94). The importance of Henrich's interpretation lies in his ability to demonstrate that Kant's analysis must rest on more than the logical conditions for possible self-consciousness (p. 83), and must involve an account of the subject's actual consciousness of itself. Or: "The identity of self-consciousness, which we *actually* think *a priori*, could be thought impossible in this way, unless it included the thought of necessary rules, under which all appearances are subsumed, insofar as they are thinkable at all" (p. 92). My problem with this interpretation will be how we are to understand the term "all appearances" in this quotation.

15. We know already something about how the former problem is to be solved. It involves the "clue" that *all* thinking is judging.

vanish and return irregularly, if inhaling on my cigarette sometimes produced smoke coming out of my ears, sometimes caused the *Jupiter* Symphony to play in my head, Kant has a strong case that we could not ever be said to have *an* experience of objects, but rather just isolated, undescribable, momentary experiences. Instead of an experience of one object which we could collect together with other like objects under a common description, we would have only ineffable glances at always unique Xs, hard even to describe theoretically.

However, so far, such claims just get us to the demand that we find some way to establish this "separability" of the experiencer from the objects experienced. In Strawson's terms we seem thus far (until, at least, the beginning of the "objective version" of the Deduction in A) just to have argued for an indispensable distinction between a "recognitional" and a "referential" component in all experience, without establishing yet either that certain very general recognitional components (categories) must be involved in the discrimination of *any* experience, or that their being so involved allows us to say we have distinguished a subjective from an objective component in experience and have so made the categories responsible for the objective component.

Simply put, having argued that there must be a unity of consciousness, that this unity must be effected and is not "received," that such a unifying is a connection of representations according to rules, Kant must now prove that some such rules must prescribe a general and necessary order to all representations and that this provides a ground for distinguishing objective from subjective connection. His argument to that effect begins at A121 and involves his rejection of the possibility that such rules for connection could be entirely subjective, "based" only on the order or representations we usually experience. In short, he will argue that the association of representations depends on some ground for their associability, their "affinity," and that this requires "objectivity rules."

He first argues that since this combination of representations must occur for us to be able to ascribe such representations to ourselves, there must be some agency or "faculty" which does the connecting. Kant names such a faculty the imagination and then points out that there must at least be some subjective rule which directs such connecting so that some representations are remembered and reproduced with some others in one representation. Such a merely empirical connection Kant calls the association of representations. Then comes the decisive phase of the argument. He claims that if there were only such an empirical association of representations, without a "transcendental ground" for their affinity in the first place, a possible self-ascription of representations, and so experience in general, would not be possible. His argument here is dense enough to warrant a long quotation.

> There must, therefore, be an objective ground, that is a ground comprehensible a priori before all empirical laws of the imagination, upon which rests the possibility, indeed the necessity, of a law extending through all appearances, a ground for regarding all of these appearances as such data of the senses which are in themselves associable, and subject to universal rules for a thoroughgoing connection in reproduction. This objective ground of all the association of appearances I call the affinity of the manifold. (A122)

Kant thus here considers the possibility that the connection and order he has argued indispensable for any experience could be supplied by rules with a wholly empirical origin. We note also again that Kant has as yet made no reference to Strawson's "weighty" sense of object, no claim that what the above asserts is that experience must be experience of objects, that is, items distinct from states of consciousness. His language instead is about "grounds" for connecting "representations," and will in fact proceed, *by virtue of a claim* about the necessary connection of such representations, *to* a claim that this *is* what counts as there being a distinction between wholly subjective and objective experience.

For the moment the problem is to discover exactly what is supposed to be impossible about an experiencer formulating rules for associating representations wholly on the basis of their occurrence in his consciousness, rather than on the basis of some "transcendental affinity." Once again, the basis of that claim is that, in such a candidate for an experiencer, there could be no unity of apperception. Here is the argument for why that would be the case.

> For even though we should have the power of associating perceptions, it would remain entirely undetermined and accidental whether they would themselves be associable; and should they not be associable, there might exist a multitude of perceptions, and indeed an entire sensibility, in which much empirical consciousness would arise in my mind, but in a state of separation, and without belonging to a consciousness of myself. (A122)

This argument then continues the kind of claim made against a conception of experience in which no recognitional component was admitted. There Kant claimed that without such a component, and at least a distinction between an object as content of consciousness and our view of it as such and such, individual experiences would be ineffable, ultimately incoherent. Now he claims that much the same thing would occur if groups of representations were associated without any ground for their connection other than the empirical order of their occurrence or subjective invention. A *kind* of "empirical consciousness" could arise in this case, but it would still be impossible to ascribe that consciousness to myself, since, again, it would be impossible to distinguish what happens to me from what is the case, to distinguish this mere association of random representations *from me,* and thus to have a genuine unity of one consciousness. Put schematically, instead of a model which looks like this

$$\left(\begin{array}{c} S \\ \diagup\mid\diagdown \\ R \quad R \quad R \end{array} \right)$$

we would have one that looks like this

and so on. As before, this latter model could not count as representations belonging to me, but to as many me's as there are arbitrary rules for association.[16] It is thus that Kant can claim:

> the unity of apperception is thus the transcendental ground of the necessary conformity to law of all appearances in one experience (A127)

and can thus, in a very introductory but nonetheless decisive way, appeal to the categories as the basis of such a ground.

> These grounds of the recognition of the manifold, so far as they concern solely the form of an experience in general are the categories. Upon them is based not only all formal unity in the synthesis of imagination, but also, by means of this synthesis, all the empirical employment [of that synthesis] . . . in connection with the appearances. (A125)

However, aside from the general line of this argument much remains unclear. There are indeed aspects of this proof which seemed to bother Kant himself a great deal in the period between the two editions (elements especially prominent in the *Prolegomena*) and which reappear in much more complicated ways in the second edition version. In particular, the broad methodological questions we are interested in here seem to have received initial but not yet satisfactory answers. That can be seen especially by considering two of the most important aspects of Kant's overall proof.

16. It should be admitted immediately here that there is no a priori reason why experience *could* not possess this fragmentary quality. It may be, in other words, that when I am aware of my self, I am so only because I am able to subsume my representations under a nonempirical rule of connection, but nothing is thereby established about the requirements for the *continuing* identity of the *same* self. (Cf. the development of the problem below.) This possibility and its relevance for Henrich's interpretation, is clearly pointed out by Paul Guyer in his review of *Identität und Objektivität, Journal of Philosophy* 76, no. 3 (1979): 163–64.

In the first place, one can ask how Kant thinks he has attained a "perspective" comprehensive enough to formulate requirements for any possible experience; that is, to exclude formally, and not simply ad hoc, other, perhaps skeptically based accounts of experience.[17] Clearly the central argument in his attempt to reach that perspective is his claim that all the contents of my consciousness must be bound up in a unity, must be ascribable to one consciousness, and that this condition could not be satisfied unless there were a priori rules governing the "binding up" or uniting of such contents. Now it has been clear throughout the above summary of the proof that much of this claim rests on other assumptions already worked out elsewhere in the *Critique*, particularly the doctrines of sensation, intuition, appearance, and concept. Accordingly much of Kant's defense for such claims as these rests on showing that his account of possible experience is the only one which could be asserted consistently, together with these other claims. Further, if his claim can be so supported, it can formally exclude other "candidates" for possible experiencers by revealing inconsistencies with these requirements. An attempt to explain, for example, the unity of consciousness by virtue of an appeal to the *directly* perceived, complex unity of the object-apprehended is excluded as dogmatically ungrounded, in violation of Kant's requirements that all perception of complexity is the result of an active ordering and unity of a complex of perceptions, and in violation of his characterization of the understanding. Likewise, an account of the required unity of consciousness which relied on empirical principles of association can be shown to depend on some prior ground or prior rules for determining which impressions are to be associated with which. However, in order for Kant's argument not to proceed in a case-by-case way, analyzing competing claimants as they appear, he must be able to show generally that no account of awareness could successfully explain the unity of consciousness, unless there were a priori rules prescribing such unifying. Support for such a claim cannot only come, in other words, from an overview of the difficulties of competing accounts. Some general point needs to be made against all such accounts.[18]

17. That is, since the "new way of ideas," the problem of skepticism had been to try to find some "divine" perspective from which idea and object could, in general, be compared. Kant, in establishing a transcendental perspective, denies that such a divine point of view is necessary, and claims that the objectivity of human knowledge can be defended wholly in terms of the *subject's* conditions for knowledge. Whether this attempt establishes anything more than indispensable elements in what we *think* of *as* objective is, of course, another, longer story.

18. The possibility that any transcendental argument can do *this* has been denied by Richard Rorty. He argues that the "only good transcendental argument is a parasitism argument," one directed only at some specific version of skepticism. See his "Verification-

In effect, what I shall claim occurs in sections of the second edition version is just such an attempt at formulating this response to all other candidates for possible experience. Kant appears to think that the only general reason any competitor could appear reasonable is if it could be established that contrary to his claim, I could be aware of some content of consciousness "immediately," directly, or, in general, independent of the conditions Kant claims in force for all experience. Since the most plausible case where that occurs, the one which provided so much common beginning ground for the rationalists and empiricists before (and after) Kant, is my experience of *myself,* my immediate experience of my own thoughts as mine, that will be the battlefield where Kant will have to struggle. What that amounts to in the second edition is showing that even "I" am only aware of myself as I "appear," that I can also only make "mediated" judgments about myself. More specifically, he will attempt to prove that all awareness of "inner sense" also presupposes apperception. As we shall see, that will be his much more general attempt to exclude all possible alternate explanations of the unity of experience and so establish his transcendental perspective.

Moreover, the second edition also offers a more extended analysis of why a claim about a necessary unity among our representations *is* a "knowledge of objects," that the requirements for a unity of apperception are *all* that we could mean by a knowledge of objects. In short, it is not at all immediately obvious why the unity among representations required for self-consciousness should be the criterion for knowledge of objects, and that too, I think becomes an extended theme in the second edition version.

THE SECOND EDITION DEDUCTION

1. Kant's Strategy

The preceding general summary of the first edition version of the Deduction has obviously still left many questions unanswered. I have interpreted the nerve of Kant's argument to be: No account of human experience can fail to explain the identity[19] of a single subject of experience throughout the combination of various different representations; the

---

ism and Transcendental Arguments," *Nous* 5 (1971): 3–14, and "Strawson's Objectivity Argument," *Review of Metaphysics* 24 (1970): 207–44.

19. Again, this requirement should be understood to mean the subject's possible awareness of its identity as the same subject of various different states. It certainly does not involve any claim about "personal identity." All Kant is arguing is that a subject must be capable of being aware that it is the same subject through many representations, it need not be aware of anything specific about this subject. This is why Kant encourages us not to identify "apperception" and "inner sense," as we shall see.

combination which makes such identity possible is always an activity of the subject (synthesis or judgment); this activity would not be possible were the subject not capable of following rules, which distinguish subjective association from objective connection; these rules could not be wholly derived from experience; therefore there must be some rules which a priori prescribe an objective combination for all possible contents of consciousness.

Before proceeding with the two questions mentioned earlier, I should point out what this interpretation of the deduction does not involve. I do not think, as some recent commentators have suggested, that Kant is, in effect, arguing here that we could not use the concept of the self unless we had or could use the concept of an object.[20] Kant does argue for something like that in the Refutation of Idealism, but such is not the argument of the Deduction. As I have stressed throughout, however "formal" Kant's methodology is, it is not limited to an analysis of the relations between concepts. For one thing, such a strategy cannot deal effectively with skepticism (a skeptic is always able to deny the necessity for any use of the concept of self);[21] for another, Kant is quite clear that he wishes to establish necessary conditions for the possibility of *experience*.

But major problems still remain. As I have suggested, if this view of Kant's strategy is correct, a good deal more needs to be said about the status of a claim for the "unity of apperception." It is not clear yet what it means to say that all my representations *must* be bound up in a unity, nor especially, exactly how much we can derive from this requirement, nor, finally, what the results of this derivation amount to.

The second edition version sheds a good deal more light on these issues, but contributes its own, new obscurities. In the first place, the strategy of the Deduction seems to have shifted and to proceed now in a

20. Strawson's attempt, in *Bounds of Sense,* is the most famous. One of the more detailed and convincing criticisms of this approach is that offered by Rorty in "Strawson's Objectivity Argument." In his own voice, however, Rorty remains close to the spirit of Strawson's strategy, disagreeing mainly about results. See p. 231: "All that transcendental arguments . . . can show is that if you have certain concepts, you must have certain other concepts also." For further discussion of Strawson's strategy, see the following: Graham Bird, "Recent Interpretations of Kant's Transcendental Deduction," *Akten des 4. Internationalen Kant Kongress, Teil I* (1974), pp. 1–14; Henry Allison, "Transcendental Idealism and Descriptive Metaphysics," *Kant-Studien* 60 (1969): 216–33; T. E. Wilkerson, "Transcendental Arguments," *Philosophical Quarterly* 20 (July 1970): 200–212; Ross Harrison, "Strawson on Outer Objects," *Philosophical Quarterly* 20 (July 1970): 213–21; A. Phillips Griffiths, "Transcendental Arguments" (1), and J. J. MacIntosh, "Transcendental Arguments" (2), *Aristotelian Society,* Supplement, vol. 43 (1969): 165–93; Jonathan Bennett, *Kant's Analytic* (Cambridge: Cambridge University Press, 1966), pp. 153–201; and "Strawson on Kant," *Philosophical Review* 77 (1968): 340–49.

21. This is pointed out by Guyer in his review of *Identität und Objektivität,* p. 161.

clearer fashion. It is true that much of this version seems to rely much more on an analysis of the logical requirements for any judgment than it does on "transcendental psychology," or even, apparently, on the general requirements of a unity of apperception. Kant seems here to come closer to a view of the Deduction he casually tossed out in the *Metaphysical First Principles of Natural Science,* when he asserted that that argument

> can be carried out almost in a single step from the precisely specified definition of a *judgment* in general (as an action through which given representations first become knowledge of an object).[22]

However, close attention to the details of the second edition clearly reveals that Kant still thinks that no "precise" definition of judgment can be given without an explanation of the requirements for an "objective unity of apperception." The connection between the possible objectivity of judgments and this requirement is quite clear at B134–35, B140, especially B141, and in all of section 20.

But these qualifications just return us to the problem of what this requirement amounts to, how many and exactly what sort of claims can be derived from it. I have suggested that these issues can best be approached by trying to understand the nature of the comprehensiveness Kant's formal perspective demands. That means trying to understand two important features of Kant's claim; just how Kant's understanding of the requirement for a unity of apperception excludes any other candidate description of experience (and so does this formally), and how those requirements are to be interpreted, whether the argument does amount to a proof that the categories have "objective reality."

Of course, it is also the case that these two questions are related. In *principle,* they are different since there is no apparent reason, prima facie, why conditions indispensable for our *experience,* even if indisputably established as necessary conditions, should also be taken to be rules which prescribe what experience of *objects* is. This is true even if part of what we show in the former proof is that the meaning of these rules involves a distinction between merely associated and rule-governed unity. That would still seem only to prove something about our requirements for experience, about what we must think, rather than a direct proof about "objects." However, the questions are also linked in that, should the former proof establish this "comprehensive perspective" and so establish from this perspective that no experience of objects considered independent of all possible experience is coherent, and that yet a distinction between subjective or ungrounded, merely associated experience and

22. Kant, *Metaphysische Anfangsgründe der Naturwissenschaft,* vol. 4, pp. 476–77. This remark has, I believe, been seriously misinterpreted by Ralph C. S. Walker, *Kant* (London: Routledge & Kegan Paul, 1978), p. 20 and pp. 74–86.

rule-directed, transcendentally grounded experience can be made, an objection based on any other notion of objectivity will have been thus formally
excluded. In fact, then, what these twin questions point to is nothing more or
less than the twin claims of the Deduction itself, a duality Kant himself often
stresses; namely, that the Deduction must prove both that the categories *are*
objective by being conditions for the possibility of experience, and that
concepts can *only* be objective in terms of some possible object of experience. Proving the first proves that the categories are necessary conditions for
experience, and proving the second proves that no other notion of objectivity than the one established could make sense; that, if you will, we have thus
established the "meaning" or "limits" of objectivity for experiencers like us.

To begin this closer look at Kant's comprehensive case for the conditions for any possible experience, we should also recall explicitly the most
important feature of his general theory of consciousness and the one that
has figured most prominently in his attempt to describe the forms of such
conscious experience — his claim that consciousness should always be
understood as a kind of activity, that to *be* conscious of anything always
means to have brought some content to consciousness in a determinate
way. In general this means that *all* experience is an apperception,
speaking loosely, a self-affection.[23] That is, to be aware of anything is to
"take something up" and "run through" such a content, to use Kant's
earlier, psychologistic metaphors, but what is taken and run through is
clearly itself, in *some* sense, a content for consciousness, an element in
our intuited manifold and not a "thing in itself," a thing considered
independently of any relation to consciousness. All combination of the
manifold is an act of spontaneity and, as we have seen in some detail, the
materials for such spontaneity must themselves be considered elements in
a subject's experience. To experience is thus always to "act" upon oneself
in a certain way, to "bring" to explicitness, conceptual definition, and
discrimination some element of our immediate awareness. Now, of
course, even though all consciousness is in *this* sense apperception, that
does not mean that all experience is an explicit awareness of my *self*, as
the notion of apperception might suggest. It is still the case that the "I
think" must always be *able* to accompany every conscious representation,
but the reason it must be able to do so is that all experience is a
determination by the subject of its own contents.[24] Because all experience
is self-affection, no theory of experience which could not account for the
possibility of the self's relation to its own contents, the possibility that the
"I think" *could* accompany its representations, could be a successful one.

23. Cf. G. Krüger, "Über Kants Lehre von der Zeit," in *Philosophie und Moral in der
kantischen Kritik* (Tübingen: J. C. B. Mohr, 1967), pp. 269–94.
24. Cf. Henrich's discussion, *Identität und Objektivität*, pp. 71–76, p. 84 ff.

With this principle accepted, we can proceed to the second edition version of the Deduction.

The actual course of the proof in the second edition at the beginning proceeds in a noticeably more "step-by-step" way than in the first, with Kant saving some of his more important digressions and explanations for later in the discussion. Again we find the central claim of his theory of synthetic unity, "we cannot represent to ourselves anything as combined in the object which we have not ourselves previously combined" (B130). He quickly then raises the problem of the "ground" of this combination, the basis not for this or that connection, but for connection of representations in general, the "ground . . . of the very possibility of the understanding." Again this ground is argued to be the unity of apperception, (section 16), is claimed to be the "supreme principle of all employment of the understanding" (section 17), and when the question of the "objectivity" of this unity is raised (section 18) such objectivity is shown to be possible only by virtue of the a priori applicability of the categories (section 20).

After this initial "beginning," however, this version of the Deduction becomes so distinctive since Kant introduces into the discussion both a more detailed explanation of his theory of apperception, and he divides the whole proof into two separate sections or steps, introducing in the latter (after section 20) a more concrete discussion of the problem of objectivity "for us" given our forms of receptivity. Through both of these discussions, he becomes more explicit about how an objective unity of consciousness can be distinguished from a subjective, and how he can support such comprehensive claims as:

> The synthetic unity of consciousness is, therefore, an objective condition of all knowledge. It is *not merely a condition that I myself require in knowing an object,* but it is a condition under which every intuition must stand in order to become an object for me. (B138) [my emphasis]

Clarification of the notion of a formal unity of consciousness occurs when Kant begins to contrast his own theory of what is required for a unity of consciousness and so for experience with the "subjective unity of consciousness, which is a determination of inner sense" (B139). Again, in making this distinction, Kant means to argue that such a purely empirical association of representations *could* not stand as a possible model of experience, that it presupposes "the pure synthesis of understanding which is the a priori underlying ground of the empirical synthesis." In section 18, he had said that the "empirical" or "subjective" unity of consciousness is "derived" from the original, or "objective" unity of apperception, or that it has its "ground" in the latter. He is thus insisting that his analysis of the requirements for such an "original" unity do not hold *only* in order to explain "knowledge of objects," as if we could have a subjective or merely empirical unity of representations, subject only to laws of association, and on the other hand, independently, could also have a representation of an object, which latter could only occur if the categories were objectively valid. Even prior to section 18, he had already made clear that the original unity of apperception is a "condition" for *all* awareness. At B132–33 he had asserted that representations "must conform to the condition under which alone they can stand together in one universal self-consciousness, because otherwise they would not without exception belong to me." The point is stressed again at B134, "only insofar as I can grasp the manifold of representations in one consciousness do I call them one and all mine. For otherwise I should have as many-colored and diverse a self as I have representations of which I am conscious to myself." Finally, at B136, he states clearly that "the supreme principle" of the understanding is that "*all* the manifold of intuition should be subject to conditions of the original synthetic unity of apperception" (my emphasis).

As his argument has been presented here, it is entirely appropriate for Kant to insist on the comprehensiveness of this "supreme principle" and not to argue conditionally, to assert only that we must combine our representations in ways specifiable a priori, only in order to have objective knowledge. Such an account of formal conditions would be far too conditional unless it also showed that such knowledge, or a distinction between objective and subjective connection, were itself necessary for a unity of apperception. And that is clearly what Kant is trying to do by insisting that any account of the combination of different representations into one consciousness would not be possible unless that combination were subject 'to the conditions for an "objective" unity of apperception, and so the categories.[25]

But just this insistence on such comprehensiveness causes serious problems. Just how are we to understand this notion of a subjective unity of consciousness "depending" on, being "derivable" from, or being "grounded" in an objective unity? Without such an explanation, we would not know what it would mean for Kant's supreme condition to be formal, to be comprehensive enough to exclude any other possible account of experience (say, one which claimed all unity was effected only according to empirical rules).

Now, as Prauss has shown,[26] this issue bothered Kant in the period between the two editions of the *Critique,* as is especially clear in some

25. Cf. Bernard Roussett's discussion, *La Doctrine kantienne de l'objectivité* (Paris: J. Vrin, 1968), p. 55.
26. G. Prauss, *Erscheinung bei Kant* (Berlin: de Gruyter, 1971), pp. 102–38.

very puzzling discussions in the *Prolegomena* (1783). Fortunately, there is a discussion in the Deduction which seems to me a direct attempt to deal with the problem.

2. The Comprehensiveness Problem

From B152 to B159, without subtitle or transition, Kant launches into a separate, apparently parenthetical discussion of what he terms "a paradox which must have been obvious to everyone in our exposition of the form of inner sense." This supposed paradox arises from Kant's claim that I only know myself as an appearance, or only as I am affected by myself, "and this would seem contradictory, since we would then have to be opposed to ourselves as passive."[27] To avoid this paradox (whatever it is), some systems of psychology, Kant goes on to report, identify "apperception" and "inner sense" — a wholly mistaken thing to do, as he attempts to show in the remainder of the section.

By attempting to clarify the relation between apperception and inner sense, Kant is attempting, I believe, to address directly the issue raised above — how we are to understand the *relation* between an awareness of the mere subjective "stream" of representations in inner sense and the apperceived unity constituted by the understanding in judgment — and thereby to make clear why no experience *could* be just a direct awareness of the stream of representations in inner sense. (I take it that it is this last argument which is what Kant is up to when he says that a subjective unity of apperception "depends" on an objective. This digression is his most direct defense of that claim.)

Moreover, this attempt involves much more than a technical clarification of Kant's doctrine of inner sense. It should be stressed that some very important, foundational elements in his whole theory here receive a crucial test. The most important results of Kant's argument in the *Critique* depend on his distinction between the understanding and sensibility. It is because the human mind is, by itself, "closed off" from independent knowledge of the world, because the mind can only organize the material of sensibility, that philosophy can only attain a priori knowledge about these "ways" or forms of organizing, and not about the world. From this flows the entire criticism of the metaphysical tradition. But it certainly seems as if I must be able to know *myself* without the aid of sensation, by pure reflection alone. To preserve his theory of philosophical formality and his characterization of mind, Kant must deny that

---

27. This is the literal translation of B152. The German text is, "indem wir uns gegen uns selbst leidend verhalten müssten." The critic Kant is probably most worried about here is one of his ablest, Pistorius. See Kemp Smith, *A Commentary*, p. 323.

this appearance is correct. To do so he comes up with his dark theory of "inner" sense, and tries to argue that in this case too, the mind does not know itself directly, but only as affected by the contents of inner sense. Thus the results of the Deduction will have been preserved; not only will *all* experience be subject to the categories, even my apparently direct experience of myself, but the theory of understanding, and formality, and so the foundation for the Dialectic will also have been decisively and comprehensively defended. We need, then, to look closely at the details of this defense.

Kant takes it that he has proved that all the contents of consciousness are apprehensible only as described (judged about or *brought* to some unity, apperceived) and that some description rules specify a necessary unity to all representations. It is in this context that the problem of comprehensiveness arises. Does all this mean that I know my *own* mental states and am aware of the connection between *them* also only by making objective judgments about these states? Can it be shown *in concreto* that awareness of the unity of mental states is subject to the same conditions as all awareness? Kant raises this issue as a problem because he is aware that, prima facie, this does not seem to be the case, that just because in this case we do not make a claim about how my representations are united (but just how they seem to me to succeed each other), there is no difference between how I appear to myself and how I am, independent of the categorical conditions, or between myself as an appearance and as a thing in itself.

Kant's discussion clearly indicates that this claim for a direct, nonjudgmental or nonapperceived awareness of self is a false solution to a nonproblem. If Kant's general theory of the necessity of synthesis is correct, so the hypothetical objectors are made to wonder in posing their supposed problem, then the same would be true of our experience of ourselves as objects of knowledge. But that would then seem to mean that, in such self-awareness, we must be both passive and active with respect to ourselves, at the same time that we know ourselves as the object of empirical attention (attending to our thoughts, emotions, etc.) even while "we" are not that object so known, but are also that determining, thinking about, and attending to such a content, so that we cannot be said to know ourselves. In the specific case where we attend to ourselves as objects of knowledge, the allegation here seems to be that Kant's theory would make impossible a reflection on ourselves as objects of awareness without positing another kind of unknown "active" self as the subject of awareness. It is to avoid this paradox, so Kant rather mysteriously reports, that some "systems of psychology" erroneously identify "apperception" and "inner sense."

To deal with this problem, Kant begins by repeating a central point in his theory of the understanding, and then applying it directly to the problem of inner sense.

> The understanding, that is to say in respect of the manifold which may be given to it in accordance with the form of sensible intuition, is able to determine sensibility inwardly. Thus the understanding, under the title of a transcendental synthesis of the imagination performs this act upon the passive subject, whose faculty it is, and we are therefore justified in saying that inner sense is affected thereby. (B153–154)

The requirement for a determination by the understanding is just as strong a requirement when the manifold is inner as when it is outer. It is just as true that

> the understanding does not therefore find in inner sense such a combination of the manifold, but produces it in that it affects that sense. (B155)

Thus, no special difficulty arises with respect to myself as object of knowledge. In such a case too, I only know myself as appearance. This does not mean that I know myself as a special appearing object, in distinction from that *object* which is the self I really am, but just that I cannot consider myself as an object of knowledge except under the conditions required for any knowledge (concepts and intuitions). So Kant complains, rather impatiently, in a footnote.

> I do not see why so much difficulty should be found in admitting that our inner sense is affected by ourselves. Such affection finds exemplification in each and every act of attention. In every act of attention, the understanding determines inner sense. (B157n)

Thus the issue of my own relation to ideas of myself should not be taken to be a special case, exempt from Kant's general theory, and casting doubt on the exclusiveness of rejection of alternate accounts of experience. That is what "psychologists" do who "identify" apperception and inner sense. They presumably assert that I can be "immediately" aware of myself in introspection, that the contents of inner sense must be taken to be either immediately perceived sense impressions (in empirical psychology) or directly apprehended ideas (in rational psychology). Kant points out that, just as we must draw a line in order to think it, or in general just as we must always determine an intuition to recognize it determinately, we could not be aware of ourselves except as some contents of intuition were brought to concepts. We thus know ourselves like everything else, and have preserved the notion of all consciousness as reflective, and so requiring Kant's rules for unity. We would thus also have strengthened the case against any possible notion of experience which tried to eliminate such regulation by the understanding. The "self that knows" thus only refers again to the logical conditions for any apperceiving or judging, and not to some substantial entity paradoxically left out of our awareness.

However, in order to come to some clearer notion of how the "formal" unity of consciousness is to be distinguished from an actual awareness of a unified self, we need to ask how this account explains such empirical self-knowledge. In the first place, such knowledge clearly involves bringing intuitions to concepts. But what exactly are we aware of if we admit that, besides the thought of myself, I also need the "intuition" of the manifold in me? Elsewhere Kant argues that the "content" of inner sense should be considered wholly dependent upon, indeed identical with, the content of outer sense, making it even harder to understand what I am aware *of* in empirical self-awareness.[28] This has led many commentators to see awareness of the contents of inner sense as a kind of awareness of awareness, a reflection on mental events as mental, even if the content of these events is supplied from without.[29] In being aware of myself, then, I would be aware of the series of episodes in my conscious life, brought to some psychological concept, and subject to the restrictions of time.

In general, then, this digression has attempted a specific clarification of what it means to assert that all awareness presupposes conditions which make a unity of apperception possible. Kant has argued strongly in the course of the Deduction that a subjective unity of consciousness, one based on the simply noticed association of representations, always depends on "transcendental" grounds of affinity. In the case of awareness of inner sense, we have found him arguing that the same conditions apply in order for there to be a consciousness of consciousness. From what we have seen, this appears to mean that I could not be conscious of the "stream" of successive representations in inner sense without juding that they are happening to me in such a successive order; that is, without carrying the representations forward and bringing them together in some

---

28. The clearest such statement is at B67. Cf. also B276.

29. See for example, T. D. Weldon, *Kant's Critique of Pure Reason,* 2nd ed. (Oxford: Clarendon Press, 1958), pp. 257–70. Weldon argues that Kant's theory of our knowledge of inner sense comes down to an awareness of *past* awarenesses of outer objects. (See especially pp. 261–62 and Weldon's case that Kant is here following Tetens, pp. 260–61.) The difficulties with Weldon's theory are: (1) It reduces all self-knowledge to knowledge of past acts of outer awareness. Surely part of our knowledge of ourselves involves such memories, but it cannot be wholly identical with it, or else we would be unable to explain why an awareness of some past, datable awareness was an awareness of my awareness. (2) His theory involves him in the difficult assertion that awareness of a spatial manifold is not originally temporal but becomes so only when I am aware of having been aware of that manifold. Cf. Wolff's discussion of this issue, *Kant's Theory of Mental Activity,* pp. 191–202, and Kemp Smith's *A Commentary,* pp. 321–31.

judgment about what is happening to me. However, all this explains what Kant calls a subjective unity of consciousness *not* as a separate kind of awareness, distinct from an objective unity of apperception, but as a subspecies of the objective unity of apperception. What is "subjective" in such a unity is just that the judgment involved is about the "subject."

We are thus still left wondering about a genuinely immediate experience *of* inner sense, an awareness which does not at all seem to be a judgment in psychology, and which led both rationalists and empiricists back to such immediate experience as a "ground" for knowledge. That is, I am certainly capable of being immediately aware of the contents of my consciousness in a way which does not amount to a judgment about myself, but is a report about *what* seems to be the case. I can be aware that this seems to me to be red without necessarily formulating a judgment about my having an experience of this seeming to me to be red. The *experience* in question is not me-having-a-certain-experience-at-a-certain-time, but just the "seeming."[30]

That is, although a unification of such states must be produced, there is no reason to claim that such unification involves the objectivity conditions necessary for apperception, unless all self-awareness were knowledge of myself as if I were an independent object of knowledge (which it is not). On the other hand, however, if self-awareness did not necessarily involve apperception and its requirements, then while it would be true that each successive mental state would be identical with "me" at that time, and different from "me" as identical with some other mental state, there is no reason why some "I" at some discrete moment could not remember and collect together such "me's" into a subjectively associated whole, and call that collection "me," at that time. Kant clearly wants to be able to distinguish a genuinely subjective unity of consciousness from an objective unity of apperception. However, I am suggesting that such passages as this digression clearly resist some of the implications of that distinction, given Kant's desire to provide formally necessary requirements for any candidate conception of experience. Within such a tension, Kant is either left opening the door to a skeptic who claims that all experience is just a subjective association, perhaps construed as objective under press of repetition, or he ends up claiming that the categories are required only in order to make a distinction between subjective and objective succession. The former, though, would give Hume too many weapons; and the latter would beg his question.

But this new "paradox" involves issues deeper than the battle with Hume. In order for Kant to conduct his analysis at a formal level, where this means not tied to any material claim about the contingent peculiarities of the human mind, he must present an argument which demon-

30. This notion of "seeming" will be discussed in greater detail shortly.

strates a condition necessary in *any* account of human experience. As he stresses in the Paralogisms, this is the "logical" requirement *that* all representations must be bound in a unity of self-consciousness.[31] He then goes on to argue that this could not occur unless some rules of unification a priori determined the general structure of all experience, and insists that nothing in this argument has said anything material about the human mind. He thereby takes it that he has shown that an exclusively empirical unity of representations could not be a candidate account of experience, that apperception could not be interpreted as the empirically apprehended stream of representations of inner sense. And all of this has made it difficult, if not impossible, to understand what this subjective unity amounts to, even if it does "depend" on objective unity.[32] Unless Kant can explain more clearly in just what sense the former "depends" on the latter (and is not identical with it), in what sense the contents of inner sense must be apperceived, there seems no reason at all to claim any a priori restriction against a model of experience which presented only an empirical unity of apperception. We could of course say that such a model would have to be skeptical about the distinctions made within it, but so much the worse for Kant's alternative, we might respond.

Now it would be unfair to Kant not to take note here of elaborations of this problem. One is provided by Kant himself, and is of little help — his discussion in the *Prolegomena* of judgments of perception and judgments of experience. The other is much more helpful, but considerably more difficult to deal with in the space of this chapter — Gerold Prauss's recent detailed reconstruction of the kind of "dependence" I argued above was central to Kant's argument. The first elaboration both confirms the problem cited here and adds to the confusion.

31. It is clear in especially the second edition version of the Paralogisms that Kant, while maintaining everywhere the nonsubstantial nature of the claim for a unity of apperception, nevertheless was bothered about just how to state that this unity "existed." He tries to sort out what this could mean in a long, fascinating note to B422.

32. This problem is similar to, but different from, issues raised in two recent commentaries, and those differences can be spelled out briefly. In "Did the Sage of Königsberg Have No Dreams?" *Essays on Kant and Hume* (New Haven: Yale University Press, 1978), L. W. Beck tries to respond to C. I. Lewis's criticism that Kant's explanation of the conditions for experience left no room for noncategorical experience, like dreaming. Beck's solution to this problem is to point out that the categories can be "required" for our dream experience without rendering that experience objective in the same way outer experience would be. He agrees with Prauss that the "judgments of perception" doctrine will not explain this possibility, and formulates an independent interpretation (p. 54). However, it seems to me that what Beck has answered is not the question, "Could Kant dream?" but, "Could Kant know that he dreamt?" He explains the possibility of knowing something objective about me (where that can include knowledge of my illusions and dreams), but not the possibility of subjective awareness itself. In sum, there is still a difference, unaccounted for by Kant, between "dreamily apprehending" and "apprehending that I am dreaming."

In the *Prolegomena* discussion, beginning in section 18,[33] Kant clearly indicates that these judgments of perception should not be taken to be judgments about perceptual consciousness (as, for example, might occur in judgments in psychology), but should be taken to be perceptual judgments, to be a form of consciousness which requires an explanation. The explanation given, though, is quite obscure. At one point, Kant asserts that such judgments do not require pure concepts of the understanding, but instead involve only the "logical connection of perception in a thinking subject." That, however, simply cannot be correct. It may be that these subjective judgments do not *assert* categorical relations, but the formulation of a determinate, even if subjective, experience would seem to require some ground of connection in appeal to categorical conditions. Otherwise the experience here being described would resemble exactly what Kant wants to rule out as an impossible account of what experience is like — a purely inner, noncategorical, direct experience of the flow of my sense impressions. The point must be here not that such an experience has no "conditions," but that the judgments in question appeal to a "ground" in a special, limited way. But while Kant's discussion sometimes approximates such an explanation, most of the time he speaks quite obscurely, in a manner I confess I simply do not understand, of such judgments "becoming" judgments of experience by the "addition" of such an appeal to a categorical ground.[34] This obscurity is deep enough, but Kant adds to the confusion by producing a series of examples of such judgments which do not appear to be judgments of perception at all, but judgments of experience formulated in terms of an empirical subject.[35]

Prauss has recently argued that, for all the obscurity of this discussion,

---

Likewise, Wolff suggests in *Kant's Theory of Mental Activity* that Kant may have proved "too much" in the Deduction, arguing that there is no such thing as subjective association (pp. 163–64). He suggests that a full account of this problem is not offered until the Second Analogy, but he himself admits that explanation only works if we can accept a problematic, hard-to-make-out distinction between a received, subjective time order and a produced objective reordering. See, for example, pp. 274–75. I think Kant does attempt a clarification of this problem, prior to the Analogies, here in the second-edition Deduction, but that this discussion fails. I have tried to indicate that this failure is tied to the deepest presupposition of the critical enterprise — the distinction between a material sensibility and a formal understanding.

33. Kant, *Prolegomena, Gesammelte Schriften,* vol. 4, p. 298.

34. To be sure, Kant said the same sort of odd thing in the first edition of the *Critique,* at A249–53, where he claimed that "appearances [*Erscheinungen*], *so far as* they are thought *as* objects according to the unity of the categories, are called *phenomena* [my emphasis]." Revealingly, Kant left this passage out in the second edition.

35. Cf. Gerold Prauss, *Erscheinung bei Kant,* pp. 187–97. Both Beck and Prauss point to the relevance of this discussion for Kant's theory of aesthetic judgments in the *Critique of Judgment* but I cannot pursue that topic here.

one can nevertheless see how Kant at least intends to make this distinction. He further claims that in the second edition Deduction, one can see even more clearly the full dimensions of Kant's solution. For my purposes here, two aspects of Prauss's account are relevant; his reconstruction of judgments of perception into "it seems . . ." judgments, and his interpretation of the Deduction based on that reconstruction.[36]

Briefly, his argument goes like this: in the first edition, Kant tended to treat the problem of mere "appearances," immediate objects of consciousness, as simply the contents of inner sense, and did not see clearly that even such contents must be apperceived, or judged about in some way, if indeed they were to be contents of consciousness. He began to see this problem in the *Prolegomena,* and even while his own discussion of the judgments of perception/judgments of experience distinction does not work, we at least begin to see how he views the problem. Such purely subjective judgments must fulfill three criteria: since such judgments are still judgments, the categories must play some role in the form such judgments can take; they must possess what Kant calls "subjective validity" (i.e., be true, even if only true-for-me); and even though the judgment is a judgment, must assert something, it must also be problematic, just in order to avoid being a standard judgment of experience.

It is important again to recall why such an account is needed. Kant is arguing that the categories are necessary conditions, a priori rules, for the combination of representations in any unified, apperceived experience. But as he saw, that cannot mean that all experience is a judgment about some internal or external object.[37] Now, to understand just what is, in the face of this problem, the "dependence" of such subjective awareness on objective conditions, Prauss proposes that we understand Kant's attempt in terms of "it seems to me . . ." judgments. He argues that Kant should not have used his examples of tasting and feeling in the *Prolegomena,* but

36. For a somewhat fuller summary of Prauss's book, see my review in the *Journal of the History of Philosophy* 12 (July 1974): 403–5. For a separate discussion of *Wahrnehmungsurteile* and *Erfahrungsurteile,* cf. Theodore E. Uehling, "Wahrnehmungsurteile and Erfahrungsurteile Reconsidered," *Kant-Studien* 49 (1978): 341–51. Uehling summarizes a number of recent discussions of the problem, but for some reason leaves out a consideration of the most detailed and subtle, Prauss's. Cf. also Bird, *Kant's Theory of Knowledge* (New York: Humanities Press, 1973), pp. 140–48.

37. Henrich, for all the power of his interpretation in *Identität und Objektivität,* admits defeat on this issue, p. 95: "Kant verfügt allendings über keine konsistente Theorie der Wahrnehmung." He does not go into much detail about the consequences of this failure. Guyer, in his review, suggests the problem can be solved if we realize that judgments about my own states of consciousness may be "anchored in categorical judgments about objects without being equivalent to any body of such judgments" (p. 160). Prauss's account is the only one known to me which tries to account for this anchoring, but it does not, I suggest here, succeed.

should have explained judgments of perception as seeming judgments, and in that way explained their dependence on judgments of experience, without making them equivalent to such judgments. Thus, a subjective unity of apperception is an awareness *that*, say, it seems that the sun warms the stone, which is a judgment about neither me nor the sun and the stone. (Prauss goes to great lengths to explain that such judgments should not be confused with similar types, such as "It seems to be raining," when we mean, say, to express surprise that *is* raining, or when we mean it looks as though it's raining but I know it isn't. Rather, we just mean to report about our awareness without making any claim about what *is* happening).

In effect, then, such judgments problematically invoke and so depend on categorically prescribed unity, but they do not assert that unity.[38] It is Prauss's contention that we could not formulate these judgments about subjective unity without knowing what would be the case if they were straightforwardly asserted, and so have preserved the Deduction's force, its claim that there can be no immediate knowledge of the contents of consciousness, contra the model of sense-data phenomenalists, that all awareness for an identical subject requires categorical rules, and that we have done so without turning all awareness into awareness of objects. In whatever way "*es scheint . . . Urteile*" can be said to "depend" or be "derived from" or have their "ground" in the judgments rendered problematic by the *es scheint,* so can it be said that a subjective unity of consciousness depends on the transcendental, or objective unity.

Prauss's account is a good deal more involved than I have indicated here, but even from this crude sketch, I think one can see that we are still left with our earlier difficulty about comprehensiveness. First of all, Prauss does not explicitly tie his discussion to the strategy of the Deduction. He seems to argue that if it is true that the categories are the only way we could explain the unity of self-consciousness, then: here is a way for understanding what Kant might have meant by a unified awareness of mere appearances. But from what Prauss says, there is no reason why the kinds of connections between representations about which we want to say, "It seems that . . . " could not be wholly noncategorical. No "dependence" on the categories is involved *necessarily* in such judgments; I might just as easily claim, "It seems to me that impressions of warmth follow upon impressions of light" as "It seems to me that the sun warms the stone." There is nothing about an analysis of subjective awareness itself which suggests that such could not be what all awareness really is, upon inspection. Prauss presents no case to show that I could not

38. Prauss, *Erscheinung bei Kant,* makes a good deal of Kant's "buchstabieren/lesen" metaphor to help account for how this could be. See A314, and Prauss, pp. 38–57.

formulate this particular kind of judgment unless the categories prescribed rules for all combinations of representations, which combinations I problematically invoke in *"es scheint"* judgments, and I cannot think of one independently.

That is, Prauss has shown just what apperceived awareness of the content of inner sense must be like if such awareness is not to collapse the distinction between apperception and inner sense into some kind of immediate awareness, *and* is not to be a species of object-awareness. "It seems . . ." judgments are not objective judgments about me, nor an "immediate" form of, say, sense-data awareness. But just to the extent that Prauss is successful, the necessary "dependence" of such judgments on categorical forms of combination becomes obscure.[39] It *would* be possible to understand the claim that no experience would be possible unless subject to the categories if it were true that all awareness of the contents of inner sense were a judgment about me, as an object.[40] But Prauss's whole analysis shows that there are certainly forms of subjective awareness which do not involve judgments about the empirical subject. However, if there are such forms of awareness, all they seem to "depend" on is *some* imposed combination of the elements of awareness, not, necessarily, categorical combination. We are again left, it seems to me, with no formal delineation of the limits of any possible experience. Of course, we are still left with some powerful arguments against, generally, an empiricist model of experience, and a forceful case for the necessity of the active role of the understanding in any experience, combining elements in ways that cannot be wholly derived from experience; but it is hard to see how any formal limitation to the possible structure of that experience can be set. If we do want to specify what these forms or rules are, we need to appeal to more than the conditions for a unity of apperception.[41]

39. He tries to make it clearer by distinguishing between an *"Anwendung"* and a *"Gebrauch"* of the categories. Cf. especially sections 15 and 16, pp. 272–321.

40. Wilfrid Sellars, in ". . . this I or he or it (the thing) which thinks . . .," *Proceedings and Addresses of the American Philosophical Association* 44 (September 1971): 5–31, offers an interpretation which begins with the same point of view adopted here, that "the recognition of the radical difference between categorical forms and matter-of-factual relationships is the *pons asinorum* of the Critical Philosophy" (p. 4), but he goes on to give an intriguing, hypothetical materialist interpretation to what is, basically, Weldon's interpretation of the inner-sense doctrine. See paragraphs 30 and 43–47, and especially his dissatisfaction with the Kantian "passive" model for inner sense, par. 52 ff.

41. As mentioned earlier, much of the current debates about the possibility of the transcendental deduction itself are related to the problem of comprehensiveness as developed here. See Stephan Körner, "The Impossibility of Transcendental Deductions," *The Monist* 51 (1961): 317-31, and the effective reply to Körner by Eva Schaper, "Arguing Transcendentally," *Kant-Studien* 63 (1972): 101–16; also Jay Rosenberg's attempt to relativize Kant's strategy in "Transcendental Arguments Revisited," *Journal of Philosophy* 72

But all of this also brings us to our second problem. However these limits are "set," formally or nonformally, do they establish the general structure any *object* of experience could have for us, or only some very basic rules which seem indispensably involved in the way we have to "think" about objects? How exactly are we to construe the results of the Deduction? More specifically, what now are we to make of Kant's most important claim about the formal results arrived at, that "the conditions for the possibility of experience are at the same time the conditions for the possibility of objects of experience"?

3. The Objectivity Problem

We have already partly seen how Kant wants to address this question in the Schematism. But a large part of his discussion of the issue occurs in the second half of this version of the Deduction, after section 20, where Kant seems to want to extend the results of the Deduction in a self-consciously radical way. He says that, although he considers himself to have proven that "the manifold in a given intuition is necessarily subject to the categories," he also considers that thereby only "a beginning is made of a deduction of the pure concepts of the understanding." The restrictions on the proof thus far, restrictions which explain why this has only been a beginning, are clear in the German text when Kant explains that the "manifold" proven to be subject to the categories is to be considered only "insofar as it is given in one (or even a unified) intuition [so fern es in Einer empirischen Abschauung gegeben ist]." The unusual capitalization of the article stresses that some aspect of the "unity" of a manifold intuited has been presupposed, as is indeed admitted in a note: "The ground of the proof rests on the represented unity of intuition, which includes in itself a synthesis of the manifold given for an intuition, and already contains the relation of the latter to the unity of apperception" (B144n). In the text of section 21, Kant says again that he has "abstracted" from the manner in which some intuition is given, and in the following (section 26) such abstraction will be corrected, and he will show that *our* manner of empirical intuition can have no other unity than that which the categories prescribe.

As so stated, this second step is clearly related to the interpretation and problem developed above. One aspect of Kant's proof is to show that there are a priori rules for any possible experience, and we have found difficulties with the formal specification of and proof for those rules. But

(1975): 611–26, and Barry Stroud's equally effective response to Rosenberg, in "Transcendental Arguments and 'Epistemological Naturalism,'" *Philosophical Studies* 31 (1977): 105–15. As presented here, Kant's case for comprehensiveness is, I believe, unsuccessful, but *not* because he operated with some question-begging or historically relative concept of experience.

another crucial part of Kant's proof is to prove that there is no knowledge of any kind "outside" of these limits. He must prove not just that the categories define the structure of our experience, or prescribe the unity for all experience, but that no knowledge of any other kind of unity is possible. This latter step is what Kant thinks allows him to claim that the categories are not rules for the mere "subjective" constitution of objects, but that no other knowledge of objects *could* be possible, except as subject to the categories. In the language he uses here, he has "so far" proved that any given intuition must be thought according to the categories. He will now show, given the forms of our intuition, that there could be no intuition given which would not be necessarily subject to the categories. It is this extension which allows Kant to claim what he did at B138.

> The synthetic unity of consciousness is, therefore, an objective condition of all knowledge. It is not merely a condition that I myself require in knowing an object, but it is a condition under which every intuition must stand in order *to become an object for me.* [my emphasis]

And it is this extension which lays the groundwork for the critique of pure reason itself, the Transcendental Dialectic. This argument alone will allow Kant to exclude the possibility that even though the categories determine the rules for sensible experience, there might be experience or knowledge of another kind not so subject. If he can show not just that what we do sensibly experience is subject to the categories, but that we could not have any knowledge not categorically prescribed, then the Dialectic can rest, as it everywhere does, on the conclusions of the Deduction.

How, then, does he accomplish this extension? The following plausible interpretation has been offered by Dieter Henrich.[42]

In the first stage of the Deduction (up to section 20) Kant had shown that whenever there is some unity among representations such unity is possible only if the categories prescribe a unity for all experience. But he has not specified the "range within which" unitary intuitions can be found.[43] It might, in other words, be possible that the categories would be responsible for the unity and determinacy of some, or some types of, intuition, but there might be other intuitions not so subject. There might be a "disproportion"[44] between the rules for consciousness and the given. (In the terms used here, this possibility would make Kant's idealism a

42. Dieter Henrich, "The Proof Structure of Kant's Transcendental Deduction," *Review of Metaphysics* 88 (1969): 640–59.

43. Ibid., p. 645.

44. Ibid., p. 647.

wholly constitutive idealism, with no demonstration that objects must conform to the categories, just a proof that we must think as if they do.) But, Kant goes on to show, there *could not* be intuitions which were not subject to categories, since *our* forms of intuitions are space and time and it has already been shown (vide the Transcendental Aesthetic) that spatial and temporal unification always requires the categories.[45] Accordingly, we have proved not that the categories regulate some partial human ability to establish unity in experience, but that there could be no unity in experience not subject to the categories. The foundation for the Dialectic's criticism of knowledge not subject to the forms of intuition and thereby to the categories has thus been laid.

The terminology used by Kant himself to make these points is, to say the least, obscure. He reminds us (in section 24) that he has thus far proven, so he thinks, the first leg, that any *given* manifold could not be determinately experienced except by virtue of a priori rules of unity. But he points out that this only establishes something about what he calls the "intellectual" synthesis of the manifold (B150). As stated above, this seems to mean that we have only proven that those aspects of any manifold of intuition which we are capable of understanding, of experiencing, are so understandable only if unified according to the categories. This has not eliminated the possibility that there could be elements of this manifold which are not susceptible to such categorical unity, remain unexperienceable, ineffable, and which would force us to construe the status of the categories as rules for ordering experience in ways which may be required for us, but which cannot be said to be in any comprehensive way objective.

In addition to this formal unity for the manifold, then, we need what Kant calls a "figurative" unity for objects of *our* intuition. The distinction goes as follows:

> This synthesis of the manifold of sensible intuition, which is possible and necessary a priori, may be entitled figurative synthesis (*synthesis speciosa*) to distinguish it from the synthesis which is thought in the mere category in respect of the manifold of an intuition in general, and which is entitled combination through the understanding (*synthesis intellectualis*). (B151)

Kant then muddies the waters even further by introducing the transcendental faculty of the imagination to help explain this figurative synthesis and distinguish it from the intellectual synthesis which is only the work of the understanding. What he appears to mean is that the figurative synthesis is directed at the particular form of sensible intuition which we possess and determines any possible content of such intuition, while the

45. Ibid., p. 649.

intellectual synthesis should be regarded as the understanding's uniting of any kind of already intuited manifold.

Much here is admittedly unclear, but the basic point comes through all these terminological labyrinths: that Kant wants to eliminate formally the possibility that some content of intuition could appear in a way that would not conform to the conditions for experience. To do this formally would prove not just that we impose a certain unity on experience (a model which often sounds as though claims for objectivity are really claims for indispensable subjective ordering) but that nothing could appear to-be-ordered except as already subject to such categories. One extended example of this requirement is the digression on inner sense, and we have already seen the problems with that account. Kant offers another example of what he is trying to say, and it too poses problems — his "house" example at B162.

There he points out that while an empirical perception is immediately subject to the forms of intuition and so must appear in space and time, it is also true that the "synthetic unity" of any object of intuition "has its seat in the understanding," that there could be no manifold in general about which to make a judgment (is it a house, a façade, a tobacco store, etc.) unless the manifold were already subject to the category of quantity. Kant does not explain why a manifold would be originally thought in the first place in terms especially of quantity and not some other category (that is a topic which will lead him to the Schematism and the problem of judgment), but he does clearly argue that the categories determine the very possibility of any object appearing to us and so excludes any possible objection that the categories provide only subjective or intellectual rules of thought.

This example occurs as an explanation to the final version of the deduction in section 26. Kant had pointed out in the first paragraph what we have been stressing here, that in this section of the Deduction:

> We have now to explain the possibility of knowing a priori by means of categories, whatever objects *may present themselves* to our senses, not indeed in respect of the form of their intuition, but in respect of the laws of their combination, and so, as it were, of prescribing laws to nature, and of making nature possible. (B159) [my emphasis]

The house discussion thus exemplifies this proof about what "may present" itself to our senses. In the example, Kant demonstrates his claim that not only must all experience involve a distinction between subjective and objective which only the categories can account for, but that no object could be "given" to us at all except in terms of these rules, and that *thus,* a necessary connection according to such rules could be the only meaning of objectivity for us.

However, this extension by Kant just raises again two familiar problems, and a new one. The crucial step in the extension is the argument that the "unity of an intuition," as opposed to the intellectual unity thought among intuitions, requires synthesis and so the categories. Such a claim forces us back to our earlier difficulties with Kant's theory of intuitions, and especially the problems of sensible "individuals" in Kant's theory. The role of synthesis "in" a pure intuition, and the role of pure intuition in the determination of a spatio-temporal particular, would both have to be greatly expanded before we could understand the second stage. In the Deduction itself, Kant seems to rely a good deal on the Aesthetic, as if all these problems had been worked out fully there.[46]

Moreover, the extension reraises the problem of a wholly "subjective" awareness of intuitions, and indeed adds to the problem by making all awareness sound like, necessarily, objective awareness. Indeed, the digression we just discussed occurs in the heart of the second stage.

Finally, another new problem also emerges. If there can be no intuition not subject to the categories and if no human knowledge is possible without intuition, then it follows, as Kant states in section 27, that "there can be no a priori knowledge, except of objects of possible experience" (B166). There *can* be such a priori knowledge because all intuition is subject to the categories, but there can be no such knowledge apart from the categorical conditions for possible experience because without intuitions, all human thought is "empty," or concerns only logical, not real, possibility. Now, as I have presented the results of the Deduction, it has been stressed that Kant does not want to maintain that the categories arc mere subjective rules for human thought. Instead, they constitute all that knowledge of an object could mean to us. They do not prescribe how we must think of the world, "be the *real* world as it may," but prescribe the rules for our knowledge of an objective world. Obviously, however, when Kant states the result of the Deduction, he often gives the impression that the former is exactly what he means. "We know only appearances," he says, not "things in themselves." In fact, one could say that the clearest way to put Kant's case for the formality of transcendental knowledge is simply to insist that he means thereby that we no knowledge of things in themselves. We do not know that every thing in itself exists only because

46. In effect, then this discussion would constitute Kant's contribution to the recent controversy surrounding the role of verificationism in transcendental arguments. See Barry Stroud, "Transcendental Arguments," in *The First Critique,* ed. T. Penelhum and J. J. MacIntosh (Belmont, Calif.: Wadsworth, 1969), pp. 54–69. The directness with which Kant wants to deny that he has only established "our" criteria for knowledge of objects (and so, without verificationism, has not refuted the skeptic who maintains that, for all we know, the real world may be quite different than is specified by these criteria) is already obvious in the B138 passage cited above.

of some cause, but we only know that any object in our experience is caused to exist because and only because causality is a necessary form of experience. Clearly, in order to assess finally what this restriction to "formal conditions" of consciousness amounts to, we need to turn to this account of appearances and things in themselves.

7

Appearances and Things in Themselves

The understanding, therefore, by assuming appearances, grants the existence of things in themselves also; and to this extent we may say that the representation of such things as are the basis of appearances, consequently of mere beings of the understanding, is not only admissible but unavoidable.[1]

1. Phenomena and Phenomenalism

We come now to a final and notoriously ambiguous consequence of Kant's formal idealism. Thus far we have been concerned with such questions as whether it is possible to specify pure forms for any experience, whether forms of intuition or forms of the thought of any object; how, on what basis, in what way knowledge of these forms can be said to yield synthetic a priori knowledge; and, how we are to understand the relation between such forms and the material of knowledge. This latter problem has appeared in a number of ways: as the problem of sensation and guidedness, the relation between pure and empirical intuition, the ground of determinate mathematical knowledge, the difference between general and transcendental logic, the origin of empirical concepts, the nature of transcendental judgment for both pure and empirical schemata, and finally as the problem of a comprehensive, formal attempt to demonstrate that pure rules of thought have objective validity. But there is a quite general characterization which Kant himself gives of the relation between the "forms" of experience and "what we experience." His argument is that *since* all knowledge occurs only as subject to such forms, what we know are only "phenomena," and not "things in themselves."

Stated so abstractly, such reasoning seems quite hasty. It is quite possible to maintain, for example, that an exclusive empiricism, in any significant form, is wrong; that all knowledge originally involves formal principles of organization and discrimination which themselves cannot be derived from experience, without thereby maintaining that what we know

1. Kant, *Prolegomena, Gesammelte Schriften,* vol. 4, p. 314.

by means of these forms is *not* the "world in itself."[2] Kant's claim to the contrary provides us now with the most detailed opportunity for investigating not only why Kant thinks his transcendental turn has this consequence, but especially what else we might need to say about the objects of human knowledge, and in what way, before his enterprise can be completed.

As the above quotation indicates, this last question, what we must "think about" the objects of knowledge beyond the formal anticipation of the structure of experience, is obviously quite relevant to the kinds of problems developed here previously. That is, Kant's position is not only that the mind has no independent access to things as they are in themselves, and can thus only know nature as subject to our forms of intuition and thought, as phenomena, but also that we are *nonetheless* "required" to think about such things in themselves in various way, for various reasons, just in order to be able to have coherent, systematic, phenomenal knowledge. Prima facie, this position seems inconsistent. The latter requirement seems to demand that reason, unaided by sensibility, be able in some nonarbitrary, well-grounded way to think about nature as it is in itself, not as it is known through sensibility, nor, theoretically, as it is a priori subject to necessary conditions for experience. This would seem to require a nonformal use of reason, a speculation about the possible material of knowledge which is substantially different from the only possibility for a priori reflection hitherto open to reason — a determination of itself, its own conditions for experience. As we shall see, however, consistently but quite problematically, Kant denies that this extension of reason's power is what is implied by the "requirement" that in phenomenal knowledge, we must think things in themselves. Aside from the role such reflection plays in transcendental knowledge itself, where the notion of a thing in itself has a wholly negative use — where it merely restates our ignorance of the transcendent realm — the positive function of such reflection is still, once again, understood as a kind of formal legislation by reason *to* nature; in effect, a discovery by reason of its own formal demands of (or "commands" to) nature. The nature of the "requirement" for what appears to be a transcendent, but remains a formal, subjective, reflection will be the focus for the following. Such is, I shall maintain, the clearest way to approach the age-old problem of how we can be wholly ignorant of things in themselves and yet "know" so much about them, both within transcendental knowledge (they are the "cause" or "ground" of appearances,

---

2. For the most famous example, as was noted in chapter 3, one could claim that space was a subjective form of our intuition, and yet that it was also a property of things in themselves.

must be assumed to "exist," etc.) and in rational reflection in general where the system of transcendent ideas must be assumed as regulative ideas. Kant's solution to this problem relies deeply on his claim that the latter kind of reflection is, again, wholly formal, and so does not involve an inconsistent, metaphysical leap into transcendent reality. That solution will have its virtues, but it will also share many of the liabilities of such formalism developed thus far. We need first to look at the most prominent negative sense given to the notion of a thing in itself, within critical philosophy itself.

Given Kant's terminological vagueness in stating his position, it is important first of all to state, in some detail, what Kant was not maintaining by claiming that all knowledge is restricted to knowledge of phenomena. His first attempt to clarify why transcendental idealism has this consequence occurs at the end of the Transcendental Aesthetic.[3] It involves a complicated association of the notions transcendental, empirical, idealism, and realism. On the negative side, the "transcendental realist" argues that there is a world of things in themselves and that only knowledge of this world could really count as knowledge. Such a realist is thus quite vulnerable to any epistemological critique, any demand that he explain how we could know such a "transcendent" reality. Under such a conception of reality, it quickly turns out that we cannot explain any such knowledge, and we turn into "empirical idealists," forced to admit that we do not know the real world but only our own representations.[4] If "reality" is defined independently of our possible access to it, then, not surprisingly, when epistemological questions are encountered, skepticism and such idealism (or an indefensible "dogmatism") are the only results. On the other hand, the transcendental idealist admits that knowledge of "reality" can only be explained in terms of some possible experience, and thus while remaining an idealist (interpreting the meaning of claims about reality in terms of *our* experience) can also be an empirical realist, since the notion of reality involved allows him to assert that we do know the empirical world as *it* is in itself.

Stated so briefly, much of such a claim seems like an unfair play on how one chooses to define what is "real"; a transcendental idealist is free to call himself a "realist" because he has interpreted reality in a way compatible with a continuing claim that "we only know our own representations." Such of course is only the result of the brevity of such formulations and the fact that they are made before Kant has a chance to

3. The discussion of idealism and realism begins at B44 = A28, and is discussed at length in sections 7 and 8. The distinction is also the crucial element in the resolution of the Third Antinomy, B566 = A538 ff.

4. In fact, it is Kant's position that transcendental realism and empirical idealism, when pressed, must become the same position, as he says explicitly at A369.

explain fully both the necessity for such a restriction and the fuller meaning of such a notion of "reality" (explanations, as we have seen, that both occur in the Analytic). For the moment, it is mostly important to understand that Kant is not claiming that transcendental idealism means to "reduce" all claims about material objects to claims *about* sense experience. It certainly often seems as if this is what Kant intends, since he does seem to want to explain any claim about objects "in terms of" some possible experience. But we have already seen that this cannot be what Kant intends. For Kant, to argue that claims about tables and chairs really "mean," or come down to, or should be interpreted as, claims *about* sensations, or about possible sense-data experience, would make no sense. For him, such latter claims are themselves empirical claims about inner states of the subject and are quite different from, not at all equivalent to, claims about objects of outer sense. In the first place, as the contrast with empirical idealism makes clear, such a restriction is not a claim that there are not material objects, just ideas. This the center of Kant's anger over being confused with Berkeley. But in the second place, it is also not an admission that we do know external objects, and then an *interpretation* of that claim so that it ends up meaning: we know such objects only insofar as we know our own sensory representations.[5] It is still the case that knowing *such* inner states has a special meaning in Kant; it means knowing objects of inner sense, not outer sense. He does want to restrict our knowledge of outer objects so that such a claim means knowledge of objects of outer sense, and so to certain kind of representations. But, again, these representations are objects of *outer* sense and are immediately experienced as such. It is thus true to say that Kant's transcendental idealism wishes to interpret all claims about any object (inner or outer) in terms of some possible experience we could have of it, and that this experience is sensory. It is not true, though, that he means to interpret, to reduce, or in any way to understand all claims about outer objects as, when properly analyzed, claims about sensations,

5. Of course, it is true that there are as many different versions of the phenomenalist interpretation of Kant as there are interpreters who maintain it. The best-known version is Kemp Smith's, who follows Vaihinger on most important points. A great deal of the issue of whether or in what sense Kant was a "phenomenalist" comes down to an interpretation of the thorny problem of affection, and while I cannot deal with that issue exhaustively here, I shall follow the approach of commentators like G. Bird, in his critique of H. A. Prichard, *Kant's Theory of Knowledge, Ch. I*, "Phenomena and Phenomenalism" (New York: Humanities Press, 1973), Gerold Prauss's in chap. 3 of *Kant und das Problem der Dinge an sich* (Bonn: Bouvier, 1971), Henry Allison's in section 2 of his "Things in Themselves, Noumena, and the Transcendental Object," *Dialectica* 32 (1978): 61–76; and Bernard Roussett's *La Doctrine kantienne de l'objectivité*, chap. 8 (Paris: J. Vrin, 1968). I shall, however, argue that these interpretations must be supplemented by a consideration of the positive role of reason in Kant's theory.

that is, inner objects. To do so would be to collapse the whole distinction between inner and outer and retreat again precisely to empirical idealism.[6]

Fair enough, one might respond, but what precisely *is* it to interpret claims about objects as claims about our experience or possible experience of objects if not to reduce them logically to claims about our (outer) sense experience? The Kantian response must be that while experience of outer objects certainly is intelligible only in terms of sensory receptivity, such experience immediately involves something more than just sense data themselves, that a full explanation of what it means to interpret claims about objects as claims about experience of objects must involve a priori elements essential to any experience, and so an explanation that reveals how. *any* experience at all immediately involves a "reference to objects" and cannot be described in terms merely of the content of sense.

That is, the real force of the phenomenality thesis is not what we would today call phenomenalism, but instead is a consequence for Kant of the theory of the forms of experience. Any experience of objects we could have is immediately subject to such forms. We do have knowledge of external objects, but we can only understand knowledge of such objects in terms of rule-governed synthesis of representations, that is, in terms of judgment and intuition. With judgment as the essential component in all knowledge, the phenomenality thesis seems first of all to come down to a claim that we only know external objects *by* making judgments about them, based on sensible intuitions in space and time, and that there are a finite number of ways human beings can intuit and judge. Since it is logically possible for there to be other forms of intuition and judgment, we need to realize that we do not know objects in any of these other ways, and so know them only under finite restrictions. We might add, as Henry Allison has recently shown,[7] that even straightforward claims about knowledge of our own ideas and impressions, as in Berkeley and Hume, turn out to be transcendental *realist* claims, just because knowledge even of such inner objects is considered by such philosophers independently of our forms of experience.

But this is all only a small first step. It may be that Kant does not

6. It is true that Kant proposes a theory according to which "representation of an object" *is* the "synthesis of representations according to rule," but there is no reason to take that to mean that knowledge of external objects is synthesized knowledge of mental items. The representations in question, if the context is representation of an external object, are still representations of outer sense. What Kant means to emphasize by the notion of synthesis is just that no such knowledge of outer objects can be obtained by one such representation (of an outer object) alone, but must be judgmentally united with remembered or projected representations according to a rule. This is argued for persuasively by Dieter Henrich in the first part of *Identität und Objektivität* (Heidelberg: Carl Winter, 1976).

7. Henry Allison, "Kant's Refutation of Realism," *Dialectica* 30 (1976): 226 and 230.

intend that his restriction of knowledge to phenomena comes to the same thing as empirical idealism, or what we would understand by phenomenalism. But what then do we do with what he also says about things in themselves? If we can know all experienceable objects as *they* are in themselves, subject to our forms of experience, why go on to insist that we cannot know how things "really" are in themselves? Almost everyone initially sympathetic to Kant, from Solomon Maimon,[8] the German Idealists, and neo-Kantians to Strawsonian austere reconstructions, has tried to eliminate this noumenal dimension to Kant's theory. Kant himself, however, far from evidencing such tendencies, always seemed to regard the distinction as the *pons asinorum* of the critical doctrine — an insistence that has created by far the most extensive critical controversy about Kant's idealism.

2. The "Two Worlds" and the "Methodological" View

There are a variety of ways in which Kant wishes to introduce the necessity for thinking of things in themselves. The first and most controversial is what could be called the exclusively "transcendental" meaning of things in itself. In this context, Kant attempts to formulate a position about all objects considered independently of our forms of knowledge, which position is strictly implied just by critical philosophy itself. He formulates this position with a confusing flurry of terminology — thing in itself, transcendental object, noumenon — which would take a study in itself to disentangle.[9] But the force of that position comes from the meaning of the *contrast* between knowledge of phenomena and of things in themselves as that contrast is a thesis of transcendental philosophy itself. It involves him in all the famous problems of affection, noumenal causality, "double" affection, and so forth. Second, he introduces a requirement for thinking things in themselves as regulative ideas necessary for science itself. Third, and with the most variations, he introduces this requirement for practical or moral reasons; he wants to open the possibility, and argue for the practical necessity, of thinking of ourselves

8. Maimon's attempt is actually quite interesting and is the beginning of what would become the neo-Kantian attempt to construe the thing in itself as a *"Grenzbegriff."* For Maimon, the critical concept of a thing in itself was an *undetermined concept* of an object, an idea of an indefinite synthesis, not a metaphysical concept, or a concept of an *undetermined object*. He runs into trouble when trying to account for affection and sensation, resorting to a theory he calls the "infinitesmals of sensation." See *Versuch über die Transzendentalphilosophie,* in *Gesammelte Werke* (Hildesheim: Georg Olms, 1965), pp. 27, 31–32.
9. Three detailed attempts to do so are Allison, "Things in Themselves, Noumena, and the Transcendental Object"; Prauss, *Kant und das Problem der Dinge an sich*; and Roussett, *La Doctrine kantienne de l'objectivité.*

as moral or noumenal agents, of the world in itself as teleologically ordered, and so on.[10] The first two such requirements for thing-in-itself talk are most relevant here for the problem of formality.

What Kant says about things in themselves as a critical philosopher is the hardest to understand. Given many of the things he says, it is impossible to deny that he intended *some* positive role for the concept, a role most often expressed by his discussion of "thinking" of the "ground" of the appearances. On such a view, for example, with respect to Kant's theory of empirical affection, it appears that Kant wants to claim that "things in themselves" are *responsible* for the determinacy of a sensed manifold, and thus for the particular, determinate character of an empirically apprehended spatial manifold, without it being the case that we know anything about such things *in themselves*. Stated positively, things in themselves can be said to be the "ground" of appearances as we apprehend them, even while, stated negatively, these things in themselves are only noumena, for us meaningful only negatively, beyond our "veil of perception."

As so stated, the familiar difficulty with this duality is also apparent. Put simply, the positive role that things in themselves occasionally are asserted to play in Kant's theory of affection (as well as the very fact that they are asserted to *exist*) does not seem consistent with the negative role assigned to noumena. How is it possible that we know something about things in themselves (that they are the ground of appearances) while at the same time a central result of the critical philosophy is the assertion that we know nothing at all about things in themselves? Looked at in terms of this well-worn paradox (stated by Jacobi very soon after the appearance of the *Critique*),[11] the problems with Kant's notion of appearance multiply, and paradox can be made to follow non sequitur quickly. The relation between things in themselves and appearances seems to be described often by Kant in terms of causal interaction, yet we know that causality is a condition only for relations between appearances; claims like, "Things in themselves are not in space and time" seem to violate directly the *Restriktionslehre*; the phrases "outside us" or "independent of our representations" acquire, in the light of these difficulties, hopelessly ambiguous nuances, and so forth.

Of course, had Kant been a skeptic about knowledge of the external world, or a straightforward phenomenalist, and interpreted claims about objects as claims about possible sense ideas, none of these problems

10. Kant himself makes what amounts to this threefold distinction at B385–86 = A308–29.

11. F. H. Jacobi, *David Hume über den Glauben, oder Idealismus und Realismus, Über den transzendentalen Idealismus, Werke,* vol. 2, ed. F. Roth F. Köpen (Darmstadt: Wissenschaftliche Buchgesellschaft, 1968), pp. 291–310.

would arise. Instead, he claims that knowledge of objects should always be understood in terms of the formal structure of our experience, requiring both intuitions and concepts, that within this structure we do know external objects, not exclusively our own ideas, *but* that we do not thereby know things in themselves. It is the presence of all these claims taken together which generate all the above problems. And again, even a fairly detailed and sensitive reading of the *Critique* could easily convince one that, whatever the difficulties, Kant does indeed want to claim that there *are* things in themselves, but that we don't know them, and that *instead* of knowing them, we know only our own representations ("in us").[12] The (for Kant) unusually poetic image which begins his discussion of the distinction between Phenomena and Noumena[13] suggests quite strongly that, beyond the safe island of truth we have discovered and charted in the Analytic, there exist other things to be known if we could but make our way through the fog banks and "swiftly melting" icebergs of the Dialectic. Such an image of limits beyond which we may not safely venture sounds like the old "veil of perception," and is often reinforced by introducing the notion of a being not so limited as us, possessing other kinds of intuitions, who *can* thus know those things in themselves which we, in our finitude, cannot. On this view, with respect to affection, we have to say that we know only the effects of the interaction between our selves and such things in themselves, although we thus also must admit that such things exist and cause our representations to have the character-

12. A look at the literature on this issue quickly shows a number of commentators who want to distinguish a proper, truly Kantian sense for talk about things in themselves, and some different sense, either appropriate in another context, or not at all what Kant meant. See for example Bird and "transcendental" and "empirical" points of view, Prauss on the same, as well as an additional distinction between "transcendental-philosophic" and "transcendent-metaphysical," Allison on a similar set of distinctions, Rolf Meerbote on an "ontological" perspective, and an "epistemological" use of "thing in itself," in "The Unknowability of Things in Themselves," *Proceedings of the Third International Kant Congress*, ed. L. W. Beck (Dordrecht: Reidel, 1972), pp. 414–23; Stephen Barker on "Appearing and Appearances," in *Kant Studies Today*, ed. L. W. Beck (La Salle, Ill.: Open Court, 1969), pp. 274–89; and Roussett on "transcendent" and "transcendental" conceptions, *La Doctrine kantienne de l'objectivité*, p. 171. In a number of these discussions, the crucial point of interpretation is simply whether one thinks Kant is claiming we know things in themselves *as* they appear to us (but do not know them apart from our forms of experience), or whether we know a different object, mental representations, and not external causes of perception. I am agreeing fully with those commentators cited here who try to construct an interpretation based on the former claim, and who then try to incorporate many of the confusing things Kant says into that interpretation, but I will add that we still need to consider how we are to understand the force of the contrast between phenomena and noumena within that interpretation, and how we should take the positive role of regulative ideas within Kant's theory.

13. B294 = A236.

istics they do have.[14] Such a familiar "two worlds" view of this problem is at least one way to interpret the meaning of the following claim made in the *Critique*.

> How things may be in themselves, apart from the representing through which they affect us, is entirely outside our sphere of knowledge. (B235 = A190)

> The nonsensible cause of these representations is completely unknown to us, and cannot therefore be intuited by us as an object. For such an object would have to be represented as neither in space nor in time . . . and apart from such conditions we cannot think any intuitions. (B522 = A494)

And perhaps the most direct confirmation of the "two realms" view:

> Now we must bear in mind that the Transcendental Aesthetic already of itself establishes the objective reality of noumena and justifies the division of objects into a world of the senses and a world of the understanding (*mundus sensibilis et intelligibilis*) . . . For the senses represent something to us merely as it appears, this something must also in itself be a thing, and an object of a nonsensible intuition, that is, of the understanding. (A249)

Even as so stated, however, doubts begin to arise immediately about the correctness of such a view of the *Restriktionslehre*. For one thing, the last quotation, while it seems to warrant dividing up the world into two sorts of objects, one set of which we cannot know, also seems to define this division *in terms of* the faculties of knowledge, and so to effect the division methodologically (or, in the terms used here, formally) by considering an object in terms of its accessibility to forms of knowledge. This view of the matter would make possible a theory which, while clearly Kantian, would seem to avoid many of the causality, interaction, and knowability problems which plague the two worlds view. We could now say that there is only one set of objects for knowledge, but these same objects can be considered from two different perspectives; that we can, theoretically, consider a sensed object *as* the object of a nonsensible intuition and so define this considered object as a "thing in itself," for us only a noumenon, even though theoretically possible.[15]

---

14. A most valuable introduction to the literature on the problem of affection is provided by Herbert Herring, *Das Problem der Affektion bei Kant, Kant-Studien Ergänzungshefte*, no. 67 (Bonn: Bouvier, 1953). Building on Vaihinger's interpretation, Erick Adickes has provided one of the most complicated interpretations of this problem, *Kants Lehre von doppelten Affektion unseres Ich als Schlüssel zu seiner Erkenntnistheorie* (Tübingen: J. C. Mohr, 1929). Although a neglected feature of such discussions, it is also important to incorporate what Kant says about *inner* "affection" into such a discussion. Roussett, *La Doctrine kantienne de l'objectivité*, tries to do this; p. 178 ff.

15. Moltke Gram, in "How to Dispense with Things in Themselves (1)," *Ratio* 18 (June 1976): 1–15, has noted this distinction between a "two worlds" and what he calls a "Two Description" Theory. He advances some interesting criticisms of the latter, but his discus-

These "two realms" and "methodological" views of Kant's doctrine can both be supported by any number of seemingly conclusive quotations. Especially when discussing the problem of affection, Kant seems to leave little doubt that his theory of experience requires two separate objects — things in themselves as ground, and appearances as effect of affection. Just as decisively, when emphasizing the unknowability of such things in themselves, their character as noumena, Kant seems to insist that there is only one set of objects to be known, and that when we, reflectively, consider those objects insofar as they can be known by us, given our finite capacity to know, such objects should be called appearances, and when we consider these same objects independently of our modes of knowledge, perhaps as the object of a nonsensible intuition, they should be called things in themselves, or noumena.

As in all such disputes about interpretation, the decisive factor is always which version makes more sense of most of the things Kant has to say about appearances and things in themselves, where "makes more sense" includes both making sense of Kant's intentions and making sense of the issue itself, arriving at the most reasonable philosophic position when faced with a body of conflicting texts.

On the face of it, what has here been called the received or two world view of the *Critique,* despite its decisive, not to say fatal, difficulties, appears to have most if not all of the classic commentaries lined up behind it.[16] Recent commentators, however, have not been so pessimistic, or so confusing. In advancing the "methodological" view of the *Critique*'s task, many of the older problems have been dealt with much more successfully. Graham Bird, Gerold Prauss, Bernard Roussett, Henry Allison,[17] and others have proposed a theory of Kant's *Restriktionslehre*

sion is limited in that within the latter camps he only includes Dryer, Adickes, Paton, Schrader, Bröcker, and Westphal, and for some reason does not consider the much more detailed interpretations of Prauss, Roussett, Bird, Allison, and others. One can only get a hint of a possible response to these interpretations in some final remarks on Meerbote, p. 16n.

16. Cf. note 5. It is also a position one finds attributed to Kant in very recent commentaries. Bennett, while he does not make Kant an idealist, does make him a phenomenalist, as on. p. 22 of *Kant's Analytic* (Cambridge: Cambridge University Press, 1966): "Kant thinks that statements about phenomena are not merely supported by, but are equivalent to, statements about actual and possible sensory states." R. P. Wolff attributes to Kant the "double affection" theory which seems to arise when Kant's alleged phenomenalism is pressed, *Kant's Theory of Mental Activity,* p. 168 ff.

17. Graham Bird, *Kant's Theory of Kowledge*; Gerold Prauss, *Erscheinung bei Kant* (Berlin: de Gruyter, 1971) and *Kant und das Problem der Dinge an sich*; Roussett, *La Doctrine kantienne de l'objectivité*; Henry Allison, "The Non-spatiality of Things in Themselves for Kant," *Journal of the History of Philosophy* 4 (1976): 313–21, "Kant's Refutation of Realism," *Dialectica* 30 (1976): 223–53, "Things in Themselves, Noumena, and the Transcendental Object," *Dialectica* 32 (1978): 61–76. Also definitely in this camp,

which seems to avoid many of the thornier problems implied by the earlier interpretations.

Such interpretations argue that much of the distinctiveness of Kant's case is lost or confused if many of his claims about appearances are not seen in their proper "epistemological" context. Of particular importance is the difference between two different ways we can consider Kant's claims about appearances: "transcendental" and "empirical."[18] When Kant says, for example, that all our knowledge is restricted to appearances, he does not mean to suggest that we are thus limited in actual, empirical knowledge either to a second-rate kind of knowledge — a knowledge of a "shadow reality," some pale version of the way things really are — nor that we are limited to a purely "internal" set of objects as the intentional correlates of knowing. Such a confusion is precisely, according to these interpretations, a confusion of transcendental with empirical perspectives. That is, amplifying now the kinds of claim made in section 1 of this chapter, empirically considered, viewed in terms of empirical knowledge, Kant is generally quite clear that we can know two kinds of appearances, inner and *outer* objects, and when we speak of knowledge of outer appearances there is no reason at all not to say that we know the *empirical* world as *it* is "in itself." There is ample evidence gathered by Bird that in the context of empirical knowledge, Kant was quite concerned lest his position be taken to mean that we cannot know outer objects as appearances of outer sense. The Refutation of Idealism and the General Note to the System of Principles stress such a point repeatedly. On the other hand, looked at "transcendentally," we must also admit that we only know these outer objects *as* appearances, as *conditioned* by the forms of space and time, and thought only by means of the categories. Such a reflective, second-level consideration (i.e., a reflection *about* empirical knowledge) restricts our knowledge to knowledge of objects insofar as they can be known by us (and thus denies us knowledge of these objects *considered* independently of how they are known by us), but this claim does not imply that, again empirically, we cannot know outer objects.[19]

There are, further, good reasons for adopting this view of the method-

with some intriguing suggestions of his own to make, is Arthur Melnick, in *Kant's Analogies of Experience* (Chicago: University of Chicago Press, 1973), pp.136–64, especially p. 152.

18. I am provisionally adopting Bird's terminology here, though the point can be made in several ways. See *Kant's Theory of Knowledge,* chap. 3.

19. I disagree with Bird's statement of what, from a transcendental perspective, we should say about ideas and objects. He argues that, if we consider two claims: (1) that there are external objects of which we have knowledge, and (2) that we are immediately aware only of our own ideas, or representations, then (1) is transcendentally false and empirically true, while (2) is false empirically but true transcendentally (p. 44). It seems to me that there is an appropriate, transcendental sense in which (2) is false, though not in the same way as such an empirical claim would be false. See above, chap. 2, chap. 3.

ological conception of the appearance doctrine, the view that the notion of a thing in itself is just that — a notion, a concept of an object theoretically considered ("transcendentally" considered) apart from any way we could know it. In the concluding remarks to the Transcendental Aesthetic, where Kant first tries to explain his theory of appearance, he mentions quite directly a "merely empirical" distinction between the way objects "really" are and the way they appear to us (B62 = A45). He then contrasts this distinction with the transcendental one between things in themselves and appearances, and warns that his position will be much confused if such a difference is not kept straight. There is also much evidence for this view, as Bird helpfully points out,[20] in the Fourth Paralogism. In this sense, the doctrine of things in themselves is simply a restatement of the central teaching of the transcendental turn itself. Further, once we make this turn, we have to realize that we are explaining these objects in two different senses, at two different levels. We are considering the relation between objects and ourselves as finite knowers both in terms of the general transcendental theory of knowledge and in terms of actual, empirical knowledge.

In this dual sense, for example, the problem of "affection" ceases to be the difficulty it was for Jacobi. The supposed problem of the "causes" of appearances arises as a problem only through a confusion of these two different perspectives. Considered as empirical events, our representations can be, without paradox, viewed as caused by outer objects, so long as the empirical nature of that relation is clear, the fact that we are considering the outer object and inner event as events in time subject to the law of causality like any other series of events. Kant's empirical realism clearly distinguishes between inner and outer appearances, and there is no reason not to regard, say, a science of psychology as capable of describing this relationship in some detail.

On the "transcendental" level, on the other hand, no talk of the *cause* of appearances is possible. From that point of view, considering all appearances, both inner and outer, together, we simply have to admit that our access to objects is always conditioned by the form of knowledge we have, and that thus we can have no knowledge of an object considered independently of such forms.[21]

But as the last statement of the methodological position[22] should make

20. Bird, *Kant's Theory of Knowledge,* p. 21 ff.

21. This seems to be Prauss's position in *Kant und das Problem der Dinge an sich,* and to some extent, Bird's. Its limitations are suggested by Allison in "Things in Themselves, Noumena, and the Transcendental Object," p. 68 ff. For a summary of Prauss's whole interpretation, see my review of his book in the *Journal of the History of Philosophy* 14 (July 1976): 374–78.

22. The position is called methodological because the concept of a thing in itself is considered as a consequence of, or indeed, an elliptical statement of, Kant's methodology,

clear, we are still left with a serious general problem. In the first place, the interpretation seems to have been *too* successful in explaining a mistaken "transcendent-metaphysical" conception of things in themselves for a correct "transcendental-philosophic" meaning.[23] If the methodological view is correct, we might still ask, What force is there left in the distinction between phenomena and noumena? This can be asked with respect especially to the first two of the three distinctions drawn earlier (p. 193). It does not at all appear that when Kant speaks of things in themselves as the ground or cause of appearances, he always means that question empirically, as the relation between empirical things in themselves and empirical appearances. Affection is still a transcendental as well as an empirical problem and must still be so addressed. Second, and in many ways more important, Kant is quite interested in arguing for the "necessity" for some determinate connection between the thought of things in themselves and phenomenal knowledge itself, as his position on regulative ideals make clear. Some basis for that determinate connection must be laid.

In fact these problems, while formulable in different ways, are deeply related. On the one hand, it is true that, transcendentally considered, the concept of a thing in itself should be considered wholly negatively. It is possible to consider any phenomenal object "as it is in itself." The force of doing *that* is just to emphasize the wholly indeterminate results. When we do attempt to think any such object "noumenally," we end up only with the empty thought of the "transcendental object = X." But there is another type of reflection on things in themselves, whereby we do not consider phenomenal objects as *they* are in themselves, but we consider types of objects which, by their very definition, could not *be* phenomenal objects. Such objects are just those defined in the system of Transcendent Ideas, and it is possible to consider *them* as the "ground" of appearances, although in a very special, indeed "formal" way.

It is this second possibility which the methodological interpretation cannot eliminate and which in fact explains the different things Kant does say about both the negative, or let us say wholly transcendental, meaning of things in themselves, and the regulative function of that same notion. Without the introduction of this regulative meaning for things in themselves and an integration of what Kant says about it with his repeated claims for the necessity of the admission of noumena, not only would a great deal of the text simply look contradictory (instead of, as it does, discussing reflection on things in themselves in the two different senses just defined),[24] but the whole force of the phenomena-noumena distinc-

"transcendental reflection" (B316 = A261 ff.) A thing considered in itself is thus just a way of making a point about the results of that methodology.

23. These terms are Prauss's in *Kant und das Problem der Dinge an sich*.

24. Kant comes the closest to distinguishing explicitly the "transcendental-negative"

tion would be lost, and that in the following way. If the contrast between noumena and phenomena is to be a true *contrast,* it must be possible for us to abstract in some way from the whole context of phenomenality and consider, at least theoretically, what knowledge of noumena would be like. To do this the notion of noumena would have to have some meaning independent of its contrast with phenomena. That is, if the concept of noumenon only means a phenomenal object considered independently of any way we could know it, then the supposed contrast between phenomena and noumena is hardly a contrast between what we can know and *what* we cannot know, but is instead just a difference between knowledge in general and the rather abstract notion of not-knowing at all. If the notion of noumena is indeed meant to express what we can't know, and thus to have a real restricting role in this account, the concept must mean something more than entertaining the sterile suggestion of not knowing anything at all.[25] But herein lies the familiar paradox again, since to establish something about noumena independently of this merely negative contrast with phenomena would violate the very restriction the whole phenomenality thesis is meant to establish. On the one hand, the contrast must involve more than the expression of the difference between knowledge and ignorance. If it didn't, for one thing, later claims about "thinking" noumena would have only the fallacious status of reasoning from ignorance (on the order of: since it can't be proved one way or another, since we are ignorant, we might as well believe there is a God, or "fairies at the bottom of my garden," for that matter). On the other hand, establishing something more than this merely negative contrast involves us in the Hegelian problem of "seeing both sides of the boundary" and so overstepping it, just to set the boundary.

3. How to Think about Things in Themselves

With such an interpretation of objectivity, we thus return to our problem of exactly what role the concept of noumena is supposed to play in the

---

meaning of thing in itself (in that sense often called the transcendental object), and the "regulative-positive" meaning (the "intelligible character" of appearances, or "thing in itself") at B566–68 = A538–40.

25. This point is made quite well by Gerd Buchdahl, *Metaphysics and the Philosophy of Science* (Cambridge: M.I.T. Press, 1969), pp. 532–43. It should also be stressed here, as Buchdahl does, that one way of interpreting in what sense we are "required" to think about things in themselves would be to argue that "mechanistic" explanations must be incomplete, that scientific "explanation" itself *requires* teleological interpretation. There are certainly suggestions of this necessity in the *Critique,* but they are not fully worked out. See Buchdahl, pp. 490–95, and Melnick, *Kant's Analogies of Experience,* pp. 121–30. A very general suggestion about the relevance of transcendent ideas, especially God, to science, has been offered by R. C. S. Walker, *Kant* (London: Routledge & Kegan Paul, 1978), pp. 165–77.

critical theory. Simply and finally put: If "appearances" do not at all mean a special kind of object of knowledge, but instead mean a way of considering any object which we could know (in terms of some possible experience or other), we still have to ask: Why introduce the notion of that which we could not know by means of any experience? Without that question, the claim that we "do not know noumena" would not at all be a restricting claim on what we can know, but merely a needlessly involved way of insisting that we cannot know what we cannot know.

Of course, we can immediately admit that the negative function of the strictly transcendental doctrine depends heavily on the restricted sense of "know" involved in the claim. The important aspect of the transcendental doctrine, its nontrivial aspect, is first of all clear in its denial of any *knowledge* other than that gained by experience, or demonstrable in terms of possible experience (as the categories are "known"). Viewed this way, the transcendental claim about not knowing noumena is not only not trivial, it represents the most important aspect of Kant's break with the metaphysical tradition. There are scores of instances in the rationalist tradition preceding Kant where philosophers claimed that the whole notion of knowledge by means of experience was incoherent unless we assumed *knowledge* not gained by experience alone. Of course, Kant himself seems to say much the same thing in his proof for synthetic a priori knowledge, but he now denies that such a priori knowledge is a knowledge of any special object, beyond any we could experience in sensation, but only of formal conditions for the possibility of subjective (that is our) experience. The restriction of knowledge to phenomena thus does restrict both empirical and philosophical knowledge to a kind of experience and a type of proof which strongly contrasts with previous attempts. Indeed, it is in just this sense that the noumenal is meant to restrict and contrast our knowledge. The contrast in question is not between what we know empirically and what we can establish in transcendental philosophy and some other domain of objects just outside our grasp. The contrast is transcendental, not metaphysical. It is a contrast between possible theories of knowledge, not a contrast within Kant's theory of knowledge.[26] When the Platonic Socrates argues in the *Phaedo* that to know equal things in our experience we must already know Equality itself, or when a proposer of the Ontological Argument attempts to establish a necessarily existing being, or when Leibniz attempts an account of the properties objects *must* have independent of any way we could experience those characteristics, Kant's claim that such thinkers have overstepped the boundary between noumena and phenomena is a

26. A characterization similar to this occurs in Melnick, *Kant's Analogies of Experience*, p.155.

claim against the concept of knowledge involved in such accounts. From the viewpoint of transcendental philosophy, it is an illusion to think that reason can know things in themselves not so much because such things must remain forever beyond our knowledge, but because the attempt to know such objects in that way arises from an illusory, and indefensible, conception of knowledge.

However, as has been argued, such a negative function is nowhere near the whole story of the place of the doctrine of things in themselves in Kant's theory. Although he attacks any conception of knowledge which claims knowledge of objects considered apart from our possible experience of them, he does quite clearly continue to assert as an important element of critical philosophy itself, that it is not only possible but necessary to think such things in themselves. What then can such a claim mean, if not a reintroduction of the two world view that causes so many problems? Such a claim about "thinking" directly about objects which *could* not be experienced in fact opens up a very large topic, and forces one to come up with some interpretation for the many passages in the *Critique* where so considering the "supersensible substrate" of appearances appears a positive, not merely a restricting or negative, possibility, according to transcendental philosophy itself.

There have of course been many attempts to interpret this clear positive function in Kant. They vary from Kant's allegiance to his "private" metaphysical views,[27] the presence of precritical doctrines in the patchwork *Critique*,[28] a desire to leave some place for his doctrine of freedom and morality,[29] to simple charges that he was confused,[30] did not think through the implications of his own methodology,[31] or, like anyone else, simply had a few bad arguments for doctrines he should not, by his own account, have held. I certainly would not want to claim that there must be another kind of interpretation here because Kant could not have been careless or mistaken, but I do think there is another explanation for such passages, one based on an internal necessity in critical philosophy itself.

27. George Schrader, "The Thing in Itself in Kantian Philosophy," in *Kant,* ed. R. P. Wolff (New York: Doubleday Anchor, 1967), pp. 172–88, and Josiah Royce, *Lectures on Modern Idealism* (New Haven: Yale University Press, 1964), pp. 36–40.

28. Norman Kemp Smith, *A Commentary to Kant's Critique of Pure Reason* (London: Macmillan, 1923), p. 404 ff.

29. Heinz Heimsoeth, *Transzendentale Dialektik,* vols. 1–4 (Berlin: de Gruyter, 1969), and Gerhart Krüger, "Der Masstab der kantischen Kritik," in *Philosophie und Moral in der kantischen Kritik* (Tübingen: J. C. B. Mohr, 1967).

30. S. Barker, "Appearing and Appearances in Kant," in *Kant Studies Today,* ed. L. W. Beck, H. A. Prichard, *Kant's Theory of Knowledge* (Oxford: Oxford University Press, 1969), J. Bennett, *Kant's Analytic.*

31. Prauss, *Kant und das Problem der Dinge an sich.*

Thus far, I have argued that the contast between apperances and things in themselves cannot be explained on any two worlds view, one which holds that things in themselves affect our sensory apparatus and remain forever hidden behind the veil of perception. Such a view makes a confusing shambles of much of Kant's transcendental theory, and is unnecessary to explain either affection or objectivity. However, I have further argued that a purely "methodological" view of this doctrine, an interpretation of things-considered-in-themselves, is also incomplete as an explanation of the doctrine. A purely negative view of noumena on such a theory ends up leaving the whole "contrast" at the heart of Kant's *Restriktionslehre* unexplained, and more important, leaves too much of the actual text unexplained.[32] Some kind of positive role for the doctrine of things in themselves is clearly at work in such passages as Bxxvi:

> Though we cannot know these objects as things themselves, we must yet be in a position to think them as things in themselves; otherwise we should be landed in the absurd conclusion that there can be appearances without anything that appears.

For, while we can duly note how careful Kant is in such formulations, reminding us that we cannot know phenomenal objects *as* things in themselves, and not simply asserting we cannot know things in themselves, we are still left with no positive way to interpret what "thinking" of things in themselves might mean. To anticipate, such a claim doesn't mean thinking of objects other than in terms of their appearances; it seems to mean thinking of appearances in terms which themselves cannot be submitted to empirical scrutiny.

It is this latter sense of thinking of things in themselves as the ground of appearances which Kant appears to have in mind in discussing the work of "reason," particularly in its "regulative" use. That is, there are clear indications that he realizes that the notion of the ground or cause of appearances can be taken in (1) an empirical sense, where we adopt a point of view wholly within experience and consider the relation between object and, say, sensation as an empirical relation and investigate the cause of inner objects of perception just as we would any other cause; (2) a wholly transcendental sense, where reflection on some phenomenal object, when considered independently of its relation to our forms of experience, yields only the negative notion of a transcendental object

---

32. A problem similar to the one raised here for the methodological interpretation — whether it trivializes the negative meaning of noumena — has been raised in a different way by Erik Stenius, "On Kant's Distinction between Phenomena and Noumena," *Philosophical Essays Dedicated to Gunnar Aspelin on the Occasion of His 65th Birthday* (Lund: C. W. R. Gleerup, 1963), pp. 231–45. See also Allison, "Things in Themselves, Noumena, and the Transcendental Object," p. 60 ff., for a discussion relevant to this point.

= X, or as he says, just the "indeterminate" notion of a "something in general";[33] or (3) a regulative sense, where such reflection can and indeed must somehow issue in "positive" results. This third possibility is discussed frequently throughout the Transcendental Dialectic, but especially in three passages: the entire series of introductory remarks for the Transcendental Dialectic (B350–96 = A293–338), wherein Kant explains his theory of Transcendental Ideas; the explanation of Transcendental Idealism as the Key to the Solution of the Cosmological Dialectic (B518–95 = A490–567), especially the last part of this discussion, beginning at B570 = A542; and the Appendix to the Transcendental Dialectic (B670–732 = A643–704), wherein Kant discusses the Regulative Employment of the Ideas of Pure Reason and the Final Purpose of the Natural Dialectic of Human Reason.

In a number of passages in these sections, Kant uses the same language he had earlier used at the end of the Analytic, where reflection on nonsensible objects, considered in terms of possible *human* knowledge, had yielded only the negative notion of a thing in itself. But here he uses that language to stress that, from another point of view, such an object *can* be considered positively, indeed even when considered the "ground" of appearances.

> If, in connection with a transcendental theology, we ask, *first,* whether there is anything distinct from the world, which contains the ground of the order of the world and of its connection in accordance with universal laws, the answer is that there *undoubtedly* is. For the world is a sum of appearances; and there must therefore be some transcendental ground of appearances, that is a ground which is thinkable only by the pure understanding. (B724 = A696)

Shortly thereafter, in explaining why we must presuppose such a ground, he says that in doing so we presuppose a "transcendental object," adding yet another, now positive, meaning to that already ambiguous term.

Of course, Kant carefully circumscribes the proper context for such positive reflection on things in themselves, and in doing so points out clearly the different senses of illusion possible when doing so and so the different senses of reflection on things in themselves sketched above. At B352 = A295ff. he reminds us that there is one type of illusion that concerns only the "misapplication" of the categories, an error of the faculty of judgment when not properly curbed by criticism. To correct this error we make use of what has been called here the transcendental notion of a thing in itself. That is, this context is wholly epistemological, and concerns a dispute among possible theories of knowledge, wherein, for example, one may agree that everything which exists has a cause, but

33. A252.

interpret that as knowledge about things in themselves. We correct that theory by means of criticism, an explication and defense of the forms of experience, and so argue that in that epistemological context, discussion of things in themselves is wholly indeterminate. From this Kant distinguishes dialectical illusion proper, wherein we claim to have knowledge of *objects* which transcends the limits of any experience whatsoever, objects like the soul, God, or the totality of some set of appearances. He goes on to point out, however, that it is not postulation of these objects themselves which is illusory, but a misunderstanding of their use (B761 = A643), and proposes to offer a theory about the proper, "immanent" use even for such transcendent principles.

That theory is his theory of transcendental ideas, sometimes called "concepts" or "maxims" of reason. According to this theory, reason has a particular task to play *within* the knowledge of appearances itself, a task defined at B365 = A307 as "to find for the conditioned knowledge obtained through the understanding the unconditioned whereby its unity is brought to completion." It is this unconditioned totality, conceived necessarily as outside or beyond any series of appearances we could apprehend, that constitutes the content of any positive reflection on things in themselves. Kant then goes on to argue that there are a number of specific ways in which such an unconditioned for the series of conditioned appearances can and must be thought, ways he designates "transcendental ideas." These are defined at B377 = A320: "A concept formed from notions and transcending the possibility of experience is an *idea* or concept of reason." And later,

> I understand by idea a necessary concept of reason to which no corresponding object can be given in sense experience. Thus the pure concepts of reason, now under consideration, are *transcendental ideas*. They are concepts of pure reason in that they view all knowledge gained in experience as being determined through an absolute totality of conditions. (B383–84 = A327)

The first thing one is struck by in reviewing the passages where Kant describes the meaning of thinking of appearances nonempirically (provisionally interpreted here as thinking of what we do experience in terms of "conditions" which are themselves not derived from nor *directly* meaningful in terms of actual or possible experience) is the strong "necessity" with which he characterizes the move to this way of thinking. In the Introduction to the Transcendental Dialectic, he first makes this point by speaking of a "subjective necessity," which we may misinterpret as objective, but which is still subjectively necessary in some way (B354 = A297). This regulative direction of the understanding is also said to be "indispensably necessary [*unentbehrlich notwendig*] if we are to direct the understanding beyond every given experience" (B673 = A645, and again at B705 = A679). Many other such passages abound in the Appendix to the Transcendental Dialectic. One of the strongest occurs at B679 = A651.

> For the law of reason to seek this [unity] is necessary, because without this law we would have no reason, but without reason we would have no coherent use of the understanding, and in the absence of this *no sufficient criterion of empirical truth,* and so in respect of this latter we must assume the systematic unity of nature as objective and necessary. [my emphasis]

So far, then, thinking of things in themselves is supposed to mean thinking of appearances in terms of a systematic unity which, while it cannot be itself experienced, nor apparently *directly* proved to be an indispensable condition of any experience, is nevertheless "subjectively" necessary, especially if we are to direct the understanding "beyond any given experience" or if we are to have a "criterion of empirical truth."

Clearly, two questions arise. What is the nature of this claim for the "necessity" of such a mode of reflection, and what, specifically, is such an assumption of ideas supposed to amount to? The answer to the first question depends on Kant's doctrine of the distinction between the understanding and reason, and especially on the limitations of the understanding in empirical knowledge.

As in many places in the *Critique,* Kant's neat divisions between various faculties can be more confusing than clarifying, but the general sense of this *Verstand/Vernunft* distinction is clear enough. The task of the understanding is most often described in terms of the discrimination and unifying of our sensory experience, our experience of sensory particulars. On the other hand, the task of reason is defined in terms of the results of the understanding's labor; Kant often says that while the understanding has appearances as its object, reason has the understanding itself, and its concepts, for *its* object.[34] Stated very generally, and without a sharp division of faculties, the tasks of our intellectual or conceptualizing grasp of the world is different when we are presented with a sensed particular and must think it together with other objects according to a rule in order to discriminate it conceptually, and when we wish to systematically think together the results of such discrimination in some interconnected system. In the latter case we shift our interest from "understanding" some sensory appearance to "conceiving" the connections among a variety of individual experiences in laws of higher generality. In the *Critique of Judgment* Kant gives, I believe, a somewhat more satisfactory explanation of such different goals in distinguishing between determinate judgments, which seek to include particulars within universal

34. As at B361 = A305 and B362 = A306.

concepts already possessed, and reflective (in the language of the *Critique*, "ascending") judgments which, when presented with a variety of particular experiences, seek a universal within which to organize these experiences.[35] Although he is somewhat inconsistent about this latter characterization in the *Critique*, such a difference between reason and the understanding is clearly present at B394 = A336. We should note immediately that one result of this description is that it seems to lead to the conclusion that such universal-seeking activities as empirical concept formation must themselves be understood as the work of reason and so founded on this "subjective necessity," whatever it turns out to be.

In one sense, then, this distinction is, as Bennett, following Swing,[36] has called it, a difference in degrees of conceptualizing, with reason involving conceptualizing at an "at least fairly high level." But the distinction also involves more than such a difference in degree. Most important, the greater degree of generality demanded by reason creates a qualitative break with the understanding; we now demand some kind of extension beyond the "limits of experience" just in order to have this greater degree of generality. That is, to invoke earlier language used here, it also involves a difference in the source or ground of conceptualizing itself. The *basis* of reason's attempt to unify experience must be understood differently than the understanding's, a difference most of all visible in the limited *kind* of "conceptualizing" involved in the understanding.

To make this limitation clear, we need to recall the limitations of the Deduction's proof about concepts. Even if the extension of the Deduction's argument in the Second Analogy goes through, we have only proved thereby that in our empirical investigation of the phenomenal world, we are *warranted* in looking for causal connections, and that this warrant has a higher authority or "more dignity" than Hume thought it did. In fact, if we did not assume that some distinction could be made between subjectively associated and objectively connected events, experience would be impossible. But the question such a theory raises for the understanding's actual, not merely possible, discrimination of the world is how we know not just that experience stands in some causal order but that it stands in this or that *general* order. Commentators, and often Kant himself, toss off that "our experience" should answer such a question, but at this point in the explanation, the whole situation is much too underdetermined to allow such a casual appeal. The understanding's pure con-

35. Kant, *Kritik der Urteilskraft, Gesammelte Schriften,* vol. 5, p. 179. This same faculty, reflective judgment, is called "wit" in the *Anthropologie,* section 42.
36. J. Bennett, *Kant's Dialectic* (Cambridge: Cambridge University Press, 1974), section 83. The quotation is on p. 263. See T. K. Swing, *Kant's Transcendental Logic* (New Haven: Yale University Press, 1969), p. 229 ff.

cepts do, perhaps, provide the rules for the unification and discrimination of some manifold, and the schemata for such concepts, perhaps, provide a way of actually applying such concepts, but it still remains the case that the actual system of causal laws and explanations of the physical world can still proceed in any number of internally consistent ways. This indeterminateness is as true of the various ways we can determinately understand our everyday sense experience as it is true of various theories and systems of science. And it is just this indeterminateness that the system of regulative ideals is supposed to help determine.

This point about the limitations of the understanding can be put in the following, familiar way. The Second Analogy, let us assume, has established that, given any singular event, E, it is necessarily the case that E is connected causally to some other event. In some particular experience, however, given this event, E, we must invoke some determinate empirical law and judge ("determinately") that E is caused by, say, the singular event A. Clearly, though, we can make this judgment only if, as Kant had stated in the B679 passage quoted above, we have already "gone beyond any *given* experience," and formulated ("reflectively") some universal rule along the order of: E-type events are caused by A-type events. What Kant is now arguing by so strongly asserting the necessity for reason's reflective yet immanent role in knowledge is that in order to formulate this rule, we must assume an order and regularity to nature which we cannot experience directly, but which is required for any systematic knowledge. Indeed, consistent with what was said in Chapter 4, the very concept of an E-*type* event is itself an empirical specification of a presupposed, species unity and so itself evidences the necessary, regulative use of reason.[37]

Indeed, Kant is willing to state the necessity for this involvement by reason in empirical knowledge itself in very strong ways. When characterizing "concepts of reason," he points out that though "no actual experience has ever been completely adequate to it, yet to it *every* actual experience belongs" (B367 = A310–11).[38] Indeed, he says at B691–A663,

---

37. As already mentioned in the discussion of empirical concepts in chapter 4, one of the best discussions of the limitations of the actual "proof" for the causal maxim can be found in Buchdahl, *Metaphysics and the Philosophy of Science*, especially, pp. 651–65. Paton had already noticed those limitations, *Kant's Metaphysics of Experience*, vol. 2 (New York: Macmillan, 1936), p. 276. A very clear, though brief, discussion of the point can be found in Melnick, *Kant's Analogies of Experience*, pp. 89–97. For an attempt to interpret Kant on the problem of induction which makes less use of regulative principles than the above, and more use of the arguments of the First and Second Analogies, see Gordon G. Brittan, Jr., *Kant's Philosophy of Science* (Princeton: Princeton University Press, 1978), pp. 188–208.

38. The distinction between the "indispensability" or subjective necessity for regulative ideas and the role of the categories as necessary conditions for the possibility of experience

The remarkable feature of these principles . . . is that they seem to be transcendental, and that although they contain mere ideas for the guidance of the empirical employment of reason — ideas which reason follows only as it were asymptotically, i.e., ever more closely without ever reaching them — they yet possess, as synthetic a priori propositions, *objective but indeterminate validity,* and serve as *rules for possible experience.* [my emphasis]

So it is this restriction on the understanding's capacity, the fact that the understanding can only judge by means of concepts, and, strictly speaking, cannot originate concepts, that makes the assumption of organizing ideas necessary, ideas which in themselves transcend the limits of experience and legislate comprehensively *to* experience. That is, such a necessity is, like many other uses of the term in Kant, conditional. That condition is the desire for a more integrated and unified system of knowledge than can be provided by the understanding alone. Of course, Kant also thinks that, in science, particularly in mathematical physics, a number of specific laws can be determined by "thinking through" the concept of matter in terms of the categories (basically, again by means of pure intuition), but it is still true that the organization of these laws into comprehensive systems of different sciences, and further subdivisions within the sciences ruled by such prescriptive, a priori principles, are only possible on the assumption of a certain natural orderliness, an assumption which amounts to thinking appearances as things in themselves, an invoking of an idea which transcends any possible experience. Simply put, we do not experience the order of nature, but without the assumption of such an order, our view of science would have to be one of, say, statistically correlated relations between individual events, and *not* one with generally explanatory theories.

It is this notion of "regulatively" thinking of appearances that appears to be what Kant means by claiming that there must be a "supersensible" ground for appearances, that things in themselves can be thought to be the intellectual substrate of phenomena. Such language refers only to a regulative way of *thinking* about appearances, a noncognitive assumption made for the sake of systematic efficiency and even the extension of empirical knowledge, but not meant to be description of some factual or metaphysical relation between appearances and things in themselves.

---

confirms a point made earlier here: that the categories, as distinct from ideas, are not "subjectively imposed" on the material of sense, but comprehensively define the only "objective reality" we could experience. In that sense, we could not wonder if "reality" were the way our categorical structure required it to be; to stress that this is a nonsensical question is just what the negative meaning of noumena is to do. We *can,* however, wonder if reality does conform to our *systematic* demands, and that is precisely why a "critique" of teleological judgment is needed in the *Kritik der Urteilskraft.* Cf. Arthur Melnick's discussion of this point, *Kant's Analogies of Experience,* pp. 136–64.

Again, this assumption is "made necessary" by the limited role of the understanding in, especially, science. Kant's transcendental theory of experience, looked at closely, really does not go very far toward explaining many of the aspects of knowledge which we would normally be interested in in a comprehensive epistemology; it particularly does not explain such things as theory formation in science, the determinate system of empirical concepts ("natural kinds") used in a science, or the relation between various theories in different sciences. He appears to want to discuss many such topics under the heading of "regulative ideas."

Given that desire, we now need to turn to which regulative ideas are necessary to assume, why these and no others, and what kind of help they are supposed to provide (especially since it is described as indispensable help) in a scientific account of phenomena. The above account, subject to particular difficulties which we haven't discussed, is relatively plausible, and given its apparent commitment to a kind of underdetermination in the formation of such systematic theories, and the fact that these organizing ideas and the theories they lead to are much more a result of pragmatics, logic, and even semantics than induction, might get a sympathetic hearing today. But with these questions, the situation gets much more murky and much less plausible.

First, Kant sometimes gives the impression that, either as determined by the three forms of syllogistic inferences or as determined by the three kinds of relational syntheses (he is just not clear here),[39] there are only three kinds of regulative ideals which we "must" assume: the mind as a simple, intelligible substance (the soul); an endless continuity in the system of appearances (the world); and a highest, self-sufficient, creative, purposively ordering ground for the totality of appearances (God). However, all attempts known to me to understand how just these three organizing principles arise from the limitations of the understanding, or even how they actually do help organize appearances in useful ways (particularly the first), have not been particularly successful.[40] What is more important here is the principle of these ideas in general. However shaky Kant's derivation of these ideas[41] may be, they reveal his continuing allegiance to a "formal" conception of both the origin and role of such concepts, his notion that such legislation arises from reason itself and legislates to experience, that the content of such legislation is supplied secondarily.

Such a formal derivation of these regulative notions is clearly very hard

39. Cf. Bennett's discussion, *Kant's Dialectic,* pp. 258–80, esp. pp. 267–70.

40. Cf. Walsh's discussion, *Kant's Criticism of Metaphysics* (Edinburgh: Edinburgh University Press, 1975), p. 248, and Swing, *Kant's Transcendental Logic,* pp. 229–244.

41. Kant himself speaks of a "deduction" of the ideas at B698 = A670, and "tries to make this clearer" at B700 = A672 ff.

to defend whenever we look at any context wherein they are actually supposed to prescribe some kind of order. If we are in fact "called on" to make assumptions about experience, which assumptions can direct but whose terms transcend such experience, then *which* assumptions would seem to be much more a result of reflection on the actual, scientific investigation of the world, and the kinds of specific scientific questions asked in various contexts, than on the formal nature of human reason. If in fact this were true, then it would also follow that the more effective such "holistic" assumptions were, especially in increasing actual empirical knowledge, the more inclined we would be to treat such assumptions less as regulative maxims, and more as correct explanations of nature. Following such suggestions through would serve to break down Kant's unnecessarily strict alternative, that reason *either* "commands" or "begs"[42] in respect to nature, but it would also tend to blur some of the more basic distinctions upon which much of the critical philosophy is based — for example, between the a priori and a posteriori.[43]

To return to the specifics of Kant, it is not difficult to establish that he himself does have a far more flexible view about the assumption of certain ideas. Although he does believe that there must be some foundational rules of reason which tell us, in effect, how to make specific general assumptions, the principle for such assumptions, while the same throughout, allows a wide variety of "reflective" determinations of experience. This breadth and the extent of reason's actual role in science is much clearer in the *Critique of Judgment,* particularly in the first Introduction,[44] than it is in the architectonically baroque *Critique.* Freed of such architectonic restraints, Kant's description of the role of reason in theory formation there includes a good deal more.

It is important as well, though, also to emphasize how committed Kant was to his "formal" method of arriving at such determinations. He appears particularly worried, as well he might be, that the subjective source of such principles should be interpreted to mean that, freed from the constraints present in the Deduction for claims about pure concepts, we can simply formulate all sorts of various ways of thinking of appearances as "in themselves."[45] He remarks instead that these concepts of reason

42. B681 = A653.

43. Said another way, such a more "reciprocal" view of the relation between what transcends and what is immanent in experience would also undermine much of the task of a "transcendental logic" itself, Kant's attempt to begin with subjective rules of thought and then attempt some proof for their "transcendence," their applicability to an objective world. Such a criticism seems close to Hegel's view of the problem, and thus to his own claims for a "dialectical," not a "transcendental," logic.

44. Kant, *Kritik der Urteilskraft, Einleitung (Erste Fassung), Gesammelte Schriften,* vol. 20, pp. 193–251.

45. Although Kant himself regularly invokes the notion of think of nature "as if" it had a

are not arbitrarily invented; they are imposed by the very nature of reason itself, and therefore stand in necessary relation to the whole employment of the understanding. (B384 = A327)

He also cautions against regarding these principles as exclusively heuristic devices. If such were the case, of course, we could materially decide which ideas to postulate on the basis of their function, on what results they led to. But, according to Kant,

> The formulation of these laws is not due to any secret design of making an experiment, by putting them forward as merely tentative suggestions. Such anticipations, when confirmed, yield strong evidence in support of the view that the hypothetically conceived unity is well-grounded; and such evidence has therefore in this respect a certain utility. But it is evident that the laws contemplate the parsimony of fundamental causes, the manifoldness of effects, and the consequent affinity of the parts of nature as being in themselves in accordance both with reason and with nature. Hence these principles carry their recommendations directly in themselves, and not merely as methodological devices. (B688 = A660)[46]

This requirement leads Kant to claim that such concepts of pure reason must be derived from some kind of a "deduction," "however greatly (as we admit) it may differ from what we have been able to give of the categories." (B698 = A670). This deduction will secure the objectivity of these concepts "but in an indeterminate manner (*principium vagum*)" (B708 = A680). This insistence on some ground for these concepts is particularly clear at B679 = A651), where Kant remarks:

> For with what right can reason, in its logical employment, call upon us to treat the multiplicity of powers exhibited in nature as simply a disguised unity, and to derive this unity, so far as possible from a fundamental power — how can reason do this, if it be free to admit as likewise possible that all powers may be heterogeneous, and that such systematic unity of derivation may not be in conformity to Nature? . . . Nor can we say that reason, while proceeding in accordance with its own principles, has arrived at knowledge of this unity through observation of the accidental consitution of nature. The law of reason which requires us to seek for this unity is necessary.

---

teleological order, following that suggestion can, I think, lead to the misleading notion of "philosophical fictions." That is just where it led Vaihinger. See also Eva Schaper, "The Thing-in-Itself as a Philosophical Fiction," *Philosophical Quarterly* 16 (1966): 233–43. A more interesting suggestion occurs in Sellars's discussions of theoretical entities (in principle unobservable) and the thing in itself, *Science and Metaphysics* (New York: Humanities Press, 1968), chap. 2.

46. Of course, there are several places where Kant does describe such principles as heuristic, but that has nothing directly to do with their derivation, as this passage shows.

Again and again, however, when called on to present this nonempirical ground, Kant retreats to some conception of reason's self-imposed demands. His final explanation of how it is that nature can be said to "fit" or accord with such demands is always an insistence that that occurs because we "dictate" such an order *to* nature. The clearest statement of this thesis occurs at B576 = A548:

> Reason does not here follow the order of things as they present themselves in appearances, but frames for itself *with perfect spontaneity* an order of its own according to ideas, to which it adapts the empirical conditions, and according to which it declares actions to be necessary, even though they have never taken place, and perhaps never will take place.[47] [my emphasis]

This most radical extension yet of the transcendental turn claims that it is a misunderstanding to ask how our conception of the order, connectedness, and unity of nature can be confirmed *by* our experience of nature. Such concepts even "of pure reason" are still said to determine the very sense of nature for us. However, at this point, without the use of the strong sense of "the possibility of experience" to establish this a priori determining role, we face an even more confusing explanation of which rules we do prescribe to nature. Aside from the very general claims that we must seek a parsimonious explanation for a diversity of laws, that simplicity of explanation should be a guide for the relation between empirical laws and other such maxims, once we do attempt a systematic integration of such laws into a whole of some determinate genus-species or theoretical system, the "indeterminateness" of Kant's formal account is quite striking. He seems to assume that, armed with these general "simplicity" and "unity" rules, "nature," as investigated determinately by the understanding, will simply "fall into line," that we will just tend toward some unified, single comprehensive account of the world. The possibility of internally consistent but competing "holistic" explanations does not seem to have occurred to him as a serious possibility. Indeed, such could not occur if his explanation of the formation of theoretical concepts is correct. The legislation by reason prescribes or "commands" to nature a priori and since "pure reason is in fact occupied with nothing but itself" (perhaps the clearest statement of the kind of formality involved in the whole Kantian enterprise), and since there is only one human reason, such conflicts cannot occur. It does not seem to me that developments in science since Kant have tended to confirm this view of either the origin of, or the results of, such a demand for systematic, theoretical unity.

I conclude two things from the above interpretation of the correct relations between appearances and things in themselves: first, that Kant

47. Cf. also B590 = A562.

admits that, just in terms of empirical knowledge itself, a scientific knowledge of appearances demands more than a phenomenal account together with the necessary, formal conditions for such phenomenality. But second, when confronted with explaning what such transcendent assumptions should be like, Kant's recourse to his general theory of formality is unhelpful in accounting for the ground of these assumptions. Further, though, he seems forced into such an account by the very nature of a transcendental explanation, especially by the "subjective" account of formality and apriority that makes possible so much of the *Critique*'s unique kind of philosophic explanation.

By now I hope that the nature of this type of issue in the *Critique* and the continuing difficulties inherent in the formalism of Kant's "formal idealism" have been adequately presented; at least, I would hope, sufficiently to provide the foundation for some final, somewhat speculative remarks about the implications of these difficulties for Kant's critical system and for philosophic methodology generally.

8
Conclusions: Kant's Formalism

Der Satz, daß das Endliche ideell ist, macht den Idealismus aus. Der Idealismus der Philosophie besteht in nichts Anderem als darin, das Endliche nicht als ein wahrhaft Seindes anzuerkennen. Jede Philosophie ist wesentlich Idealismus oder hat denselben wenigstens zu ihrem Prinzip, und die Frage ist denn nur, inwiefern dasselbe wirklich durchgeführt ist.

G. W. F. Hegel, *Wissenschaft der Logik*

[Die Philosophie] soll das Denkbare abgrenzen und damit das Undenkbare. / Die Grenzen meiner Sprache bedeuten die Grenzen meiner Welt.

Ludwig Wittgenstein, *Tractatus Logico-Philosophicus,* 4.114, 5.6[1]

1. Form, Mind, and Imposed Unity

Individual arguments in philosophy which purport to establish such claims as the existence of final causes, abstract entities, God, or a nonmaterial substance, or which present and defend some general characterization of being, or the order, harmony, purposiveness or beauty of nature, could be approached "critically" simply on an individual basis. It might be possible to "criticize" such arguments in a way internal to the assumptions of each, to show that even under such assumptions, conclusions do not follow from premises, to offer problematic counterexamples based on similar types of reasoning, or to show that the assumptions necessary for such arguments are internally inconsistent, dogmatically asserted, or treacherously ambiguous. However, such a characterization of a "critical spirit" in philosophy does no justice to the ambitiousness and scope of Kant's critical idealism, a dimension best emphasized, we have argued, by noticing its comprehensive formality. That is, Kant does not want to assert in isolation that the various arguments traditionally used in philosophy to support such claims as the above simply *do not* allow us to claim such knowledge of things in themselves, but that they *cannot*. And

---

1. G. W. F. Hegel, *Wissenschaft der Logik,* vol. 1 (Hamburg: Felix Meiner, 1932), p. 145; Ludwig Wittgenstein, *Tractatus Logico-Philosophicus* (London: Routledge & Kegan Paul, 1961).

establishing the latter is only possible by virtue of some success in determining what the "forms" of our possible knowledge are.

Even so, of course, the methodology used to establish this formal dimension can itself be characterized in a number of ways. Many such reconstructions could end up similar to a more contemporary understanding of such formalism. Kant's transcendentalism could be interpreted simply as a limited epistemology, understood as an analysis of the conceptual presuppositions of what is accepted as objective knowledge, or perhaps, more adventuresomely, as an account, by means of some "transcendental argument" of which concepts one must be able to "use" in order to use others. Certainly such an understanding of a formal methodology is part of what Kant is attempting. But it has been demonstrated above that Kant also thinks that such an analysis itself must be, when finally completed, at the same time an account of the "subjective" forms of experience, a specification thereby of the *limits* of any possible experience, and so an account of all possible objects of experience when considered in terms of such forms. It is his claim that the former, exclusively "meta-level" notion of formality could not establish any significant results without including the latter, subjective interpretation of form.

The connecting link in this mostly implicit argument about methodology is, throughout, the valuable problem of skepticism. A complete *logos* of *epistēmē* must, for Kant at least, find some way of dealing effectively with the *quid iuris* question raised by skepticism.[2] Attention to that question is what distinguishes transcendental philosophy both from conceptual analysis alone and from a psychological account of mental activity. What must be proved is that knowledge of objective reality, especially a type of a priori knowledge, is possible, if skepticism is to be dealt with effectively, and that cannot be done by a strictly formal account of the presuppositions of various claims to know, or various, specific denials of knowledge. But just such a *quid iuris* defense commits us, as transcendental philosophers, to some account of what count as the forms or rules for our knowledge of objective reality, and why. As we have seen, Kant here "turns" away from any hypothetically "divine" perspective in order to construct such a defense, that is, away from any attempt to assume a philosophic perspective from which our forms of knowledge and reality "in itself" could be "compared." What we understand *as* objective reality must be uncovered *and defended as objective* "from within," somehow, from the standpoint of our modes of thinking about (or "speaking about") objective reality. Thus, to separate the "metaphysics of transcendental idealism" — with its account of the special object of transcenden-

2. As at B116 = A84 ff.

tal inquiry, the subjective forms of experience — from Kant's "theory of
knowledge" is to deprive the transcendental turn of its very force, its
interest in defending such forms of "our" mental activity as forms of
knowledge. In sum, transcendental formalism *is* a "meta-level" analysis
of the modes of knowledge, but must *thereby* be an account of *our* way of
understanding knowledge of objective reality, and *because* of this restriction in standpoint, also must include an attempt at some defense of these
formal, nonderived rules, *as* forms of knowledge, as more than merely
"our" ways of organizing and discriminating experience. That *quid iuris*
question forces any epistemology to show that certain claims about
objective reality, when properly understood and delineated, are well
founded; to do that, something, however indirectly and subjectively
based, must be said about objective reality, just so that we do know that
certain kinds of claims are justified; and, for Kant, this demands a
comprehensive attempt to determine what can count as experience of
objective reality "for us."[3]

To accomplish this task, however, raises, as we have seen, endless
complications involving the subjective status of our rules for understanding objective reality. If we do attempt to defend some synthetic a priori
judgment by appealing in some complex way to how we understand (or
even "must understand") objective reality, then, we have asked here in a
variety of ways, how *do* we also establish that these "ways" or forms
correctly discriminate, or prescribe an *objective* order to nature? When
the problem is posed in this way, we are naturally led to one of the most
familiar interpretations prominent in many commentators who take
Kant's notion of subjective forms as seriously as has been done here —
that these subjective modes of understanding are "imposed" necessarily
on experience, that the *mind* imposes *its* own rules of unification on any
material contributed by sensory experience.

I have tried to argue that transcendental idealism, when interpreted as
formal idealism, is not only a central aspect of Kant's theory, but that the
above general arguments for such an "idealism" are quite reasonable.
However, I have also suggested that the above "imposition" model is too
simplistic to express adequately how Kant wants to argue for the "objectivity" of our "subjective" understanding of reality. These objections to
the "imposition" can now be summarized as follows.[4]

In the first place, we must be careful in any talk about the structure of

3. In effect, Kant's epistemology thus rejects both strategies open to him as possible
responses to the *quid iuris* question: "foundationalist" approaches in the empiricist tradition, and the search for a supreme "guarantor" of some kind of our "ideas."
4. I am concerned here with objections to this notion as a correct interpretation of Kant.
There are, of course, objections which can be raised directly against the very notion. See
J. Bennett, *Kant's Dialectic* (Cambridge, Cambridge Univeristy Press, 1974), p. 54 ff.

the "mind" being imposed on reality, and careful about understanding the relation between forms of thought and intuition and the mind. Kant does want to interpret the formal structure of our understanding of objective reality as "subjective," that is, as defensible only as "human," and so as a restricted mode of understanding. But he does not thereby understand these forms as "mental" dispositions, or structures of the mind. As was clear in chapters 3 and 4, Kant is interested in rules for conceptual *activity,* the forms of objective judgment, and this interest allows him, so he believes, to be neutral metaphysically about "what it is" which thinks, or about the "metaphysical" status of these forms. Likewise, in chapter 6, it was apparent that when Kant calls the unity of apperception required for any experience "formal" he means to assert only *that* judgment, or any cognitive activity, and so any experience, would not be possible unless elements of consciousness were brought to a unity. This expresses a formal demand or a "supreme law" for what must be *done,* and, again, does not express any claim about the mind as some special, perhaps nonmaterial object. A claim about what, intellectually, we do is not the same as a claim about what the mind is, and the forms of such activity are thus not special mental objects, a special mental structure, or dispositions, or psychological laws, but rules, normative restrictions on various activities ("whatever" the mental subject of those activities is).[5]

Now, of course, from the Dissertation on, Kant does speak of laws of the mind (*Gemüt*), but in those contexts he is almost always thinking of the mind just as *Spontaneität,* as intuiting and judging activity. The Paralogisms supply ample evidence of this desire not to follow, let us say, the Cartesian route in philosophy, where a priori concern with what can and cannot be known ended up as a metaphysical theory about the mind (as mental substance) which knows and about "its" objects. Kant claims to be interested in the structure of knowing, not in the knowing subject.[6]

However, it must be quickly admitted that this kind of interpretation and defense of Kant's understanding of subjective forms is quite limited. Some of those limitations were apparent in his account of the formal nature of the unity of apperception, and especially in his attempt to distinguish apperception from self-knowledge. More broadly, however, Kant's account of mental activity must be committed to *some* claim about

5. The tendency to speak in "mentalistic" terms in interpreting Kant is prominent in Vaihinger, Kemp Smith, and Weldon, and is responsible, in part, for nineteenth-century psychologistic Kantianism. These erroneous interpretations are yet another reason to keep the formal nature of Kant's idealism prominently in mind, especially the analogy with the formalism of general logic.

6. This distinction is the central theme of the Paralogisms, particularly as restated in the second edition. See especially his introductory remarks B406–413, B421, and B426–28.

the *possibility* of such a unique type of activity, and those sorts of claims would necessarily be metaphysical, or substantive. That is, the whole notion of "following" a rule implies an ability to decide which (empirical) rule is to be followed and an ability to understand some empirical situation in terms of some a priori principle.[7] It is hard to see how a number of elements in Kant's theory could be preserved if, say, a materialist theory of mind, and especially cognitive activity, were true.[8] (It would be particularly difficult to explain the possibility of "judgment," as it was interpreted in chapter 5.) In other words, while Kant's theory itself is not, I believe, *about* the structure of the mind, it is true that some claim about the metaphysical possibility of cognitive activity is assumed by that theory.

The relationship between such assumptions and transcendental philosophy itself is not, I admit, pellucid. There is, though, quite a bit of evidence that Kant himself was at least willing to speculate about that relationship and even occasionally to attempt some bridge between the speculative requirements for his transcendental philosophy, and his practical philosophy. That bridge depends on the notion of "freedom" required for the cognitive understanding of *Spontaneität* to be consistent.[9] I won't pursue that connection here, except to suggest that even though Kant's view of the forms of mental activity is intended to be a metaphysically neutral understanding of rules, a complete account would have to include some explanation of the subject of thinking. Moreover, just that requirement alone demonstrates one significant area, quite important for the German Idealists after Kant, where an "epistemological theory" depends on "metaphysical" presuppositions (or is itself a kind of metaphysics).[10]

7. At least, on Kant's understanding of "following a rule," however that notion is understood by others. It is apparent throughout Kant's account that for him the normative dimension to questions of knowledge always prevents a psychologistic (or behavioristic) "reduction" of such questions.

8. Cf. again though some alternative suggestions in Sellars's ". . . the I or he or it which thinks . . . ," *Proceedings and Addresses of the APA* 44 (September 1971): 11 ff.

9. Such speculation begins at a footnote to B158, where Kant discusses "representing" myself as "Intelligenz." He continues to argue that man's capacity for apperception itself establishes that he is "a purely intelligible object" at B575–A547, and recalls the same kind of argument, but again without much development, in the *Grundlegung, Gesammelte Schriften*, vol. 5, pp. 447–48 and especially p. 452. Exactly how Kant wants to make this bridge from his theoretical to his practical philosophy is obscure, and he himself, some commentators argue, drops the attempt by the time of the *Second Critique*. There is an analysis of the attempt in R. P. Wolff, *The Autonomy of Reason* (New York: Harper & Row, 1973), p. 9 ff., but Wolff's account is quite speculative and does not, I think, establish a connection between transcendental apperception and moral freedom.

10. There is a clear link in German philosophy after Kant, especially throughout the work of Fichte and Hegel, established by a common attention to the implications of defining

But the "mind-imposed unity" model is simplistic not only because of the metaphysically neutral notion of intellectual activity at the heart of Kant's project, but mainly because of the limitations of the "imposition" metaphor itself. Kant's frequent formulations notwithstanding, it is especially clear from his account of "transcendental judgment," as interpreted here in chapter 5, and from the second part of the Deduction, as presented in chapter 6, that Kant does not think that subjective rules of unification are imposed on the material of sensation and in any direct or simplistic way determine objective reality for us, "be the real world as it may." The error of this view was also, I believe, clear from close attention to what is and is not implied by his appearance/thing-in-itself doctrine, as presented here in chapter 7, and by considering the difference between *admittedly* "imposed" regulative ideas and the quite different explanations for conditions for the possibility of experience.

What, in general, distinguishes his position on form from that imposition interpretation is a twofold qualification. In the first place, Kant does argue that our understanding of the general structure of phenomenal reality can only be defended as "our" understanding of such reality, but he goes on to show that and why no other possible account of experience *could* account for the unity of apperception essential to any experience. Kant's attempt at comprehensiveness, both with regard to our forms of thought and especially our forms of intuition, is an attempt to exclude regarding pure forms of experience as one of many possible ways of organizing experience which we just happen to possess and "blindly" impose. Of course, everything thus depends on how, by appeal to what, he means to exclude the other options as "transcendentally" if not logically impossible, and we argued that there were serious problems with that attempt. But his intentions are, at any rate, straightforward. As the B138 passage makes clear, if he can establish not just what "I require" in order to know an object, but what is required for *anything* to be an object, then it will have been established that such formal unity is not imposed on our experience, but expresses the structure any experience of an object could have. In this sense, if such a comprehensive perspective could be attained, then it could be said that our forms of experience just *are* the only terms in which "relation to objects" could be established by human knowers. This formal unity is not imposed; it just is the only type of unity we could understand in our experience.

But besides the attempt at comprehensiveness — or more correctly as an important, unique feature of that case — we have Kant's intriguing

---

man's rational nature as *Spontaneität*. It is prominent in Fichte's early (1794) discussions of *Tathandlung* and is central to any understanding of Hegel's notion of *Geist*. For more on the issue, see W. Janke, *Fichte: Sein und Reflexion* (Berlin: de Gruyter, 1970), p. 69 ff., and Dieter Henrich *Fichtes ursprüngliche Einsicht* (Frankfurt: Vittorio Klostermann, 1967).

account of judgment (*Urteilskraft*) as further evidence against the imposition model. I suggested above that Kant *intends* both transcendental and
empirical judgment to account for the application of concepts, and so to
distinguish this application from simple imposition. Although Kant's
theory of judgment has been quite neglected in commentaries, it not only
provides, I have suggested, an attempt at avoiding the "subjectivist" and
"constructivist" interpretations of the relation between the form and
content of experience, but also reveals a serious instability in the under-
standing/sensibility distinction so very essential to the *Critique*. Being
able to provide a "schema" for both pure and empirical concepts *would*
establish the relation between concepts and objects in a way based on
some view of both objects of intuition and concepts (and thus again
would distinguish a "guided" application from imposition). But Kant
cannot, I also suggested, carry out this demand without a serious qualification on fundamental presuppositions elsewhere in the *Critique*. Instead, Kant either reverts to his even more obscure theory of pure
intuition (which itself stresses all over again a more constructivist theory
of phenomenal unity)[11] or mysteriously hints at a hidden art lying in the
depths of the human soul. In short, the schematism and the theory of
transcendental judgment should be the center of any correctly Kantian
understanding of the subjective status of forms of intuition, and of their
application, and it does clearly evidence Kant's intention to avoid the
"imposition" interpretation, but it fails to support the weight of so much
of the critical edifice. It must be admitted, though, that however much
attention to these dimensions of Kant's theory of form can help to clarify
his intentions, and establish the proper context for evaluating his results,
it also begins immediately to reraise many of the problems which often
occurred in preceding chapters. Indeed, a summary look at those problems suggests at least two general, continually apparent difficulties with
Kant's formal methodology.

2. Kantian Difficulties

The first set of problems stems directly from Kant's claim about the
priority and independence of transcendental philosophy itself. He argues
that any individual claim to know, whether in metaphysics or science, is
intelligible not only in terms of rules which determine what could count
as knowledge or not, that we could not determine truth and error on the
basis of evidence and argument except in terms of rules for what counts
as evidence in the first place. But in order to know what could or couldn't
be known in general, a transcendental foundation for all knowledge must
be laid, and the limits of knowledge thereby established prior to, and

11. Cf. chap. 3, p. 84 ff.

independent of, actual attempts to know. But conceived in even this abstract way, it is obvious that, somewhere, Kant will have to face the problem of what we *do* have to "know" in order to specify, with the authority of necessity and universality, the forms or modes for any knowledge claim. Knowing in general both *that* there are, necessarily, subjective forms of experience, knowable a priori, and knowing determinately *what* they are, raise the problem of what such knowledge of forms is "based on," what is "appealed to" in order to establish them.

The second problem arises once we accept some provisional version of Kant's formal idealism. If we accept his claim that his idealism is not wholly "constitutive" (in the sense in which Kant himself seems to have regarded Fichte's),[12] but that the forms of experience must be applied to an empirically apprehended "matter," then we need to provide some less metaphorical interpretation of just what this relationship consists in. That is, I have argued, Kant's theory of *empirical knowledge* is quite an important feature of his transcendental enterprise; or, at least, until we understand it throroughly, we will not have understood his notion of form.

The first problem is especially important in trying to understand just how "transcendental philosophy" differs from traditional philosophic methodology. After all, Kant claims that the *Critique* just *is* an essay on methodology, and its manner of achieving its formal results is intended to be a radical departure from the attempts at synthetic a priori knowledge (and the attempts at an exhaustive denial of the possibility of such knowledge), prior to this attempt. Accordingly, it is even more important to understand, in some general, "strategic" way, *how* Kant means to establish his "merely" formal a priori results, especially because he still intends those results to *answer* many of the questions posed by his predecessors. That is, when he says that his transcendental methodology will achieve "more success" in the tasks of metaphysics, he does not only mean that it will place traditional metaphysical questions in their proper "practical" or regulative context,[13] but also that the *Critique* itself will provide an interpretation directly responsive to many such traditional questions (e.g., the nature of space and time, the problems of substance, permanence, alteration, causality, actuality, necessity, etc.)

In this sense, it could certainly be said that Kant is indeed still interested in providing some general *explanation* for, speaking quite broadly now, "why things are as they are." Now, to be sure, a good deal

12. Kant's most famous denunciation of any Fichtean interpretation of idealism occurs in his open letter of 7 August 1799.

13. Krüger in "Der Masstab der kantischen Kritik," in *Philosophie und Moral in der kantischen Kritik* (Tübingen: J. C. B. Mohr, 1967), goes so far as to claim that "die Kritik auf einer theologischen Metaphysik der Welt berüht" (p. 248).

of his most explicit attempts to deal with that kind of a question directly involve him in problems of teleology, but teleology is meant to explain the order and systematic unity of different aspects of part of nature, and Kant is interested as well in explaining or accounting for the formal structure of nature itself, understood as any object of experience, prior to a concern with the systematic unity of various natural laws.[14] To offer such an explanation, however, he argues for a Copernican revolution in philosophy, a transcendental turn to issues of prior importance in methodological terms than had been appreciated by much of the tradition. His theory in this way will present a new *type* of philosophic explanation, self-consciously different from that offered by, especially, the most important representatives of the two previous modern examples of such explanation, Leibniz and Hume. Simply put, he replaces Leibniz's appeal to God and the Principle of Sufficient Reason as an "explanation" for why, in general, the world is as it is (or is at all), and not some other way. Leibniz had offered that explanation to account for the difference between logical possibility and reality, to *account* for the difference between how things might have been and how they are. At the heart of Kant's theory, on the other hand, is a more complicated difference between logical possibility and "real possibility," an a priori determination of what could be possible *for us*. This formulation of the really possible also counters the antimetaphysical attack of Hume, who had argued that an understanding of nature could only occur actually, in terms of empirical experience alone; that no a priori reflection about the "ground" of nature was possible. In other words, Kant follows Leibniz in denying that our explanations of nature, as philosophers, need be exclusively tied to a theory about the actual apprehension of nature, but he replaces a metaphysical appeal to God, sufficient reason, compossibility, and so forth with this account of what is "really possible" for us.

   And of course, all our difficulties have arisen in trying to specify just how this "real possibility" is to be determined and defended. As we have seen, Kant intends to argue that an initial, independent, formal reflection

14. On this point, compare Gerd Buchdahl, *Metaphysics and the Philosophy of Science* (Cambridge: M.I.T. Press, 1969), pp. 20–62, and Hans Graubner, *Form und Wesen* (Bonn: Bouvier, 1972), pp. 59–92. In more traditional terms, Kant's revolution involves a complicated reassessment of the relation between the notions of a *ratio cognescendi* and a *ratio essendi*. The traditional understanding of that relation had allowed Descrartes to doubt whether our being able to *conceive* the soul clearly and distinctly as a separate, nonextended substance allowed us to say that the soul *was* such a substance. Kant wants to argue in a roughly similar way that we could *only* understand the experienceable world as, say, causally ordered, but to claim as well that establishing such an "only" *counts* as providing a *ratio essendi* for the phenomenal world, as proving that it *is* so ordered. To establish the latter in effect involves him in arguing *for* the transcendental turn, a difficult methodological task, as has been apparent at a number of points in the preceding.

on what could or couldn't be known by humans sets the "limits" of real
possibility, and thus by understanding exhaustively the forms of our
experience, we are able to understand, at least in some initial way, why
nature is as it is, "for us." We do not know why our forms of experience
are as they are, but we do know that understanding such a formal
structure *is* what accounts for such reality (again "for us"); that it does so
more satisfactorily than any appeal to a "supreme" ground of all being,
and more consistently than any account based on actual experience alone.
Kant, in the middle between these two positions, so he thinks, argues
that if the forms of any experience can be determined and established as
necessary conditions for any experience then no appeal to a metaphysical
ground of explanation *is needed* to counter doubts about the status of
these forms, *and* thus no skepticism results as a consequence of the
absence of such an appeal. The possibility of experience, or a rational
determination of real possibility, allows us to say that "for us" the
conditions for the possibility of experience are at the same time the
conditions for the possibility of objects of experience, or, recalling his
formulation in "Von einem neuerdings erhobenen Ton in der Philosophie," "*forma dat esse rei,*" where such forms are understood as our
forms of experience.[15] Thus, in sum, reflection on what could be known
by us, if that is possible, *is* a determination of what nature or being is like
for us, because it can be shown that such forms of experience comprehensively restrict any understanding of nature we could have. A philosophic
explanation of what there is can thus be shifted from a "divine" perspective to a human one without falling victim to an empirical skepticism, or
some merely pragmatic or conventional explanation for, and defense of,
our understanding of nature.

It is this line of argument which raised the question of the "ground" for
these forms of knowledge themselves, that to which we appeal to determine (to *know*) what they are. In general, establishing such forms
determinately by appeal to what is presupposed by "experience" always
runs a great risk, as we have seen, of begging the whole question of
"necessary" conditions by assuming a concept of experience which would
presuppose them. Attempting to begin with some minimal notion of
"being aware," on the other hand, runs the risk of ending up maintaining

15. When, however, Kant argues that "in der Form besteht das Wesen der Sache," he is
consciously restricting his understanding of what *Form* will account for (*Wesen*), and
implicitly denying the other traditional formula, "forma est differentia specifica." That is, as
Graubner puts it, "auf der transzendentalen Form beruht das 'esse' des Erscheinungsdinges.
Der Satz, 'forma est differentia specifica' aber kann in dieser Philosophie keine Beziehung
auf das 'esse rei,' also keinen ontologischen Sinn mehr behaupten" (*Form und Wesen*,
p. 52). Graubner does not, though, go on to ask what does account for such a "differentia
specifica."

that all forms of experience require objectivity rules, or forms of knowledge, even experience which *is not* "knowledge." Finally, any simplistic resort to the imposition metaphor is inconsistent with much of what Kant says about his results.[16]

But this problem arose in a number of specific contexts as well. We found it hard to understand, for example, just how appeals to "pure intuition" were to establish *determinately* the legitimacy of any mathematical concept. Kant's commitment to prior-to-experience "constructability" or even intuitability, construed broadly, seemed quite abstract and so tenuously tied to some related account of the forms of sensibility as to end up quite an empty explanation. There was in short, *no* explanation for the source of, or limits for, constructability or intuitability itself. And, I have maintained, such a problem is not, as it is often interpreted, simply a consequence of an archaic Kantian commitment to "sensible picturability" as a criterion for mathematical legitimacy, but must be seen directly as a consequence of the self-imposed limits of his formal methodology itself.

This problem about the origin of specific forms was even clearer in the case of empirical concepts. Given Kant's understanding of formality, such an explanation could establish the general legitimacy of, say, the use of the concept of cause or substance in the formal organization and explanation of the empirically apprehended world, but the situation is quite indeterminate and confusing beyond that. This particular issue raised quite well the overall problem of where to "stop" in "giving an account of" (a "by what right" defense of) *our* "modes of knowledge." Kant seems to think that a philosophic explanation is adequate when the general rules for any concept-acquisition are given, but, as I tried to show in chapter 4, too many other issues are involved for that limitation to be reasonable. In that discussion particularly, there was a difference between understanding the role of some rule of recognition in our knowledge and understanding why any particular rule should *count* as a rule for knowledge of the empirical world. Such a "warrant" for legitimate entry into the conceptual order seemed to require a more extensive explanation than Kant's formal discussion of categories and regulative ideas allows. Many of the problems he himself raises are inadequately dealt with if he "stops" his account of "our mode of knowledge" at such a formal level.[17]

16. I think, but cannot here demonstrate, that similar kinds of problems in transcendental reasoning occur in more contemporary versions of "what must be the case arguments," e.g., the private language argument, or various transcendental arguments in Strawson and Shoemaker. For a general discussion of some of these problems (although a discussion weak on Kant and his idealism) see Ross Harrison, *What There Must Be* (Oxford: Clarendon Press, 1974), especially the first two chapters, pp. 1–50.

17. L. Wittgenstein, *Blue and Brown Books* (New York: Harper & Row, 1958), suggest a

This problem was also clearly present in chapter 5, where, as indicated in the preceding section, Kant's account of judgment most clearly indicates that some kind of knowledge of such a "warrant" is required not only in order to know that a rule *is* a "correct" rule, but also to know how to "apply" such empirical rules. Finally, the whole issue is most apparent where the legislation and even imposition metaphors are strongest, in the account of regulative ideas. Thus, in general, *how* and especially by what right we "come up with," and correctly use, pure intuitions, concepts, schemata, and ideas must remain quite dark, so long as our philosophic attention is restricted to our "modes" or forms of knowledge alone.

Indeed, at the heart of this problem, sensibility and understanding are understood as such a strict dichotomy by Kant that the second major problem in his transcendental methodology was often apparent — how we are to understand the relation between the forms and the matter of experience. Virtually every aspect of his account of the matter of experience is understood wholly in terms of his formal presumptions, making it hard to understand such notions as sensory guidedness, the relation between pure and empirical intuition, the application of concepts in judgment, the difference between inner awareness and apperception, and the conformity of nature to regulative ideas. In sum, however much Kant intends to avoid the "imposition" interpretation, it is still the case that, to use his own favorite metaphor for his formalism, reason legislates to nature, or even commands to nature, *so* formally, so independently of any "material" reflection about nature, that the very possibility of "obedience" to such laws, or the role of reason's "subjects" in formulating them

---

solution to this problem. He writes at p. 5: "The mistake we are liable to make could be expressed thus: We are looking for the use of a sign, but we look for it as though it were an object coexisting with the sign. (One of the reasons for this mistake is again that we are looking for a 'thing corresponding to a substantive.')" Indeed, Wittgeinstein's whole attempt in this section of the *Blue Book* is to deny that explaining "following a rule" (of language) requires any prior image or intermediate entity or "seeing" that which allows us to formulate the rule. Following a rule is thus something we do, and is not like applying *something*. So, the notion of rule is not meant to account for such a standard; it is just meant, if correctly understood, to show how senseless asking for such a standard is.

But it doesn't seem to me that this is what we have done. We have not made the mistake of looking for the "use" of a rule as if *it,* or the rule itself were "a substantive." We have asked instead for an explanation of the *ground* for the rule's acquisition (and use) and an explanation of this rule's relation to judgment. Neither question confuses a rule's use *with* a substantive; both just ask how *that use* can be *explained* without such a substantive. Further, it has been shown that (at least) *Kant's own case* for rules cannot go through without such an explanation. The use of rules in Kant occurs in judgment and it is this, above all, which requires some account of how rules for such judgments are (nonarbitrarily) acquired and how we explain their possession and application. For more on the relation between Kant and Wittgenstein, see Hubert Schwyzer, "Thought and Reality: The Metaphysics of Kant and Wittgenstein," *The Philosophical Quarterly* 23 (1973).

seem considerations much too abstractly excluded. It is not incidental, I would suggest, that something of the same problem can be said to emerge in Kant's moral, aesthetic, and teleological formalism.

However, I do not want here to recapitulate the individual difficulties of the preceding chapters, nor to venture into the relation between those problems and other aspects of Kant's formalism. I think it has been established that many of those theoretical problems are consequences of Kant's formal methodology itself, his attempt to specify a priori, formally, independently of any material or metaphysical commitments, the subjective structure of our experience of the world. The ground appealed to in order to establish these forms, and the problem of how we are to understand the application of such conditions, are both questions that at least strongly suggest, I think, that Kant's account, limited as it is to an exclusive concern with our "modes of knowledge," itself requires a more complicated account of the relation between form and a perhaps metaphysical "content" then his transcendental methodology allows. However, whatever difficulties are inherent in that methodology, attention to the formal nature of that enterprise has also shown that those difficulties are not those of a phenomenalistic idealism, theories of "mind-constructed nature," psychologistic epistemologies, or strictly conceptual, analytic versions of transcendentalism.

Admittedly, of course, the idea of "breaking down" Kant's sensibility/understanding dualism, or "opening the door" to a fuller explanation of the substantive or metaphysical foundation for pure intuition, concept, schema, and idea, or even just recognizing the necessity for a substantive account of the subject which thinks rather than just the rules of its thinking, are all fairly abstract conclusions to draw from the problems presented here. One might admit, to paraphrase one recent reviewer of Sellars' Kantianism, that the "epistemological chicken" *did* "hatch out of the metaphysical egg,"[18] that our philosophic knowledge of "basic principles" is not *based* on a reflection on the rules of language or thought, but, in some complicated way, that *the situation is the other way around,* and still reasonably ask what such an admission comes to concretely, particularly if such reflection is to be more substantive, to require more direct metaphysical commitments — to mathematical objects, sets, abstract entities, natural kinds, minds, the whole — than Kant's admission about regulative ideas allows. I cannot, of course, provide such an answer here, and can only repeat that this kind of reflection on the limitations of Kant's methodology can itself only be regarded as a "Prolegomena" to any future metaphysics. One can,

18. Keith Lehrer, review of *Science, Perception and Reality, Journal of Philosophy* 43 (1966): p. 277.

though, appreciate the force of the whole problematic presented here by noticing, in conclusion, the philosophic legacy left by Kant's enterprise and the persistence of those limitations.

3. Kant's Legacy

"The Father of Modern Philosophy," it is said, is Descartes. To a large extent, such a characterization is meant to express the influential, indeed founding role of Descartes in the "epistemological turn" so overwhelmingly influential since his time — the turn to epistemology *as* the center of philosophy itself, or to a theoretical philosophy everywhere determined and restricted by prior, independent reflection on what is or could be known. Descartes's obvious distate for scholastic dogmatism led him to philosophize one step earlier, methodologically, than much of the tradition, with a prior concern for the nature and possibilities of knowledge itself. However, as was apparent at a number of points in the preceding discussion of Kant's similar interests, such a concern, precisely because it originates in a radical doubt, or uncertainty about what can be known, immediately *itself* faces the problem of securing some foundation for its results. To claim that we *cannot* know final causes, or the nature of the soul, and not just that the various arguments thus far presented in philosophy do not establish such conclusions, means that some formal determination of the nature of knowledge itself must be presented, *and* some defense offered for claims about what, in general, can be known. Descartes's inability to complete the "epistemological" turn systematically is obvious at just that point however. Depending on how one interprets his sincerity,[19] he either had to appeal to God to support such claims as knowledge of continuing existence, the external world, or even the veracity of the criterion of knowledge itself, clarity and distinctness (an appeal which clearly reraises the issue of by what right we can claim to *know* God's existence and his goodness, and thus the impossible circularity problem), or he must appeal to noncognitive "reasons" for the adoption of certain standards for knowledge and no others, wholly practical reasons, based on the *teachings* of nature and not the *lumen naturale*.

It is Kant who attempted the resolution of the problems implied by any insistence on "epistemological priority," and who thus richly deserves Hegel's description as "the Enlightenment made methodical."[20] The foundation for our modes of organizing and discriminating the world

19. On the problem of just how Descartes does "ground" his epistemology, see Hiram Caton, *The Origin of Subjectivity* (New Haven: Yale University Press, 1973).

20. G. W. F. Hegel, *Vorlesungen über die Geschichte der Philosophie, Werke,* vol. 20 (Frankfurt: Suhrkamp, 1971), p. 333.

could be sought in the discoverable requirements for any experience whatsoever. In this sense it could fairly be said that Kant's most influential legacy to philosophy is just the problematic of critical philosophy itself.

By problematic, I mean that any conception of methodology which considers itself initially critical, which begins with an independent attempt to determine the forms of our knowledge, the limits on possible meaning in discourse, must face many of the same problems faced by Kant. More specifically, such enterprises must offer some independent reasons for accepting some account of our modes of intellectual activity or speech as modes of possible knowledge or meaningfulness if some *general* restriction about what can and cannot be known is to be established. Indeed, the same problematic emerges in the most prominent contemporary manifestation of Kant's transcendentalism, the "Linguistic Turn," where the questions shift to a determination of the possible meaning of discourse.[21] There too, at least *if* we want to avoid merely describing various standards for various types of discourse, or the difficulties now well known in verificationist defenses for theories of meaning, or conventionalist theories of such standards, or pragmatic, wholly noncognitive, Carnapean defenses of such external criteria, then we again face the problems of formalism and comprehensiveness apparent at so many crucial points in Kant. The broad problem at stake in all such critical enterprises is how to determine *in general* proper "account-giving" in philosophy, and indeed in all knowledge or discourse. To make such a determination implies some sort of comprehensive perspective on what can or cannot be said, or known; to know *that* is quite a different thing from knowing any one element in terms of some standard for knowledge or to say any one thing meaningfully by virtue of some criterion for meaningfulness. I have suggested that, however important and interesting many of Kant's reflections on the problem of form are, this comprehensiveness is not attained. This is true with respect to the large-scale strategy of the Deduction as well as with respect to his attempts to argue for what could and could not be known through sensation, a determination of the ground of intuitive knowledge in mathematics, his theory of empirical concepts, and in other specific arguments.

Now, certainly, none of this means that it follows that, given the difficulties of establishing such formal limits, it must be possible, a fortiori, to know what Kant said we couldn't — God, an infinite series, the soul, and so forth. In fact, many of Kant's most persuasive arguments

21. I have tried to indicate the relevance of these problems in Kant to the Linguistic Turn in my "Critical Methodology and Comprehensiveness in Philosophy," *Metaphilosophy* 9 (1978): 197–211.

in the Transcendental Dialectic, while they refer to his notion of the limits of experience, are often based on a direct consideration of arguments for the soul or God, and it would still be true that any claim in philosophy to know anything would still be subject to the same type of internal "criticism." More important, though, it would *also* not follow that, given the problem in Kant's attempt at a formal delineation of the structure of all human experience, such an attempt at "comprehensiveness" itself should be abandoned. It is still the case that the intelligibility of any one element of our experience or discourse is so only in the light of, if you will, "intelligibility" as such, and for philosophy to lose sight totally of "the whole" structure of possible intelligibility in this or any other sense, would be quite indefensibly myopic.[22]

At least, that guiding assumption about the necessity for some such account of the comprehensive features of experience has been quite prominent in another tradition in philosophy heavily indebted to Kant. Thus far, the major Kantian element identifiable in post-Kantian (and especially Anglo-American, or analytic) philosophic methodologies has been the assumption that a determination of what could or could not be a meaningful assertion could, in advance as it were, let us know what could or could not be a legitimate philosophical, moral, religious, or scientific question. I have suggested, though hardly demonstrated, that many of the problems encountered here with Kant might develop as well, in different ways, in attempts to determine formally and comprehensively such Kantian-like limits. However, there were several attempts, mostly in the European tradition after Kant, to deal with this problem directly, and to transform the Kantian methodology at its foundation in order to deal with it.

For example, although a great many of Hegel's claims about "Absolute Knowledge" are often taken to be claims for a knowledge of some God-like "Absolute Spirit," it seems to me that many of those formulations can better be seen as an intensification of Kant's problem, as developed here, with an "absolute standpoint," a point of view, or perspective, by virtue of which intelligibility itself could be uncovered and defended, and from which the unity of all forms of "spiritual" activity could be understood. Hegel's enterprise could thus be seen as a direct attempt to solve many of the problems of "formalism" in Kant's enterprise, both by arguing for a different, more intimate connection between the speculative role of reason and the analytic function of the understanding than did Kant, and by trying to solve the problem of the "ground" of form by the introduction of the broader notion of "negative activity" (Hegel's version of *Spontaneität,*) or finally the "history" of spirit as a way of accounting for the origin, determinacy, and extent of such forms.[23]

22. Ibid., 208 ff.
23. The relation between Hegel and Kant is of course much more complicated that can

But such suggestions about the persistence of Kant's problematic can at this point only serve as proposals for further interpretation. While the problem of formalism is, I think, by far the most important in understanding German Idealism, and especially in helping to establish the legitimacy of its idealistic concerns, no such detailed demonstration can be given here.[24] I've wanted to establish how important the problem of form is in correctly understanding the nature of transcendental philosophy, how difficult that notion has proven to be in Kant, and how difficult it can be in successors working directly in the tradition of his Copernican revolution. Finally, that is, I think it can fairly be said that Kant's theory of form, and especially the limitations of that theory, simply set the agenda for any philosophy influenced in any way by his extraordinary turn to the activities of the transcendental subject as the proper object of philosophic reflection.

---

be indicated here. I have tried to spell out that connection in more detail in my "Hegel's Phenomenological Criticism," and have tried to suggest how some of Kant's problems linger on in Hegel's *Science of Logic* in my "Hegel's Metaphysics and the Problem of Contradiction," *Journal of the History of Philosophy* 16 (1978): 301–312.

The best treatments known to me of Hegel's "formalism" occur in Dieter Henrich, "Hegels Logik der Reflexion," in *Hegel im Kontext* (Frankfurt: Suhrkamp, 1967), p. 95 ff, and Peter Rohs, *Form und Grund* (Bonn: Bouvier, 1969). Finally, the problems inherent in any attempt at a comprehensive understanding of the "whole" of human experience are self-consciously taken up by Heidegger when he distinguishes between "ontological" and "ontic" concerns. The obvious ancestor for such a distinction is Kant on "transcendental" and "empirical."

24. It is also the issue which informs much early discussion in phenomenology about a "material" a priori, particularly in Scheler, Lask, Reinach, and, of course, Husserl.

Bibliography

PRIMARY TEXTS

Kant, Immanuel. *Critique of Pure Reason,* trans. N. Kemp Smith. New York: St. Martin's Press, 1929.
———. *Kant's gesammelte Schriften,* ed. Königlich Preussischen Akademie der Wissenschaften. Berlin, Leipzig: de Gruyter, 1922.
———. *Kritik der reinen Vernunft,* ed. R. Schmidt. Hamburg: Felix Meiner, 1954.
———. *Prolegomena to Any Future Metaphysics,* trans. L. W. Beck. Indianapolis: Bobbs-Merrrill, 1950.
———. *Werke in sechs Bände,* ed. W. Weischedel. Wiesbaden: Insel, 1960.

SECONDARY LITERATURE

Adickes, Erich. *Kant als Naturforscher,* 2 vols. Berlin: de Gruyter, 1924.
———. *Kants Lehre von doppelten Affektion unseres Ich als Schlüssel zu seiner Erkenntnistheorie.* Tübingen: J. C. B. Mohr, 1929.
———. *Kant und das Ding an sich.* Berlin: Pan, 1924–25.
Allison, Henry E. "Kant's Concept of the Transcendental Object," *Kant-Studien* 59 (1968): 165–86.
———. "Kant's Critique of Berkeley," *Journal of the History of Philosophy* 11 (1973): 232–44.
———. "Kant's Refutation of Realism," *Dialectica* 30 (1976): 223–53.
———. "Kant's Transcendental Humanism," *The Monist* 55, no. 2 (April 1971): 182–207.
———. *The Kant-Eberhard Controversy.* Baltimore: The Johns Hopkins University Press, 1974.
———. "The Non-Spatiality of Things in Themselves for Kant," *Journal of the History of Philosophy* 4 (1976): 313–21.
———. "Things in Themselves, Noumena, and Transcendental Objects," *Dialectica* 32 (1978): 61–76.
———. "Transcendental Affinity — Kant's Answer to Hume," *Proceedings of the Third International Kant Congress,* ed. L. W. Beck. Dordrecht: Reidel, 1972, pp. 203–11.
———. "Transcendental Idealism and Descriptive Metaphysics," *Kant-Studien* 60 (1969): 216–33.
Ameriks, Karl. "Kant's Transcendental Deduction as a Regressive Argument," *Kant-Studien* 69 (1978): 273–87.

234

Bibliography

Aquila, Richard. "Kant's Phenomenalism," *Idealistic Studies* 5 (1975): 108–26.

———. "Kant's Theory of Concepts," *Kant-Studien* 65 (1974): 1–19.

———."The Relationship between Pure and Empirical Intuition in Kant," *Kant-Studien* 68 (1977): 275–89.

———."Two Kinds of Transcendental Arguments in Kant," *Kant-Studien* 67 (1976): 1–19.

Ballauf, Theodor. *Über den Vorstellungsbegriff bei Kant.* Berlin: Verlag für Staatswissenschaft und Geschichte, 1938.

Barker, Stephen. "Appearing and Appearances," reprinted in *Kant Studies Today,* ed. L. W. Beck (see below), pp. 278–89.

Beck, Lewis White. "Can Kant's Synthetic Judgments Be Made Analytic?" reprinted in *Kant,* ed. R. P. Wolff (see below), pp. 3–22.

———. "Did the Sage of Königsberg Have No Dreams?" reprinted in *Essays on Kant and Hume* (see below), pp. 38–60.

———. *Early German Philosophy.* Cambridge: Harvard University Press, 1969.

———. *Essays on Kant and Hume.* New Haven: Yale University Press, 1978.

———. "Kant's Strategy," reprinted in *Essays on Kant and Hume* (see below), pp. 3–19.

———. (ed.) *Kant Studies Today.* La Salle, Ill.: Open Court, 1969.

———. "Kant's Theory of Definition," reprinted in *Kant,* ed. R. P. Wolff (see below), pp. 23–34.

———. (ed.) *Kant's Theory of Kowledge.* Boston: Reidel, 1974.

———. "Towards a Meta-Critique of Pure Reason," reprinted in *Essays on Kant and Hume* (see below), pp. 20–37.

Bennett, Jonathan. *Kant's Analytic.* Cambridge: Cambridge University Press, 1966.

———. *Kant's Dialectic.* Cambridge: Cambridge University Press, 1974.

———. "Strawson on Kant," *Philosophical Review* 77 (1968): 340–49.

Bird, Graham. *Kant's Theory of Knowledge.* New York: Humanities Press, 1973.

———. "Logik und Psychologie in der Transzendentalen Deduktion," *Kant-Studien* 56 (1965–66): 373–84.

———. "Recent Interpretations of Kant's Transcendental Deduction," *Akten des 4. Internationalen Kant-Kongress, Teil I* (1974): pp. 1–14.

Bossart, William. "Is Philosophy Transcendental?" *The Monist* 55, no. 2 (April 1971): 293–311.

Brittan, Gordon G., Jr. *Kant's Theory of Science.* Princeton: Princeton University Press, 1978.

Bröcker, Walter. *Kant über Metaphysik und Erfahrung.* Frankfurt: Klostermann, 1970.

Bubner, Rudiger. "Kant, Transcendental Arguments and the Problem of Deduction," *Review of Metaphysics* 28 (1975): 453–67.

———. "Zur Struktur eines Transzendentalen Arguments." *Akten des 4. Internationalen Kant-Kongress, Teil I* (1974), pp. 15–27.

Buchdahl, Gerd. *Metaphysics and the Philosophy of Science.* Cambridge: M.I.T. Press, 1969.

Caird, Edward. *The Critical Philosophy of Kant.* Glasgow: J. Maclehose, 1909.

Cassirer, Ernst. *Substance and Function.* Chicago: Dover, 1953.

Caton, Hiram. *The Origin of Subjectivity*. New Haven: Yale University Press, 1973.
Chipman, L. "Kant's Categories and Their Schematism," *Kant-Studien* 63 (1972): 36–50.
———. "Things in Themselves," *Philosophy and Phenomenological Research* 33 (1972–73): 489–502.
Clarke, Romane. "Sensuous Jugments," *Nous* 7 (1973): 45–56.
Cohen, Hermann. *Kants Theorie der Erfahrung*. Berlin: Dümmler, 1871 (2nd ed. 1885).
Collins, James. "Kant's Logic as a Critical Aid," *Review of Metaphysics* 30 (1977): 440–61.
Crawford, Patricia. "Kant's Theory of Philosophical Proof," *Kant-Studien* 53 (1961–62): 257–68.
Cummins, P. "Kant on Inner and Outer Intuition," *Nous* 2 (1968): 271–92.
Daval, Roger. *La Metaphysique de Kant*. Paris: Presses Universitaires de France, 1951.
Delekat, F. *Immanuel Kant*. Heidelberg: Quelle and Meyer, 1966 (2nd ed.).
de Vleeschauwer, H. J. *La Deduction transcendentale dans l'oeuvre de Kant*. Paris: La Hage, 1934–37.
Dryer, D. P. *Kant's Solution for Verification in Metaphysics*. London: Allen & Unwin, 1966.
Earman, John. "Kant, Incongruous Counterparts and the Nature of Space and Space-Time," *Ratio* 13 (1971): 1–18.
Ebbinghaus, Julius. "Kants Lehre von der Anschauung a priori," reprinted in *Kant*, ed. G. Prauss (see below), pp. 44–61.
Economos, John J. "Kant's Theory of Concepts," *Kant-Studien* 64 (1973): 63–70.
Fink, Eugen. *Alles und Nichts*. The Hague: Nijhoff, 1959.
Foster, L., and Swanson, J. W. (eds.) *Experience and Theory*. Amherst, Mass.: University of Massachusetts Press, 1970.
Friedman, Lawrence. "Kant's Theory of Time," *Review of Metaphysics* 7 (1954): 379–88.
Funke, Gerhard. "Der Weg zur ontologischen Kantinterpretation . . . Heinz Heimsoeths historisch-systematische Interpretation der kritizistischen kritik über Metaphysik," *Kant-Studien* 62 (1971): 446–66.
Garnett, Cristopher. *The Kantian Philosophy of Space*. New York: Columbia University Press, 1939.
Gram, Moltke. "Categories and Transcendental Arguments," *Man and World* 6 (1973): 252–69.
———. (ed.). *Disputed Questions*. Chicago: Quadrangle, 1967.
———. "How to Dispense with Things in Themselves (I)," *Ratio* 18 (1976): 1–15.
———. *Kant, Ontology, and the A Priori*. Evanston, Ill.: Northwestern University Press, 1968.
———. "Must Transcendental Arguments Be Spurious?" *Kant-Studien* 65 (1974): 304–17.
———. "Must We Revisit Transcendental Arguments?" *Philosophical Studies* 31 (1977): 235–48.
———. "The Crisis of Syntheticity: The Kant-Eberhard Controversy," *Kant-Studien* 71 (1980): 155–80.

———."The Myth of Double Affection," in *Reflections on Kant's Philosophy,* ed. W. Werkmeister (see below), pp. 29–26.

———. "Transcendental Arguments," *Nous* 5 (1971):15–26.

Graubner, Hans. *Form und Wesen: Ein Beitrag zur Deutung des Formbegriffs in Kants Kritik der reinen Vernunft.* Bonn: Bouvier, 1972.

Grayeff, Felix. *Deutung und Darstellung der theoretischen Philosophie Kants.* Hamburg: F. Meiner, 1966.

———."The Relationship of the Transcendental and Formal Logic," *Kant-Studien* 51 (1959): 349–52.

Griffiths, A. Phillips. "Transcendental Arguments (I)," *Proceedings of the Aristotelian Society* 43 (1969): 145–80.

Guyer, Paul. *"Identität und Objektivität,"* a review, *Journal of Philosophy* 76 (1979): 151–67.

———. "Kant on Apperception and A Priori Synthesis," *American Philosophical Quarterly* 17 (1980): 206–12.

Hacker, P. M. S. "Are Transcendental Arguments a Version of Verificationism?" *American Philosophical Quarterly* 9 (1972): 78–85.

Harrison, Ross. *On What There Must Be.* Oxford: The Clarendon Press, 1974.

———."Strawson on Outer Objects," *Philosophical Quarterly* 20 (1970): 213–21.

Hartmann, Klaus. "On Taking the Transcendental Turn," *Review of Metaphysics* 20 (1964): 223–49.

Hartmann, Nicolai. "Diesseits von Idealismus und Realismus," *Kant-Studien* 29 (1924): 160–206.

———. *Kleinere Schriften,* vol. 1–3. Berlin: de Gruyter, 1955–58.

———. "Wie ist kritische Ontologie überhaupt möglich?" in *Kleinere Schriften,* vol. 3 (see above), pp. 268–313.

Hegel, G. W. F. *Enzyklopädie der philosophischen Wissenschaften.* Hamburg: Felix Meiner, 1969.

———. *Glauben und Wissen,* in *Werke,* vol. 2. Frankfurt: Suhrkamp, 1970.

———. *Wissenschaft der Logik,* 2 vols. Hamburg: Felix Meiner, 1971.

Heidegger, Martin. *Being and Time,* trans. J. Marquarrie and E. Robinson. New York: Harper & Row, 1962.

———. *Kant and the Problem of Metaphysics,* trans. James S. Churchill. Bloomington: Indiana University Press, 1968.

———. *Kants These über das Sein.* Frankfurt: Vittorio Klostermann, 1963.

———. *What Is a Thing?* trans. W. B. Barton and Vera Deutsch. Chicago: H. Regnery, 1967.

Heidemann, Ingeborg. *Spontaneität und Zeitlichkeit.* Köln: Kölner Universität Verlag, 1958.

Heimsoeth, Heinz. "Metaphysical Motives in the Development of Critical Idealism," in *Kant: Disputed Questions,* ed. M. Gram (see above), pp. 158–99.

———. *Transzendentale Dialektik,* (4 vols.). Berlin: de Gruyter, 1969.

Henrich, Dieter. *Identität und Objektivität.* Heidelberg: Carl Winter Verlag, 1976.

———. *Fichtes ürsprungliche Einsicht.* Frankfurt: Vittoria Klostermann, 1967.

———. *Hegel im Kontext.* Frankfurt: Suhrkamp, 1967.

————. "Hegels Logik der Reflexion," in *Hegel im Kontext* (see above), pp. 95–156.

————. "The Proof Structure of Kant's Transcendental Deduction," *Review of Metaphysics* 88 (1969): 640–59.

————. "Über die Einheit der Subjektivität," *Philosophische Rundschau* 3 (1955): 28–69.

————. "Zur theoretische Philosophie Kants," *Philosophische Rundschau* 1 (1953): 124–49.

Herring, T. *Das Problem der Affektion bei Kant.* Köln: Kölner Universitäts-Verlag, 1953.

Hinske, Norbert. "Die historische Vorlagen der kantischen Transzendentalen Philosophie," *Archiv für Begriffsgeschichte* 12 (1968): 86–113.

————. "Kants Begriff der Transzendentalen und die Problematik seiner Begriffsgeschichte," *Kant-Studien* 64 (1973): 56–62.

Hintikka, Jaakko. "An Analysis of Analyticity," in *Deskription, Analytizität und Existenz*, ed. Paul Weingartner (see below), pp. 193–214.

————. "Are Logical Truths Tautologies?" in *Deskription, Analytizität und Existenz*, ed. Paul Weingartner (see below), pp. 215–33.

————. "Kant and the Tradition of Analysis," in *Deskription, Analytizität und Existenz*, ed. Paul Weingartner (see below), pp. 254–72.

————. "Kantian Intuitions," *Inquiry* 15 (1972): 341–45.

————. "Kant on the Mathematical Method," reprinted in *Kant Studies Today*, ed. L. W. Beck (see above), pp. 117–40.

————. "Kant Vindicated," in *Deskription, Analytizität und Existenz*, ed. Paul Weingartner (see below), pp. 234–53.

————. "On Kant's Notion of Intuition (Anschauung)," in *The First Critique*, ed. T. Penelhum and J. J. MacIntosh (see below), pp. 38–53.

————. "Transcendental Arguments: Genuine and Spurious," *Nous* 6 (1972): 274–81.

Hoaglund, John. "The Thing in Itself in English Interpretations of Kant," *American Philosophical Quarterly* 10 (1973): 1–14.

Horkheimer, Max. "Traditional and Critical Theory," in *Critical Theory.* New York: Seabury Press, 1972, pp. 188–243.

Horstmann, R. P. "Space as Intuition and Geometry," *Ratio* 18 1976): 17–30.

Howell, Robert. "Intuition, Synthesis, and the Problem of Individuation in the *Critique of Pure Reason*," *Nous* 7 (1973): 207–32.

Huber, Gerhard. *Das Sein und das Absolut.* Basel: Verlag für Recht und Gesellschaft, 1955.

Hume, David. *A Treatise of Human Nature*, ed. L. A. Selby-Bigge. Oxford: The Clarendon Press, 1967.

Humphrey, Ted. "The Historical and Conceptual Relations between Kant's Metaphysics of Space and Philosophy of Geometry," *Journal of the History of Philosophy* 11 (1973): 483–512.

Jacobi, F. H. *David Hume über den Glauben, oder Idealismus und Realismus, Über der transzendentalen Idealismus, Werke*, vol. 2, ed. F. Roth F. Köpen. Darmstadt: Wissenschaftliche Buchgesellschaft, 1968.

Janke, W. *Fichte: Sein und Reflexion.* Berlin: de Gryter, 1970.

Joseph, H. W. B. "The Schematism of the Categories in Kant's *Critique of Pure Reason*," in *Essays in Ancient and Modern Philosophy*. Oxford: The Clarendon Press, 1935.

Kalin, Martin. "Kant's Transcendental Arguments as Gedankenexperimente," *Kant-Studien* 63 (1972): 313–28.

Kaulbach, Friedrich. "Dialektik und Theorie der philosophischen Methode bei Kant," *Kant-Studien* 64 (1973): 395–410.

―――. "Die kantische Lehre von Ding und Sein in der Interpretation Heideggers," *Kant-Studien* 55 (1964): 194–220.

―――. "Schema, Bild, und Modell nach den Voraussetzungen des kantischen Denkens," in *Kant*, ed. G. Prauss (see below), pp. 105–29.

Kemp Smith, Norman. *A Commentary to Kant's Critique of Pure Reason*. London: Macmillan, 1923.

Kern, Iso. *Husserl und Kant*. The Hague: Nijhoff, 1964.

Körner, Stephan. "The Impossibility of Transcendental Deductions," *The Monist* 51 (1961): 317–31.

Krausser, Peter. "The Operational Conception of 'reine Anschauung' (Pure Intuition) in Kant's Theory of Experience and Science," *Studies in History and Philosophy of Science* 3 (1972–73): 81–87.

Kroner, Richard. *Von Kant bis Hegel*. Tübingen: J. C. B. Mohr, 1961.

Krüger, Gerhard. "Der Masstab der kantischen Kritik," reprinted in *Philosophie und Moral in der kantischen Kritik*, 2nd ed. (see below), pp. 237–68.

―――.*Philosophie und Moral in der kantischen Kritik*, 2nd ed. Tübingen: J. C. B. Mohr, 1967.

―――."Über Kants Lehre von der Zeit," reprinted in *Philosophie und Moral in der kantischen Kritik*, 2nd ed. (see above), pp. 269–94.

Lachièze-Rey, Pierre. *L'Idealisme kantien*. Paris: J. Vrin, 1950.

Le Clerc, Ivor. "The Meaning of 'Spacc' in Kant," reprinted in *Kant's Theory of Knowledge*, ed. L. W. Beck (see above), pp. 87–94.

Lehmann, Gerhard. "Kritizismus und kritische motive in der Entwicklung der kantischen Philosophie," *Kant-Studien* 48 (1956–57): 25–54.

―――. "Voraussetzungen und Grenzen systematischer Kantinterpretation," *Kant-Studien* 49 (1957–58): 364–88.

Lehrer, Keith. "Science, Perception and Reality," review, *Journal of Philosophy* 63 (1966): 266–77.

Leibniz, G. W. *Die philosophische Schriften*, ed. C. J. Gerhardt. Hildesheim: Georg Olms, 1960.

Lewis, C. I. *An Analysis of Knowledge and Valuation*. La Salle, Ill.: Open Court, 1946.

MacIntosh, J. J. "Transcendental Arguments (II)," *Proceedings of the Aristotelian Society* 43 (1969): 181–93.

Maimon, Solomon. *Versuch über die Transzendentalphilosophie* in *Gesammelte Werke*. Hildesheim: Georg Olms, 1965.

Martin, Gottfried. *Immanuel Kant, Ontologie und Wissenschaftstheorie*. Berlin: de Gruyter, 1969.

Meerbote, Rolf. "The Unknowability of Things in Themselves," in *Proceedings of the Third International Kant-Kongress,* ed. L. W. Beck. Dordrecht: Reidel, 1972, pp. 274–89.

———. "Kant's Use of the Notions 'Objective Reality' and 'Objective Validity'," *Kant-Studien* 63 (1972): 31–38.

Melnick, Arthur. *Kant's Analogies of Experience.* Chicago: University of Chicago Press, 1973.

Mijuskovic, Ben. "The Premise of the Transcendental Analytic," *Philosophical Quarterly* 23 (1973): 156–61.

Mittelstrass, Jürgen. "Spontaneität, Ein Beitrag in Blick auf Kant," in *Kant,* ed. G. Prauss (see below), pp. 62–72.

Mörchen, Hermann. *Die Einbildungskraft bei Kant.* Tübingen: Max Niemeyer, 1970.

Morgenbesser, S., et al. (eds.) *Philosophy, Science, and Method.* New York: St. Martin's Press, 1969.

Nagel, E. *The Structure of Science.* New York: Harcourt, Brace & World, 1961.

Navert, Jean. "Ontologie et criticisme dans la philosophie de Kant," *Revue des sciences philosophiques et théologiques* 37 (1953): 253–55.

Olivier, J. W. "Kant's Copernican Analogy," *Kant-Studien* 55 (1964): 505–11.

Palter, Robert. "Absolute Space and Absolute Motion in Kant's Critical Philosophy," in *Kant's Theory of Knowledge,* ed. L. W. Beck (see above), pp. 95–110.

Parson, Charles. "Infinity and Kant's Conception of the 'Possibility of Experience'," reprinted in *Kant,* ed. R. P. Wolff (see below), pp. 37–53.

———. "Kant's Philosophy of Arithmetic," in *Philosophy, Science, and Method,* ed. S. Morgenbesser, et al. (see above), pp. 568–94.

Paton, H. J. *Kant's Metaphysic of Experience,* 2 vols. New York: Macmillan, 1936.

Pears, David. "The Incongruity of Counterparts," *Philosophy of Science* 25 (1958): 109–15.

Penelhum, T., and MacIntosh, J. (eds.) *The First Critique.* Belmont, Calif.: Wadsworth, 1969.

Pippin, Robert. "Critical Methodology and Comprehensiveness in Philosophy," *Metaphilosophy* 9 (1978): 197–211.

———. "Erscheinung bei Kant," a review, *Journal of the History of Philosophy* 12 (1974): 403–45.

———. "Hegel's Metaphysics and the Problem of Contradiction," *Journal of the History of Philosophy* 16 (1978): 301–12.

———. "Hegel's Phenomenological Criticism," *Man and World* 8 (1975): 296–314.

———. "Kant und das Problem der Dinge an sich," a review, *Journal of the History of Philosophy* 14 (1976): 374–78.

———. "The Kant-Eberhard Controversy," a review, *Kant-Studien* 66 (1975): 247–50.

Poincaré, H. *Science and Method.* New York: Dover, 1952.

Prauss, Gerold. *Erscheinung bei Kant.* Berlin: de Gruyter, 1971.

———. "Freges Beitrag zur Erkenntnistheorie," *Allgemeine Zeitschrift für Philosophie* 1 (1974): 34–64.

——. *Kant und das Problem der Dinge an sich*. Bonn: Bouvier Verlag H. Grund-
mann, 1974.

——. (ed.) *Kant: Zur Deutung seiner Theorie von Erkennen und Handeln*. Köln:
Kiepenhauer und Witsch, 1973.

Prichard, H. A. *Kant's Theory of Knowledge*. Oxford: Oxford University Press, 1969.

Rademacher, Hans. "Zum Problem der transzendentalen Apperzeption bei Kant,"
Zeitschrift für Philosophische Forschung 24 (1970): 28–49.

Reich, Klaus. *Die Vollständigkeit der kantischen Urteilstafeln*. Berlin: Diss. Rostock,
1932.

Reichenbach, Hans. *The Philosophy of Space and Time*. New York: Dover, 1957.

Reinach, Adolf. *Gesammelte Schriften*. Halle, 1921.

Rohs, Peter. "Beweismöglichkeiten für die transzendentale Ästhetik," *Philo-
sophisches Jahrbuch* 79 (1972): 373–85.

——. *Form und Grund*. Bonn: Bouvier, 1969.

——. *Transzendentale Ästhetik*. Meisenheim am Glan: A. Hain, 1973.

——. *Transzendentale Logik*. Meisenheim am Glan: A. Hain, 1976.

Rorty, Richard. *Philosophy and the Mirror of Nature*. Princeton: Princeton University Press, 1979.

——. "Strawson's Objectivity Argument," *Review of Metaphysics* 24 (1970):
207–44.

——. "Verificationism and Transcendental Arguments," *Nous* 5 (1971): 3–14.

Rosen, Stanley. *G. W. F. Hegel. An Introduction to the Science of Wisdom*. New
Haven: Yale University Press, 1974.

——. *The Limits of Analysis*. New York: Basic Books, 1980.

Rosenberg, Jay. "Transcendental Arguments Revisited," *Journal of Philosophy* 72
(1975): 611–26.

Roussett, Bernard. *La Doctrine kantienne de l'objectivité*. Paris: J. Vrin, 1968.

Royce, Josiah. *Lectures on Modern Idealism*. New Haven: Yale University Press,
1964.

Russell, Bertrand. *Introduction to Mathematical Philosophy*. London: Allen &
Unwin, 1960.

——. *Mysticism and Logic and Other Essays*. London: Allen & Unwin, 1959.

Schäfer, Lothar. *Kants Metaphysik der Natur*. Berlin: De Gruyter, 1966.

Schaper, Eva. "Arguing Transcendentally," *Kant-Studien* 63 (1972): 101–16.

——. "Kant on Imagination," *Philosophical Forum* 2 (1970-71): 430–45.

——. "Kant's Schematism Reconsidered," *Review of Metaphysics* 18 (1964):
267–92.

——. "The Thing-in-Itself as a Philosophical Fiction," *Philosophical Quarterly* 14
(1966): 233–43.

Scheler, Max. *Der Formalismus in der Ethik und die materiale Wertethik*. Berne:
Franke-Verlag, 1954.

Scholz, Heinrich. "Das Vermächtnis der kantischen Lehre vom Raum und von der
Zeit," *Kant-Studien* 29 (1924): 21–69.

Schrader, George. "Kant's Theory of Concepts," reprinted in *Kant*, ed. R. P. Wolff
(see below), pp. 134–55.

——. "The Thing in Itself in Kantian Philosophy," reprinted in *Kant*, ed. R. P.
Wolff (see below), pp. 172–88.

———. "The Transcendental Ideality and Empirical Reality of Kant's Space and Time," *The Review of Metaphysics* 4 (1951): 507–36.

Schwyzer, Hubert. "Thought and Reality: The Metaphysics of Kant and Wittgenstein," *The Philosophical Quarterly* 23 (1973): 193–206.

Scott-Taggart, M. J. "Recent Work on the Philosophy of Kant," reprinted in *Kant Studies Today*, ed. L. W. Beck (see above), pp. 1–71.

Seebohm, Thomas. *Die Bedingungen der Möglichkeit der Transzendental-Philosophie*. Bonn: Bouvier, 1962.

Sellars, Wilfrid. "Empiricism and the Philosophy of Mind," in *Science, Perception and Reality* (see below), pp. 127–96.

———. *Science and Metaphysics. Variations on Kantian Themes*. New York: Humanities Press, 1963.

———. *Science, Perception and Reality*. New York: Humanities Press, 1963.

———. "Some Remarks on Kant's Theory of Experience," *Journal of Philosophy* 64 (1967): 633–47.

———. ". . . this I or he or it (the thing) which thinks . . ." *Proceedings and Addresses of the American Philosophical Association* 44 (September 1971): 5–31.

———. "Towards a Theory of Categories," in *Experience and Theory*, eds. Lawrence Foster and J. W. Swanson (see above), pp. 55–78.

Sluga, Hans. "Frege's Alleged Realism," *Inquiry* 20 (1977): 227–42.

Stegmüller, Wolfgang. "Towards a Rational Reconstruction of Kant's Metaphysics of Experience, Part I," *Ratio* 9 (1967): 1–32. Part II, *Ratio* 10 (1968): 1–37.

Stenius, Erik. "On Kant's Distinction between Phenomena and Noumena," in *Philosophical Essays to Gunnar Aspelin on the Occasion of His 65th Birthday*. Lund: C. W. R. Gleerup, 1965, pp. 231–45.

Stern, L. J. "Empirical Concepts as Rules in the *Critique of Pure Reason*," *Akten des 4. Internationalen Kant-Kongresses, Teil II*. vol. 1. Berlin: de Gruyter, 1974, pp. 158–65.

Strawson, Peter F. *Individuals*. London: Methuen, 1959.

———. *The Bounds of Sense*. London: Methuen, 1966.

Stroud, Barry. *Hume*. London: Routledge & Kegan Paul, 1977.

———. "Transcendental Arguments," reprinted in *The First Critique*, ed. T. Penelhum and J. MacIntosh (see above), pp. 54–69.

———. "Transcendental Arguments and 'Epistemological Naturalism'," *Philosophical Studies* 31 (1977): 105–15.

Swing, Thomas. *Kant's Transcendental Logic*. New Haven: Yale University Press, 1969.

Thompson, Manley. "Singular Terms and Intuitions in Kant's Epistemology," *Review of Metaphysics* 26 (1972): 314–43.

Uehling, Theodor E. "Wahrnehmungsurteile and Erfahrungsurteile Reconsidered," *Kant-Studien* 49 (1978): 341–51.

Vaihinger, Hans. *Kommentar zur Kants Kritik der reinen Vernunft*, (2 vols.) Stuttgart: W. Spemann, 1881–92.

Walker, Ralph. C. S. *Kant*. London: Routledge & Kegan Paul, 1978.

Walsh, W. H. "Kant on the Perception of Time," *Monist* 51 (1967): 376–96.

———. *Kant's Criticism of Metaphysics*. Edinburgh: Edinburgh University Press, 1975.

———. "Schematism," in *Kant,* ed. R. P. Wolff (see below), pp. 71–87.

Warnock, G. J. "Conceptual Schematism," *Analysis* 9 (1948–49): 77–82.

Washburn, Michael. "Dogmatism, Scepticism, Criticism: The Dialectic of Kant's 'Silent Decade'," *Journal of the History of Philosophy* 13 (1975): 161–76.

Weingartner, Paul (ed.). *Deskription, Analyzität und Existenz*. Salzburg: Anton Pustet, 1966.

Weldon, T. D. *Kant's Critique of Pure Reason*. Oxford: The Clarendon Press, 1958.

Werkmeister, W. H. (ed.) *Reflections on Kant's Philosophy*. Gainesville: University of Florida Press, 1975.

Wilkerson, T. E. "Transcendental Arguments," *Philosophical Quarterly* 20 (1970): 200–212.

Wilson, Kirk. "Kant on Intuitions," *Philosophical Quarterly* 25 (1975): 247–65.

Wittgenstein, Ludwig. *Blue and Brown Books*. New York: Harper & Row, 1958.

———. *Philosophical Investigations*. New York: Macmillan, 1965.

———. *Tractatus Logico-Philosophicus*. London: Routledge & Kegan Paul, 1961.

Wolff, Robert Paul (ed.). *Kant: A Collection of Critical Essays*. New York: Doubleday Anchor, 1967.

———. *Kant's Theory of Mental Activity*. Cambridge: Harvard University Press, 1963.

———. *The Autonomy of Reason*. New York: Harper & Row, 1973.

Zocher, Rudolf. "Kants Transzendentale Deduktion der Kategorien," *Zeitschrift für Philosophische Forschung* 8 (1954): 161–94.

Index